The Penetrated Male

The Penetrated Male

Jonathan Kemp

punctum books ✶ brooklyn, ny

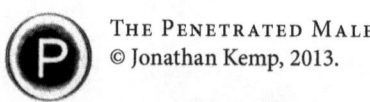

THE PENETRATED MALE
© Jonathan Kemp, 2013.

http://creativecommons.org/licenses/by-nc-nd/3.0/

This work is Open Access, which means that you are free to copy, distribute, display, and perform the work as long as you clearly attribute the work to the authors, that you do not use this work for commercial gain in any form whatsoever, and that you in no way alter, transform, or build upon the work outside of its normal use in academic scholarship without express permission of the author and the publisher of this volume. For any reuse or distribution, you must make clear to others the license terms of this work.

First published in 2013 by
punctum books
Brooklyn, New York
http://punctumbooks.com

ISBN-13: 978-0615870861
ISBN-10: 0615870864

Library of Congress Cataloging Data is available from the Library of Congress.

Cover Image: detail from Matthew Stradling, *All Fours* (1998); oil on canvas.

Facing-page drawing by Heather Masciandaro.

Table of Contents

Acknowledgements	I
Introduction	1
1. The Madness of the Penetrated Body	23
2. The Limits of the Body	71
3. The Male Body and the Outside	123
4. Writing the Behind	165
Bibliography	217

Acknowledgements

This book is based on a PhD thesis, and as such is greatly indebted to the insightful supervision provided by Professor Johnny Golding and Doctor Carolyn Brown. In addition, I'd like to thank Roy Woolley for his helpful feedback on the manuscript. Thanks to Matthew Stradling for permission to use his painting *All Fours* (1998, oil on canvas) on the cover.

This book is dedicated to the memory of my sister, Louise Kemp (1964–1992).

"The text is (should be) that uninhibited person
who shows his behind to the Political Father"
- Roland Barthes, *The Pleasure of the Text*

"Movement always happens behind the thinker's back"
- Gilles Deleuze, *Dialogues*

"Philosophy will always come in by the back door"
- Derek Attridge, introduction to Jacques Derrida, *Acts of Literature*

Introduction

> "...the man who does not *feel* his body will never
> be in a position to conceive a living thought..."
> - E. M. Cioran, *A Short History of Decay*

> "He who wishes to know the truth about life in its
> immediacy must scrutinize its estranged form"
> - Theodor W. Adorno, *Minima Moralia*

This book scrutinizes literary representations of the male body in what is perhaps its most estranged form: in the process of being penetrated. It does this both in order to suggest that penetration is a condition of modern masculine subjectivity, and to reclaim the male body as a penetrable body. It will argue that the submission by which masculinity registers within the socio-symbolic order is effected by a process of penetration that remainders the male body, marking it as waste and associating it with a pejorative femininity.

Taboos not only against anality and anal intercourse, but, by extension, against so-called passivity and powerlessness, come into play in our traditional understanding of the penetrated male body. Through the traditional cultural associations that exist between the concept *body* and the concept *woman*, the name *feminine* is given to any breach of the taboo against penetrating the male body. As will be shown, the chain of equivalences binding these two abject bodies significantly includes the notion of psychosis and waste. Through close readings of various texts from the period 1860–1947, this book aims to show how the penetrated male body figures as a site of ambiguity hovering behind the protocols of representation that govern its emergence.

THE POLITICS OF THE ANUS

Michel Foucault's work on the ancient civilizations of Greece and Rome has demonstrated how male–male eroticism was governed by a strict understanding that the penetrated partner was a non-citizen: that is, a slave, a woman, or a young boy. The civic status and political power of the *adult* male citizen was contingent upon his body remaining impenetrable, for it was understood that "when one played the role of subordinate partner in the game of pleasure relations, one could not be truly dominant in the game of civic and political activity" (Foucault 1992, 220; see also Dover 1989, 140–7; Boswell 1981, 50, 53, 184): to be penetrated was to cease to be fully human. This pattern was to re-emerge throughout Europe after about 1700, as Randolph Trumbach's work on eighteenth century sexuality shows. The only remotely acceptable form of male–male sodomy became that performed by an adult male upon an adolescent boy, who was seen to exist "in a transitional state between man and woman" (Trumbach 1993, 255), and therefore neither fully male nor fully human. Trumbach's research reveals a consolidation of gender difference taking place in the 1700s by which effeminacy became associated with anal passivity: "Adult men were deemed effeminate only when they allowed themselves to be sexually penetrated" (Trumbach 1995, 255).

By focusing on the penetrated male body, this book is thus not only highlighting the "repudiation of the feminine"[1] upon

---

[1] This phrase is from Jessica Benjamin's *The Bonds of Love: Psychoanalysis, Feminism and the Problem of Domination* (London: Virago, 1990). She argues that the boy's identity as male must

which traditional, patriarchal and heterosexual masculinity is predicated, but is also making a claim for a reappraisal of masculine pleasure, reclaiming that body as something other than grotesque or unthinkable; it might understand the penetrated male body as something other than feminine, and feminine as something other than submissive, powerless and vulnerable. But how has it come to represent these things in the first place, if not through its interpretation by a perceptual system which always already equates these terms with a highly pejorative femininity, that is, a system of mimetic identification and conceptual foreclosure?

The finitude of the flesh from which transcendence is attempted through the traditional process of disembodied masculine subjectivity is clearly linked not only with death, but also with sexuality, desire, eroticism: *le petit mort*. Erotic submission is a limit-experience. In the words of Steven Marcus, "sex ... serves as a kind of metaphor for death" (Marcus 1970, 29). The dialectic of death and desire has a tortuous and tangled history in Western thought, and it is not my intention to map it here (see, for example, Bataille 1987; Dollimore 1997). But from late nineteenth-century sexological tracts through to Leo Bersani's reflections on AIDS in "Is the Rectum a Grave?" (Bersani 1987), the anus has been explicitly linked to death and negation, not least because it is the site of decay, the egress for waste matter. The anus is permitted a single function: ejecting, not receiving; it is a way out of the body, not a way in. In the Victorian homosexual pornographic novel *Teleny*, for example, penetrative anal pleasure culminates in literal death[2]. The model for a receptive sexual orifice within our thinking remains the vagina – and this despite that orifice's own duality of functions. Yet, whilst D. H. Lawrence's remark that "Sex is a creative flow, the excrementory flow is towards dissolution" (Lawrence 1961, 69) indicates the horror

---

inevitably involve a rejection of the mother and all she represents and in this sense masculinity is a *re*active process of dis-identification.

[2] *Teleny*'s authorship is attributed, in part at least, to Oscar Wilde. See Winston Leyland's introduction (San Francisco: Gay Sunshine Press, 1984).

of mixing these two flows, it ignores the excrementory function of the genitals. As Freud remarks:

> Where the anus is concerned it becomes still clearer that it is disgust which stamps that sexual aim as a perversion. I hope I shall not be accused of partisanship when I assert that people who try to account for this disgust by saying that the organ in question serves the function of excretion and comes in contact with excrement ... are not much more to the point than hysterical girls who account for their disgust at the male genital by saying that it serves to void urine. (Freud 1977, 64)

And while Freud's words still strike a revolutionary note, they are themselves couched in terms that serve to signal Freud's anxiety over whether he himself might be accused of partisanship, accused of *knowing* subjectively the anal eroticism it is only his intention to explore under the rubric of an objective science. Rupert Davenport-Hines, commenting upon the media representation of AIDS as a punishment against homosexuals for "abusing their arses", argues that:

> Objectively the discrimination between penises and rectums is nonsense; given the greater horror that shit commands over urine in our culture, the distinction is understandable; but nonsense is still nonsense, whether acculturated, atavistic or adopted as an excuse for journalistic bullying. (Davenport-Hines 1990, 336)

Whilst the horror of shit is clearly central to the phobia surrounding sexual use of the anus, this book maintains that an equally nonsensical (though equally powerful) *gender* discrimination is at work, rendering the male anus a particularly problematical site of such anxiety. For example, the reference in some gay pornography to the male anus as a boy-pussy or man-cunt bears witness to a clear gender ambiguity attending the penetration of that orifice. Mario Mieli, an early gay liberationist, called passive homosexuality a form of feminine sexuality (Mieli 1980, 148), using an idealized concept of woman as the model for a more liberal sexual politics.

Guy Hocquenghem worked with a more usefully undifferentiated model of desire, derived from Gilles Deleuze and Felix Guattari's *Anti-Oedipus*. In that book, Deleuze and Guattari argue that the privatized anus symbolizes a more molecular approach to desire, the organic flows of the body more conducive to the amorphous manifestations of corporeal pleasure. They shatter the human body into myriad parts, and expose these parts to a multiplicity of sensations and intensities the overall experience of which results in what has been called the subject. For Deleuze and Guattari, subjectivity is the immediate residual outcome of bodily sensation.

The masculine subjectivity that has emerged within Western capitalist discourse is seen as the result of reducing bodily sensation to a programmatic model of procreative sexuality centred on genital differentiation. The penis transcends into the phallus, following the model of the privatized anus. Consequently, the phallicized penis is the only permissable site of pleasure on the male body. In this sense, a binary is established by which the penis is secondary to the concept of Phallus, just as the body is considered secondary to the mind. The anus is thus excluded altogether from the male libidinal economy, such that its erotic use immediately carries with it the threat of castration. Erotic investment in the male anus is hegemonically disavowed by branding its owners as *symbolic women*; a kind of castration is performed. Because "seen from behind we are all women", because "the anus does not practice sexual discrimination" (Hocquenghem 1990, 101), the role of the phallus is to affirm sexual difference through its presence. As such, homophobia and misogyny, as Craig Owen (1987) has argued, serve the same social function, stemming from the same fear of the penetrated/penetrable body – which thus becomes an index of femininity. Taking its cue from *Anti-Oedipus*, Hocquenghem's *Homosexual Desire* (1972) argues that the privatized anus, as employed in male homosexual intercourse, can assist in the battle against the entire armature of Western capitalist patriarchal power. Whilst similar in many respects to Mieli, Hocquenghem is far less humanist in his approach, preferring, instead of a unified notion of the homosexual, to explore the polymorphous potential of desire. In a later essay, for example, written in 1987, he states that "homosexuality is baroque, dramatic, it is an 'effect', not a principle", claiming that the term expresses "a certain 'attitude towards life' rather than an 'identity'" (Hocquenghem 2000, 71), prefiguring one of the tropes of later Queer Theory (see, for example, the introduction to Warner 1993).

Hocquenghem argues for anal pleasure not as a specifically homosexual activity, but as a way of undermining all sexual categorizations. The symbolic role of the anus is pitted against that of the phallus, the latter's private status correlated with the former's function as the public marker of sexual difference. If "the body gathers round the phallus like society round the chief" (Hocquenghem 1993, 96), it unravels around the anus. Whereas only approximately half the population have a phallus, everyone has an anus, its universal possession overriding its privatized and individuated function. In Hocquenghem's view sexual use of the anus is therefore revolutionary,[3] not simply in terms of overturning sexual categorizations but also by undermining the economic sublimation equating faeces with money.

Along with Robert Mapplethorpe's (in)famous photographs of gay fisting, and his self-penetrating self-portrait with a bullwhip unravelling like a demonic tail from his behind, the work of Mieli and Hocquenghem can be located within a geneaology throughout the 1970s and 1980s that worked alongside gay activism's promotion of sexual freedom. The advent of AIDS, however, cast a shadow within which this discourse on pleasure became viewed pejoratively as highly utopian, if not downright irresponsible. By 1987, for Leo Bersani at least, the rectum had become a grave, once more a

---

[3] In a later essay, Hocquenghem declares, "Our assholes are revolutionary". "Towards an Irrecuperable Pederasty", trans. Chris Fox, in Jonathan Goldberg (ed), *Reclaiming Sodom* (London & New York: Routledge, 1993), 236.

signifier of negation, dissolution and death. In his essay "Is the Rectum a Grave?", Bersani refers to the "seductive and intolerable image of a grown man, legs high in the air, unable to refuse the suicidal ecstasy of being a woman" (Bersani 1987, 212). Why intolerable? Why suicidal? And why a woman? This book offers a reading of the penetrated male body that suggests another way of seeing it – one which resists the non-contradictory nature of such identity thinking.

In *Negative Dialectics*, Theodor Adorno attacks identity thinking by arguing that: "objects do not go into their concepts without leaving a remainder ... they come to contradict the traditional norm of adequacy", and that this contradiction "indicates the untruth of identity, the fact that the concept does not exhaust the thing conceived" (Adorno 1996, 5). In other words, it signifies a rupture between the 'is' and the 'ought', a gulf or inadequacy between representation and the reality it claims to represent: a gulf of ideological mediation. Put yet another way, the nonidentical is a break between the singular and the multiple, the universal and the particular. In terms of certain contemporary thinkers, this gap or aporia takes on the names of pharmakon, differance, differend, even 'poetics'. This book argues that the concept *man* remainders the body, as something excessive and wasteful, in the manner described by Adorno. It maintains that central to that denial of the flesh is the conceptual attachment of the body with woman, and the status of woman within binary logic as man's other, resulting in men's inevitable *de*tachment from and domination of the body/woman/nature. Such detachment finds its apotheosis in the anxious impenetrability maintained by the German *Freikorps*, a vigilante military group who took it upon themselves to wipe out the 'red terror' of Bolshevism between the wars, and whose writings have been analysed by Klaus Theweleit in his two-volume work *Male Fantasies*[4]. The male body, according to this mode of analysis, must remain something impenetrable and unknown.

---

[4] See Chapter One for an account of Theweleit's work.

But such absolute detachment of the body is not possible, and the male body remains inherently penetrable, inherently knowable. By focusing on the penetrability of the male body – a penetrability, as this book shows, considered both fearful and fascinating – the texts analysed challenge this tradition of masculine impenetrability and detachment. In them, the male body is opened up in ways that open up masculine subjectivity, thus debunking the abstract conception of the male subject as unified and self-enclosed.

THREE SPECIFIC LEVELS

The book works with three specific levels.

1) *the conceptual level.* Primarily, what still characterizes most of our understandings of the male body is phallocentrism and phallogocentrism (Derrida 1987, 191), by which masculinist discourse insists on a binary logic that subsumes the second term to the first. However critical of the role of the phallus such readings might be, the phallus remains the determining signifier within their economies. The constitution of discourse and sexual difference is still figured by the mark of the phallus. Kaja Silverman (1993) attempted to conjure up an alternative, non-phallic economy, within which to place and regard the male body, but was only able to do so by recourse to tropes of femininity. Challenging the phallogocentrism of traditional notions of masculine embodiment and the feminine paradigm of non-phallic alternatives, this book focuses on anality as another way of looking at maleness. It aims to do this by working on the metonymic register by which the penetrated male body is brought into focus as neither feminine nor psychotic.

2) *the literary level.* It will be argued that certain aspects of modern literature constitute the male body differently by marking it as a site of penetration. In the work of Schreber, Genet and Joyce this metonymic register finds its full expression as the male body opens up, presents itself as defiantly penetrative. I want to suggest that these texts delineate a different

– non-phallic – genealogy for the male subject, by focusing on the penetrated male body. I will be considering this body not as the radical other of traditional Western masculinity, but rather as what David Savran calls its "pathologized double" (Savran 1998, 27); as that which lurks *behind* it like a shadow, though which is in no sense outside it. This pathologization will be shown as inherently coded with a debased and abject femininity that came into play most strongly towards the latter half of the nineteenth century, and which has only been placed under strutiny within the last fifty years.

3) *the corporeal level.* Why are the body's openings so disturbing to the concept of unified subjectivity? And why is their penetration considered so dangerous? Is the closed body a result of the foreclosing of language, or is language modelled on the ideality of a safely closed body enclosing a safely closed subject? Can opening one open the other? Can the movements and flows of an opened body be represented, or does representation itself only function upon a foreclosure of such nomadic flesh? On this corporeal level, the anus functions as the behind – as that which cannot be seen, but which can nevertheless be known. In this way, the term behind will make clear the link between the crisis of masculinity and the crisis of reason. In an attempt to characterize a certain anxiety that is common to both corporeal and intellectual uncertainty, the full erotic charge of the term *behind* – as a homograph that binds together a corporeal vulnerability as well as an epistemological one – will be in play throughout the book. Indeed, writing the behind will be shown to be so inherently fraught with the dangers of this *double entendre* that the foundations of masculine discourse themselves are revealed as anything but secure. The male behind and its attendant cultural anxieties are linked here to the 'behind' of discourse, to what lurks behind, and thus, by extension, to analysis itself. For isn't to turn one's back, as Jacques Derrida remarks, both "a very amorous position" *and* "the analytic position" (1987, 178)? Notice he doesn't say 'a' but 'the' analytic position. To analyse, to think, in other words, is always already to insist that in doing so thought invites an act of penetration which

occurs *behind* the thinker. Amongst other things, this book wants to stress the *anal* in *analysis*. As such, it is concerned with the claim that thought is embodied, and that, moreover, such embodiment is first and foremost erotic – first and foremost concerned with the body and its sensations.

Given that concepts are often seen somewhat simplistically as belonging in discrete pairs, like animals entering Noah's ark, belonging on either side of a boundary or division which poses them as not only opposites but also as fundamentally oppositional (a violent hierarchy) – what this book calls the logic of the either/or – then the challenge that such division is neither possible nor adequate gestures to another form of logic altogether: a logic of the neither/nor, a point I will develop throughout this book. The behind, registering as both discursive aporia and corporeal liminality, thus enables and articulates a thinking that moves beyond the either/or of traditional logic.

MOVING BEYOND THE 'EITHER/OR'

What does it mean to move beyond the strictures of the either/or logic that often obstructs critical thinking? How is such a move achieved? This concern is expressed by Lacan, Deleuze, Derrida, Foucault and Kristeva who have begun this exploration of a logic that does not reduce to a position of either/or.

This book focuses on one aspect of embodiment so far ignored or misunderstood within critical theory: that of the penetrated male body. Within the confines of a binary understanding of gender subjectivity predicated on sexual positioning, the penetrated partner – regardless of gender – becomes understood as somehow female/feminized. A discourse characterized by high levels of anxiety concerning the visibility of the penetrated male body will be shown to rely most on this feminine paradigm. But that is not the whole picture. As this book also shows, behind this discursively negative figure is another, and another. In other words, there are chains of equivalences that work against the metaphor equating the penetrated male body with femininity and psychosis. The restriction of the metaphoric association by which anus=vagina, or penetrated male body=feminine body, will be shown to be the stimulus for a poetics by which that metaphor is rendered unstable and illogical, exemplary of another form of logic. The use of metaphors such as flowers and suns to symbolize the anus, and the metonymy which links the anus to other openings in the body, all work towards destabilizing that traditional metaphor. In the novels of Jean Genet, for example, it will be seen how flowers become metonymically linked to the penetrated male anus, suggesting a fertility at odds with the traditional characterization of anality with death. In Schreber's *Memoirs*, the male anus equates with the sun, as well as with God, both cultural signifiers of the giving of life. Schreber's submission to God's will, and his subsequent transformation into a woman, are in order to create a new world, linking the penetrated male body to a Utopian dream. In Wilde's *Dorian Gray*, the male anus equates with the ear *and* flowers, delineating a process of cross-fertilization centred upon the production or dissemination of discourse. For Wilde, masculine subjectivity is only possible through a process of penetration by which the male body is inseminated. In Baudelaire's prose poem 'Miss Scalpel', the eyes become the entry point into the male body most vulnerable to such analogy. Here, the ambiguity of the gaze creates an uncertainty about subjectivity and penetrability that becomes the primary condition of his poetics. In *A Rebours*, Joris-Karl Huysmans offers the mouth as a way into the male body. In a move that renders the mouth and the anus interchangeable, Huysmans inverts the male body and disrupts the notion of a contained and stable self. In each case the anxieties surrounding the penetration of the male body will be shown to be part of a process that also includes fascination and pleasure. The conflict between anxiety and pleasure is focused, for the sake of this book, most intensely upon a body both abjected and desired.

Given that the notion of the abject developed by Kristeva names the process by which the human subject constitutes itself through ejecting the things it does not want to contain, how are we to understand the constitution of masculine subjectivity through denial of the penetrated body? These ejected things are characterized as waste and include, Kristeva argues, the experience of sensuality or *jouissance* attending the process of abjection. The reduction of anxiety that comes from the removal of those things considered horrific or abject thus comes at a price: all sensuality, all open corporeality, must also be reduced. In order to register within the symbolic order, masculinity must, of necessity, close the body down. As such closure is not possible, what Kristeva calls the semiotic lodges the body/bodily within the symbolic, outlawed by the protocols of representation, though by no means any less real for all that.

What I am calling the protocols of representation are the discursive or logistic terms by which the penetrated male body registers as somehow female; that is, it appears logically within a feminine paradigm. The chain of equivalences which bind the concept of woman to the concept of the body, and which mark the body as inherently penetrable, delineate a discursive field that implies masculine impenetrability. As Susan Bordo argues, "the deep associations of masculinity as active, constitutive (and self-constituting) subjectivity and femininity as a passive, 'natural' bodily state underlie the equation of penetrability with femininity" (1994, 288).

What constitutes the protocols of representation will be coterminous throughout this book with what Lacan calls the symbolic order. These protocols establish the terms by which representation registers as meaningful. As such, entry into the normative standard set by the symbolic order requires conformity to its protocols.

What happens, however, when such conformity is rejected? This non-conformity may take many forms. Whilst there is, undoubtedly, stigmatization through abjection, an expulsion from the body politic of those elements deemed worthless, there is also, within modernity or the modern particularly, such a high level of uncertainty over the truthfulness or usefulness of the symbolic order and its protocols, that this stigmatization itself cannot remain stable in its abjection.

As Kristeva points out, "abjection is above all ambiguity" (1982, 9).

The conformity of the either/or is challenged by the non-conformity of the neither/nor, a non-conformity which revels in wordplay, ambivalence and radical multiplicity, its suggestion of an unseen behind to every text. This ambiguity within the symbolic order's primary tool (language) allows for play. Exposing and exploring this ambiguous play of language has been the primary task of the work of Jacques Derrida. In this book, this instability or play will go by the name of the behind. Poetics will mark or signify language's ability to have a behind. As such, the poetics of the penetrated male body, it will be argued, allow for its reappropriation from the feminine paradigm imposed upon it by the symbolic order.

It is a conceptual excess that cannot be conceptualized in any discourse except through rupture. Put another way, the poetic emerges in the relationship between the commensurability of something and its incommensurability. Barthes describes it as "the violation of a limit to the signifying space" (Barthes 1979, 126). Foucault calls it the thought from outside. Lyotard calls it a differend. Derrida calls it many things: *différance* or 'trace', '*pharmakon*', 'hymen', 'supplement', and 'gram'; "a kind of *general strategy of deconstruction*" (Derrida 1981, 41, original emphasis). Sue Golding also calls this unsayable something a poetics, "a kind of dirty, bloody poetics, one which insists on, say, bodies and skin and smells and imagination in the face of it all" (Golding 2000, 286). For Golding, it is always dynamic, always political, always a risky and violent place to inhabit (Golding 2001, 52). It insists on a multiplicity or multi-dimensionality irreducible to the consolations of identity thinking and dialectical analysis.

This poetics, then, exposes the conditions of its own emergence at the risk of being rendered meaningless. It takes the substance of discourse (language) and uses it – not always knowingly or deliberately – to scramble discourse's code, rearranging it into other patterns, other codes. It differs both from Aristotle's use of the term as a form of textual analysis, and from Todorov's use of it to name a form of structuration within textual practices. These uses of the term poetics seek to unveil or expose something considered hitherto hidden. They work with metaphors of the visible. The poetics I am attempting to articulate focuses more on how what is known is contoured by what is not.

Significantly, both the ear and the anus are bodily orifices that cannot be seen directly by the subject; they are not immediately accessible through the visual. Chapter Two examines Oscar Wilde's use of the ear as a site of penetration upon the male body by which masculine subjectivity takes control, functioning, it will be shown, as a displaced anus. This metonymy of the body loosens the grip of metaphor, moving away from a logic of substitution towards one of contiguity. It is a poetic device that can be found operating predominantly in works of modern literature, specifically those examined here.

THE BEHIND

In Derek Attridge's introduction to *Acts of Literature* he remarks that Derrida's work is "*more open* to anthologizing and translation than most" (Attridge 1992, x, original emphasis), attesting to a certain slackness or openness within the Derridean text. Could this textual laxity have anything to do with Attridge's confession a page earlier that his selection of material for the anthology "constitutes my singular response, at this particular time, to the many demands – imperious, pleasurable, unfathomable – which Derrida's texts have made on me" (Attridge 1992, x)?

This confession attests to a relation between these two men in which one submits to the imperious, though pleasurable, demands of another. Similarly, Gilles Deleuze claims to have fucked the philosophers whose work he has penetrated. Explaining his process of writing about other thinkers, his strategy for getting them to say something other than what was generally assumed they were saying, Deleuze admits that

> the main way I coped with it at the time was to see the history of philosophy as a sort of buggery or (it

> comes to the same thing) immaculate conception.
> I saw myself as taking an author *from behind* and
> giving him a child that would be his own off-spring,
> yet monstrous. (1995, 6, emphasis added)

Furthermore, could this strategy of taking an author from behind be what Lyotard had in mind when, in *Libidinal Economy*, he prescribes a form of non-dialectical thinking the task of which is to "produce a philosophy of sodomists" (Lyotard 1993, 258)? And what is to be understood by Deleuze's equation of the immaculate conception with buggery?[5]

This notion of philosophy as buggery also appears in Derrida's *The Postcard*, where, contemplating a postcard showing a drawing of Plato standing behind Socrates, who is writing at a desk, Derrida writes,

> I see *Plato* getting an erection in *Socrates*' back and
> see the insane hubris of his prick, an interminable,
> disproportionate erection traversing Paris's head
> like a single idea and then the copyist's chair, before
> slowly sliding, still warm, under *Socrates*' right leg,
> in harmony or symphony with the movement of this
> phallus sheaf, the points, plumes, pens, fingers, nails
> and *grattoirs*, the very pencil boxes which address
> themselves in the same direction. (Derrida 1987, 18)

This sodomitical founding[6] moment of Western thought is something of which Derrida states "I do not know or do not yet want to see" (Derrida 1987, 18), placing this penetrated male body under erasure, characterizing it as a blind spot at the precise moment it comes to view. It is, for Derrida, "a catastrophe, right near the beginning, this overturning that I still cannot succeed in thinking" (Derrida 1987, 19); an "*overturning* and inversion of relations" (Derrida 1987, 22,

---

[5] On this point, see Chapter Three of this book.

[6] Lee Edelman calls this phenomenon of *a posteriori* thought '(be)hindsight', "in order to figure its complicitous involvement in the sodomitical encounter". *Homographesis* (London & New York: Routledge 1994), 176.

emphasis added), moreover, which could be said to be characteristic of his own deconstructive project. *Twice* Derrida refuses or is incapable of thinking such a thought (perhaps because it would involve turning over?) – but he is nonetheless forced to conclude that "there is only the *back*, seen from the back, in what is written, such is the final word. Everything is played out in *retro* and *a tergo*" (Derrida 1987, 48). What is written, it would seem, is written upon our backs, out of sight. This behind thus contours discourse whilst remaining resistant to it.

Writing the behind will be shown to bring into play troubling uncertainties between a whole host of binary oppositions. The multiplicity of language, as the motor of the poetics of the penetrated male body, works towards highlighting this uncertainty lurking behind the seemingly stable structures of discourse. As with Kristeva's 'abject', this instability that Derrida names 'deconstruction' occasions pleasure or *jouissance*: "Deconstruction perhaps has the effect, if not the mission, of liberating forbidden *jouissance*" (Derrida 1992, 56). In this sense, it connects with a utopian project of liberation the aim of which is the destabilization or deconstruction of meta-narratives.

MODERNITY AND THE 'BEHIND'

In many ways, modernity would appear to be the cultural moment or phenomenon most associated with the behind. According to Malcolm Bradbury and James McFarlane, for example, modernism is characterized by a move which aims at "taking us *behind* familiar reality", allowing for "a deeper penetration of life" (Bradbury and McFarlane 1983, 24, 25, emphasis added).[7] Modernism's rejection of the traditional correspondence between language and reality provides the

---

[7] "It has become a commonplace of criticism to argue that modernist literature is about language itself ... *behind* the façade of utility we find another language, which is the real realm of modernity", Allan Stoekl, *Politics, Writing, Mutilation: The Cases of Bataille, Blanchot,*

main route by which this discursive instability occasioned by the penetrated male body will be understood and explored in what follows. This instability is charged with an equally unsettling eroticism. Barthes' essay on Bataille's *Story of the Eye* provides a good example. In attempting to distinguish between the modernity of Bataille and the classicism of the Marquis de Sade, Barthes refers to Bataille's project of "exploring the tremulous quality of a number of objects ... in such a way as to interchange from one to another the functions of obscenity and those of substance", and this is, he believes, "a modern notion of which Sade knew nothing" (Barthes 1979, 126). It allows for what is considered to be obscene to have a substance: to be substantial. According to Barthes, Bataille's method of combining two chains of equivalence – metaphor and metonymy – marks modernity with a deeply unsettling eroticism. Bataille uses eroticism to test the limits of representation. In this way, obscenity is given a substance, and the unthought is thought and carves out a discursive space.

Similarly, the texts analysed in this book will be used to argue that the chains of equivalence which bind the penetrated male body to the feminine paradigm are also responsible for creating a space in which this negativity cannot be completely and securely distinguished from its positive others. This condition of indistinguishability is, for Barthes, characteristic of the distinctly modern notion of "a world become *blurred*", in which "properties are no longer separate" but rather "form a *wavy* meaning" (Barthes 1979, 125, original emphasis). The readings offered in this book aim to demonstrate how such vertiginousness of thought is linked to the vertiginousness of the penetrable male body. What might this abject body reveal about the aspirations of the non-abject body, and beyond that, the difficulties in telling them apart? The behind of discourse and the behind of the male body, it is suggested, are both blind spots to which discourse responds with various strategies, depending upon its character. What this book is terming the behind, in other words, constitutes something which

---

Roussel, Leiris and Ponge (Minneapolis: University of Minnesota Press, 1985), xi (emphasis added).

structures reality whilst at the same time remaining imperceptible. The uncertainty created by this conflict is one that Barthes recognizes as the main characteristic of a certain poetics, producing

> something that could never happen under any circumstances – except, that is, in the shadowy or burning realm of fantasy, which by that very token it alone can indicate. (Barthes 1979, 120)

For Barthes, the realm of fantasy – itself impossible to define ("shadowy or burning"?) – is the poetic space in which uncertainty lurks most visibly. It is a space that is, Barthes suggests, most capable of being indicated within works of imagination, within texts that *work with* the double properties and therefore the ambiguities of language. It is in poetic prose such as that found in *Story of the Eye* that Barthes finds the double workings of metaphor and metonym.[8] Indeed, Barthes argues, "this double property is the necessary and sufficient condition of every paradigm" (Barthes 1979, 120). In combining metonymy and metaphor, by recombining the chains of equivalence within poetic prose of an extremely erotic nature, Bataille manages, according to Barthes, to produce an "open literature out of the reach of all interpretation" (Barthes 1979, 123). It is a literature marked by its poetic capacity, its non-novelistic strategies, and its vigilance to the trajectory of an object rather than – as in the classical novel – subjects or characters.

AN OPEN LITERATURE

The texts analysed might be seen to be part of a similarly open literature – that is, a literature that, in the moment and movement of that uncertainty, attains its *poiesis*. The

---

[8] Barthes maintains the distinctions made by Jakobson, which state that metaphor, as a figure of similarity, is antithetical to metonymy, which is a figure of continuity.

resistance to stable meaning which Barthes finds characteristic of Bataille's novel, and of open literature in general, is part and parcel of poetics as it is being understood here. The play of the imagination beyond or behind the strictures of the binaric codings embedded in language is its primary motor. And it is this play which, in Joyce's *Ulysses* in particular (see Chapter Four), allows for a radical rethinking of the penetrated male body and, beyond that, the male body in general. It constitutes a rethinking which does not rely upon the phallus as the primary signifier of sexual difference, but rather delineates a much more diffuse understanding of (masculine) embodiment.

Julia Kristeva calls it an abject literature, and argues that

> On close inspection, all literature is probably a version of the apocalypse that seems to me rooted, no matter what its socio-historical conditions might be, on the fragile border (borderline cases) where identities (subject/object, etc.) do not exist or only barely so – double, fuzzy, heterogenous, animal, metamorphosed, altered, abject. (Kristeva 1982, 207)

It is, for Kristeva, as for Barthes, specifically within the domain of the imaginary that the abject both lurks most insidiously and takes shape most distinctly ("it is the workings of the imagination whose foundations are being laid here" [Kristeva 1982, 5]). What I am calling an open literature (after Barthes) is to be understood in similar terms. Whilst for Kristeva the abject most often takes the form of the maternal body, however, in this book it will take the form of the penetrated male body.

This book is thus not only concerned with refiguring male penetration in opposition to the negativity that has come to surround it, but, more importantly, with unpicking the discursive implementation of such negativity in the first place. It aims to restate and recharge the political implications of the penetrated male body through a recourse not to a generalized politics of identity or resistance but to a specific poetics of representation by which the entire metaphysical structure of sexual categorization is called into question. It aims to do this by focusing on the revolutionary capabilities of literature, its potential to create a space in which the unsayable can be said, or its unsayability at least remarked upon. Paying close attention to the interchanges of metaphor and metonymy within these texts, the erotic embodiments they offer can be better understood and the writing of the behind be aligned with the poetics outlined above.

The book begins with the case of Daniel Paul Schreber, focusing upon the penetrated male body as a rupture within discourse, and linking that rupture with the penetrated anus. By placing reality so unquestionably on the plane of the fantasmatic, Schreber's *Memoirs of My Nervous Illness* paradoxically throws into relief the extent to which such a position might be inherent in our standard methods of retaining and (re)producing meaning. Whilst not a literary text, it appears here under the aegis of Jean-Jacques Lecercle's claims that Schreber's text is full of the symptoms of a literary strategy in its use of metaphors and similes (Lecercle 1985, 121). The reading offered here, moreover, will show that *Memoirs* is also coded with the poetics described above. Schreber's *Memoirs* reveal a penetrated male body in its most pathologized form: a body that can only register within the protocols of representation as both psychotic and female. That is, the penetrated male body registers as a rupture or a gap within discourse. Schreber's experience of his body as penetrable constitutes a phantasmatical transformation of his sex which occasions a severe psychosis. Chapter One thus delineates the terms by which the remainder of the book will be articulated: namely, that within the protocols of representation, the penetrated male body represents reason's other; that there is a certain madness attendant upon excessive pleasure which links with passivity, submission and femininity. This excess names the meeting place of the body and language, gesturing towards the poetics of which I have spoken earlier. Using the work of Deleuze and Guattari, Foucault and Lacan, this gap or rupture within discourse so named will then be linked to the symbolic function of the anus.

Chapter Two examines other modes of penetrating the male body as they appear in three texts from the last half of the nineteenth century, a period of heightened anxiety over gender norms, as well as heightened experimentation with gender deviance. This chapter will broaden the understanding of the penetrated male body by exploring the limits of its representation. A prose poem by Baudelaire will be shown to focus upon penetration through the eyes, whilst Huysmans' novel *A Rebour* provides an example of the mouth as the orifice through which the taboo against penetrability is breached. Wilde's *Dorian Gray* offers the ear as the most dangerous and productive entry into the male body, for it is through the ear that discourse penetrates and inseminates the listener. The skin becomes a boundary both psychological and physical. In these texts, penetration of the male body is both the occasion of an intense fascination and the necessary condition for the emergence of normative masculine subjectivity. Arguing that the metonymic contiguity of the bodily orifices at work in these texts offers a different reading or poetics of the penetrated male body, this chapter sets the stage for Chapter Three's demonstration of how Jean Genet's direct buckling of the metaphor of the penetrated male body as somehow always already feminine and/or psychotic works through a similar application of these metonyms. I will demonstrate how Genet both accepts and rejects the protocols of representation – through what I call buckling the metaphor. The penetrated male body presented by Genet is explicitly replaced by a female body, only for this replacement to be put to the purpose of debunking its own claims to representation.

Finally, Chapter Four provides an understanding of the penetrated male body that moves beyond binaric logic, locating a space within representation in which the multiplicity of the body appears as a nomadic and discursive fold. The language of Joyce's *Ulysses*, and the representation of the penetrated male body found there, will be shown to occasion a more multi-dimensional sense of the body. Joyce rejects the binary logic of the either/or, articulating instead a multiplicity not reducible to the protocols of representation, but which nevertheless registers its presence through their willful corruption. The scatological link Joyce maintains between the anus and writing complicates the traditional links between anality and death, whilst his presentation of the penetrated male body as an essentially hermaphroditic gesture works against the protocols of representation by which that body must always register as female. Joyce's text, in this sense, performs a logic of the neither/nor by which the penetrated body can be reclaimed from that site of non-contradiction and understood in terms of that estrangement by which the immediacy of life might be sought.

Chapter One

The Madness of the Penetrated Body

> "Everything that's said, expressed, gestured, manifested, assumes its sense only as a function of a response that has to be formulated concerning this fundamentally symbolic relation - *Am I a man, or am I a woman?*"
> - Jacques Lacan, *The Psychoses*

> "After all I too am only a human being and therefore limited by the confines of human understanding"
> - Daniel Paul Schreber, *Memoirs*

> "[W]hat if thought were as much an affair of the skin as of the brain?"
> - Didier Anzieu, *The Skin Ego*

> "How could a discourse based on reason speak of *that*?"
> - Michel Foucault, *History of Sexuality Volume One*

This chapter reads Daniel Paul Schreber's *Memoirs of My Nervous Illness* (1903) to demonstrate the ways in which the penetrated male body registers not only as female but also, and as a consequence, as psychotic. Schreber's psychosis will help set some of the terms of this book by showing his madness to be coterminous with a penetration of the male body which, within late nineteenth century discourse, could only register as female. As such, the reason, or mind, that Schreber claims to have lost is recouped within the terms of his psychosis, which reinscribes the cultural associations of corporeal penetrability with femininity. The body's modern conceptual equivalence with 'woman', and its subsequent polarization from man, are revealed as both highly rigid and highly unstable. Moreover, the underlying sensation to which Schreber's text bears witness is a deeply troubling eroticism, or what he calls voluptuousness. Whilst this voluptuousness or excess is presented within Screber's text as the conceptual opposite of reason/rationality, it nevertheless remains the motor of his discourse, undermining the polarity by which these two concepts adhere. Lacan's notion of the *point de capiton*, or quilting point, will be used to demonstrate how the fixing of meaning and the penetrability of the male body are intertwined, and how the psychosis Schreber experiences is but an extreme form of the processes by which the male subject *means* something within the symbolic order.

Daniel Paul Schreber (1842–1911) suffered two serious mental breakdowns during his adult life, for which he was institutionalized. He worked in the German courts and was successful enough to be appointed *Senatpräsident* or presiding judge of the third chamber of the Supreme Court of Appeals at the age of fifty-one, the youngest man ever to be appointed that position. The first breakdown in 1884 followed his failure to be elected for the National Liberal Party, and his primary symptom was hypochrondria. He spent six months in a clinic run by Dr Paul Flechsig, the same doctor to whom he turned eight years later when his second breakdown occurred, which was also the outcome of a certain failure of his civic role. A month after taking up the prestigious post of *Senatpräsident*, Schreber's anxiety over his ability to perform this task was so great that hospitalization was required again, this time for a period of nine years.

His main symptoms were delusional and paranoid, and were grounded in the belief that, in the words of the medical expert's report:

> he is called to redeem the world and to bring back to mankind the lost state of Blessedness. He maintains he has been given this task by direct divine inspiration. ... The most essential part of his mission of redemption is that it is necessary for him first of all to be transformed into a woman. (Cited in Schreber 1988, 272)

Such transformation was to be achieved by an act of divine penetration, to keep it within what Schreber called the Order of the World. The fact that beyond his own mad cosmology such transformation was *not* within the order of things, but the sign of a radical psychosis, tells us as much about that order – its limits, its laws and strictures – as it does about Schreber's madness.

Upon his release in 1902, Schreber began writing *Memoirs of My Nervous Illness*, based on the notes he had been keeping since 1897. It was published in 1903, and Carl Jung gave Freud a copy in the summer of 1910. Freud published his own interpretation of the Schreber case the following year, the year Schreber died.

Schreber's text is exemplary here for a variety of reasons. Its central anxiety over gender identity, for example, allows us to explore the radical division between the public domain of masculinity and the private domain of femininity.[9] Schreber's text holds a unique position as Freud's only case history to emerge from a purely textual analysis, for Freud never actually met his patient. The *Memoirs*' ambiguous status as a hybrid text can be seen in declared confusion over the epistemological role it claims to play. It is Christian confessional and scientific case study at once; a hybrid of the religious and the sexological such as gave birth to the modern *scientia sexualis* under whose rubric the desiring subject has subsequently come to be almost universally understood (Foucault 1990, 18–25). Schreber considered his text to be "of value both for science and the knowledge of religious truths" (Schreber 1988, 31). Science and

---

[9] Today, his diagnosis may well be gender disphoria, and he would possibly identify as trans; he might even transition.

religion meet at this ambivalent juncture where their two axes cross, forming a limit that contours the language of Schreber's discourse.

The gendered implications of Schreber's psychosis make the penetrated male body both appear and disappear. In this sense, it is a limit experience, provoking the loss of that body even as it shows it in its starkest light.

Finally, the work of Lacan, Foucault and Deleuze and Guattari will provide the means by which this rupture of discourse and the holes of the male body – specifically the anus – can be linked and understood as a significant expression of something often deemed unspeakable: namely, men's penetrability or corporeal openness.

THE PARADOX OF MODERNITY

As both high court judge *and* certified lunatic, Schreber embodies – and his text mirrors – a profound uncertainty about the Law through which his words make sense, and not only or most importantly to himself. It is the Law not as merely a set of codes of punishment based on a classical understanding of what constitutes the Best for society, but the Law as a moral structure grounded in itself. According to Deleuze, this is a distinctly modern notion of The Law, by which "the object of the law is by definition unknowable and elusive" (1991, 83). As such, "the law cannot specify its object without self-contradiction, nor can it define itself with reference to a content without removing the repression on which it rests" (Deleuze 1991, 85). It will be shown in Chapter Three, in relation to Genet, that this form of the Law is best understood through transgression.

Schreber's text signals, and bridges, the radical demarcation of the private domain and the public domain, and does so through an emphasis on their highly gendered structuration. The text blurs those boundaries: there is no definitive or clear-cut division between 'judge' and 'madman', for when does one end and the other begin? How much of the latter was latent in the former? In this sense, madness is not simply reason's 'other'. Schreber's *Memoirs*, after all, were presented as evidence of his sanity to a court who subsequently released him from the asylum, a fact that is in no way diminished by its eventual fate as a statement of profound psychosis, but rather broadens the problematic of the text in fascinating and as yet unexplored ways. What is it then that the *Memoirs* can tell us, not simply about the status of language within modernity, but also its gendered limitations, its connections to the body, its mappings of a space 'outside' reason which, at the same time, casts into relief certain aspects of reason? For how can one and the same text be exemplary of both the reasoning mind and a profound loss of it? Or, in Foucault's words, "which syntax functions *at the same time* on the level of declared meaning *and* on that of interpreted signification?" (Foucault 1998, 8, original emphasis). Further: in what ways is this epistemological uncertainty associated with or correlated to the vicissitudes of the flesh? The central concern, then, will be how the Schreber case might aid the examination of the epistemological currency of certain concepts – such as 'submission', 'power', 'madness', 'reason' – in the light of their implicit associations with concepts such as 'man' and 'woman', and what role the penetrated male body plays in both consolidating and breaking these associations.

In Eric L. Santner's study of Schreber, it is claimed that Schreber's psychosis demonstrates

> what may very well be the central paradox of modernity: that the subject is solicited by a will to autonomy in the name of the very community that is thereby undermined, whose very substance thereby passes over into the subject. (Santner 1996, 145)

In Santner's account of modernity, communality is, paradoxically, undermined by autonomy. The subject appears through an appropriation of the community's "very substance". This substance *enters into* the subject in order that the subject can *be* at all. As such, Immanuel Kant's definition of Enlightenment as a break away from submissive tutelage and the development of self-reflexivity or autonomy (Kant 1959, 85) is incompatible with those symbolic resources by which the social hegemony legitimizes itself, such as law, monarchy or state. The social requires conformity to those symbolic resources in the manner of a submission to their efficacy, to the exact extent that autonomy, or Kantian Enlightenment, if achieved at all, would paradoxically undermine the social by bringing those very resources under scrutiny.

It has been well-documented how the rise of a 'private self' at the start of the nineteenth century threw into disarray the coherence of a 'public self'. As Peter Gay points out in his study of what he calls that century's "effort to map inner space" (1998, 4), the production of the modern self has led to a situation in which "the individual's imperious desires and the needs of civilisation are usually at odds" (1998, 9). There is thus a radical conflict – perhaps an incompossibility – between the impulse to be one's own person and one's duty to the societal whole, one's submission to a leader/Law. Heteronomy versus autonomy. Indeed, modernity, as Santner understands it, is precisely this conflict.

Given the highly gendered character of this public/private division, and given the tropes of submission to male rule implicit in this paradox, it is clear that for men becoming a subject inevitably involves an inescapable, though unarticulated, moment of homosexual panic[10]: can one submit to another man without losing one's manhood? The paradox of submitting to another male (God, King, *Führer*, etc.) versus 'being a man', i.e., self-governing, self-sufficient, and independent. It is a clearly profound conflict centring on the question of how to be individual (oneself) and also *an* individual (part of

---

[10] The phrase 'homosexual panic' is from Eve Sedgwick, *Between Men: English Literature and Male Homosocial Desire* (New York: Columbia University Press, 1985), where it refers to that equivocal moment where the socially drawn line between being a man's man and being interested in men becomes dangerously blurred (89). In Santner's analysis of Schreber, he uses the term to describe Freud's interpretation of Schreber's breakdown. See Eric L. Santner, *My Own Private Germany: Daniel Paul Schreber's Secret History of Modernity* (Princeton, New Jersey: Princeton University Press, 1996), 17.

a community). How to submit whilst remaining dominant? How to negotiate the symbolic order without conforming to it through a submission it demands or necessitates? The gender implications of this conflict inevitably raise the question of masculine submission, as it functions at/as the very foundation of modern masculinity.

SUBMISSIVE MASCULINITY

The concept of submission has been gendered more or less explicitly since at least the end of the nineteenth century within terms by which women submit and men dominate. The reversal of this model within *fin-de-siècle* male masochist fantasies, whilst undoubtedly challenging the naturalization of these terms, nevertheless retains the symmetry of its gendered structuration: the woman takes on the 'male' role of domination, the man the 'female' role of submission, the latter occasioning, as will be demonstrated later in Chapter Three, both a fascinating *jouissance* and an abject terror. In short, submission is always conceptualized as 'feminine', domination as 'masculine'. Moreover, submission is always conflated with passivity, whilst domination is conflated with activity. For a man to submit to patriarchy – to the father/leader – is to make himself passive, and that concept in turn, as we know, is often coded as feminine. Therefore, for a man to submit to a masculinist discourse is to render himself in some sense 'female' within the terms of the symbolic order that equate femininity with submission. A dilemma in the form of a paradox lies at the heart of that which is all too often considered most comprehensively stable.

Santner argues that this process of conformity by which the subject emerges within discourse acts not upon the mind but upon the body as the site of the performative command. Thus he argues:

> The (repetitive) demand to live in conformity with the social essence with which one has been invested, and thus *to stay on the proper side of a socially consecrated*

> *boundary*, is one that is addressed not only or even
> primarily to the mind or intellect, but to the body.
> (Santner 1998, 12, original emphasis)

However, whilst the body may well be the most significant reminder of which side of that socially consecrated boundary called gender one belongs and must remain, it is within the *mind* that that command circulates endlessly, that is, it is within discourse. Therefore, Foucault sees the primary target of the discursive command as the mind, not the body – or rather the body *through* the mind/mind *through* the body. In *Discipline and Punish* Foucault argues that the change in juridical punishment from execution to incarceration expresses a shift in discursive strategies of control that direct power's attention away from the body and onto the mind:

> It is no longer the body, with the ritual play of
> excessive pains, spectacular brandings in the ritual
> of the public execution; it is the mind or rather a play
> of representations and signs circulating discreetly
> but necessarily and evidently in the minds of all.
> (Foucault 1985, 101)

Whilst those signs circulate inside our minds, however, they nevertheless find their most visual expression on the body. Foucault insists on an inseparability of the two, arguing, in "Nietzsche, Genealogy, History" that:

> The body manifests the stigmata of past experience
> and also gives rise to desires, failings and errors.
> These elements may join in a body where they achieve
> a sudden expression, but as often, their encounter is
> an engagement in which they efface each other, where
> the body becomes the pretext of their insurmount-
> able conflict. (Foucault 1998b, 375)

For Foucault, the mind and the body are equally involved in the discursive project of subject formation – indeed the former is manifested through the latter. The body is, he claims, the pretext of this conflict of interests. The multiplicity of discourse renders the reproduction of the status quo, or the order of things, not only incomplete but radically so. The body is the site upon which these conflicts play themselves out:

> The body is the inscribed surface of events (traced by language and dissolved by ideas), the locus of a dissociated Self (adopting the illusion of a substantial unity), and a volume in perpetual disintegration.
> (Foucault 1977, 148)

Between the specifically disciplinary command to have a body and the actual sensations of the body lies a space which, for men at least, is the cause of great anxiety. That command is a highly disciplinary silencing, a denial of those sensations and a blanket refusal to concede that they play any role in our experience of knowledge: as a man, one must not 'know' one's own body. It is thus a space in which the male body vanishes if the command is to be obeyed; that is, if the body is to signify as male at all. Social bodies of men – those institutions that have tended to uphold a belief in objectivity and reason as the only reliable forms of knowledge – therefore retain and perpetuate that very domination which must be abdicated on the individual level by submission to the laws of the group upon entry to it. These laws allow that individual to exist, to signify, only so long as they are strictly followed. To be a man is to discipline and dominate the culturally coded 'private' domain of the body and its sensations. 'Manhood' is the prize bestowed upon successful completion of this task. For the sake of self-preservation, masculinity is performed, and such performativity, as Judith Butler argues, constitutes its claim to essence (Butler 1990).

Such mimicry for the sake of self-preservation, however, is a highly unstable process, for the Law contains within its performativity a necessary repetition in constant danger of mutating, of producing an alternative that, through a form of symbolic excommunication, constitutes the greatest challenge to its unquestioned immutability. In this respect, Schreber provides a unique focal point for this discursive instability, being at once judge and madman, both in the law and out of it.

Because Schreber's words were generated in a lunatic asylum, and not a court of law, the location of his discourse serves to highlight the limits of a knowledge co-opted for the justification of patriarchy and social domination. As Schreber himself remarks, "what can be more definite for a human being than what he has lived through and felt on his own body?" (Schreber 1988, 99n). Yet because his *Memoirs* served to prove in court that his powers of reasoning were intact they must in some way uphold the very thing they threaten most of all: Reason. For how can the same text, the same language, be both a cry of madness and a plea for sanity?

To recap, male subjectivity is only intelligible – paradoxically – through a penetrability it cannot subsequently concede, but must actively avoid if it is to retain its masculine status. As such, the body's inherent penetrability is overcome by a performative disembodiment promoted through the will to knowledge and achieved through the domination of, and distancing from, nature (as Other/woman/body). The skin thus functions as an epistemological limit, even in the most phantasmatic journeyings beyond it. The body is tamed and contained by a logic of the skin that embeds sexual difference within the very mappings of its surface.

THE SKIN EGO

In *The Ego and the Id* (1923), Freud attempts to trace the formation of the ego as "first and foremost a bodily ego" (Freud 1986, 451); that is, "not merely a surface entity, but ... itself the projection of a surface". In a footnote added in 1927, Freud further explains that

> the ego is ultimately derived from bodily sensations, chiefly from those springing from the surface of the body. It may thus be regarded as a mental projection of the surface of the body, besides...representing the superficies of the mental apparatus. (1986, 451)

It is worth recalling here that for Freud "the ego represents what may be called reason and common sense, in contrast to the id, which contains the passions" (Freud 1986, 450). The commonsensical ego battles with the irrational id, coding bodily sensation according to symbolic mandates which gender the conflict. These codes become codes of conduct, permitting or prohibiting what the body can do. For example, Freud characterizes Schreber's psychosis as a conflict between a "feminine phantasy" of passivity and a "masculine protest" against it (Freud 1977). For him, Schreber's paranoia is a refusal to recognize his homosexual desire to submit to another man. Homosexual desire becomes, in Freud's reading, coded as a desire to be a woman, placing Freud's analysis within the tradition of late nineteenth-century sexological theories of homosexuality as a third sex. The main problem, however, is that the gravitational pull of Freud's analysis is towards a direct correspondence between Schreber's life and the work of his *Memoirs*, a correspondence which will shortly be challenged.

The French psychoanalyst Didier Anzieu develops Freud's insights into ego-formation as bodily projection into what he calls a 'skin ego'. The skin ego, Anzieu argues, is

> a reality of the order of phantasy: it figures in phantasies, dreams, everyday speech, posture and disturbances of thought; and it provides the imaginary space on which phantasies, dreams, thinking and every form of psychopathological organization are constituted. ... The Skin Ego is an intermediate structure of the psychical apparatus. (Anzieu 1989, 4)

The skin ego refuses the Cartesian opposition between the mind and the body; it is an interface between the body as object and the mind as subject, a psychic map of sensations, of one's experience of one's own body and its place in the world, its relation to itself and things external to it, out of which thought is generated. If it is also a space of psychopathology, it must therefore represent a rupture between the world 'out there' and the inner organization of the subject.

According to psychoanalysis, the ego has no prior status, but emerges, is constructed, from experience, sensation or consciousness. Yet the ego must make sense of these sensations within the rubric of a symbolic mandate which insists on sexual differentiation as a decisive factor in the interpretation and articulation of bodily cognition. The ego must answer the question – and not only once – of whether the 'I' through which it expresses itself is male or female, for, as Lacan states in the first epigraph above, the question of gender is the basis of all meaningful expression within the symbolic order. As such, the answer to the question *Am I a man, or am I a woman?* functions as the ground for all meaning, making it function also as a limit – a limit which is also a rupture. For, finding an adequate answer to that question presupposes that the concepts 'man' and 'woman' are mutually exclusive absolutes and that locating oneself at one of those poles immediately and necessarily cancels out the possibility of being at the other: If I am a man, it is because I am not a woman, and *vice versa*.

Significantly, answering this question only serves the purposes of the symbolic order, for "[i]n the psyche there is nothing by which the subject may situate himself [*sic*] as a male or female being" (Lacan 1986, 204). The psyche, for Lacan, is radically inept when it comes to categorizing itself, be it within the rubric of gender dimorphism or otherwise. It is only in the symbolic order, only in relation to its Other, that is, only in language, that the subject emerges as an 'I' *and simultaneously* genders that 'I' as 'male' or 'female' – positions which Lacan maintains do not naturally or necessarily correspond to the biological categories which go by those same names. Nevertheless, they do name for him a relation to sexual reproduction which equates the polarity of the 'male' with that of activity and the polarity of the 'female' with that of passivity (Lacan 1986, 204). For Lacan anything passive is symbolically meaningful only as 'female', however disassociated from 'woman' that concept may be in his libidinal economy. So, whilst he breaks the biological or anatomical link between 'female' and 'woman', he nevertheless remains bound by the cultural associations that form a chain of equivalence linking the concept of 'female' with the concept of 'passivity'.

As the epigraph from Schreber suggests, however, the limit imposed by such seemingly necessary absolutism also implies a 'beyond' (or behind) for which no answers can as yet be found, a 'something' in excess of the answer itself, something in excess, that is, of being a 'man' or a 'woman'. For to answer that question is only ever to locate a limit to the event of masculinity or femininity, and therefore to reinscribe the very logic by which such an answer is provided.

Whilst Anzieu does not specifically address the question of gender in his work,[11] Klaus Theweleit's analyses of the formation of the ego of the soldier, to which this chapter will soon turn, will provide an opportunity to explore the ways in which, for men, the skin often functions as a barrier against the knowable, penetrable body. As Anzieu argues, the skin is "the interface which marks the boundary with the outside and keeps that outside out; it is the barrier which *protects against penetration*" (Anzieu 1989, 40, emphasis added). But what happens when the transgression of that boundary is experienced as pleasurable? What happens when such penetration, far from being guarded against, is instead desired – when, for example, the thought occurs to a man, as it did to Schreber, that "it really must be rather pleasant to be a woman succumbing to intercourse" (Schreber 1988, 63)? Schreber's *Memoirs* provides one answer to this question, from which much can be extrapolated.

DIVINE PENETRATION

In November 1893, just after taking up the post of the highest judicial office in Germany, Schreber embarked on a nine year period of institutionalization in mental hospitals for believing that not only was he the only man left alive, but that in order

---

[11] For this reason Judith Butler foregoes serious discussion of Anzieu's work in *Gender Trouble* (New York and London: Routledge, 1990), 163, n43.

to repopulate the planet, God had to transform Schreber into a woman and impregnate him (her?). Several months before the onslaught of his psychosis, Schreber recalls having the following experience:

> One morning while still in bed (whether still half asleep or already awake I cannot remember), I had a feeling which, thinking about it later when fully awake, struck me as highly peculiar. It was the idea that it really must be rather pleasant to be a woman succumbing to intercourse. (Schreber 1988, 63)

This lazy, hazy, half-dream of sexual submission occurs within and establishes a limit: a border zone between the unconscious state of sleep and the conscious state of wakefulness. Whilst submission is clearly aligned with 'woman', its contemplation provokes ambiguity, instability, forgetfulness ("whether still half asleep or already awake I cannot remember"). An idea considered "highly peculiar" when revisited in the cold light of day was, within the relative safety of a dream-like state, thought "rather pleasant". This zone, this 'dream', has been isolated by Freud as the cause and origin of the *Senatpräsident*'s mental breakdown, and is interpreted by him as a simple homosexual wish-fulfilment, which he derives from Schreber's delusional belief in his becoming a woman.

In his study on Schreber, Freud's interpretation unfolds within the hermetically sealed domain of the *Memoirs*, treating it as a kind of psychobiography, mapping a direct and straightforward point for point correspondence between Schreber's life and his text. As Foucault points out in an essay on Hölderin, however:

> this approach, pursued to the very heart of madness, is based on the assumption that the meaning of a work, its themes and specific domain, can be traced to a series of events whose details are known to us. The question posed by this non-conceptual eclecticism, as it derives from 'clinical' psychology, is whether a chain of significations can be formed to link, without discontinuity or rupture, an individual

life to a life's work, events to words, and the mute
forms of madness to the most essential aspects of a
poem. (Foucault 1998b, 7)

Whilst Schreber is clearly no poet – which, according to Elias Canetti, prevents us from being completely seduced by his words (Canetti 1973, 505) – his text, nevertheless, remains in some sense 'poetic'. As Jean Jacques Lecercle points out, Schreber's use of metaphors and similes marks his text with the symptoms of literary strategy, its linguistic techniques the same as those identifiable within many works of fiction (Lecercle 1985, 121). As such, Schreber's imaginative engagement with and articulation of his own 'reality' can be explored in order to work against such adequation as Freud attempts. An exploration of its ruptures and discontinuities throws up a very different picture.

For, as the citation from Foucault suggests, it is possible that instead of a direct correspondence between the work and the life out of which it was produced, there exists another, more complex, trajectory marked by discontinuities and ruptures. On this other path, madness and discourse collide in order to produce a text as a kind of excess: a phantasmatical space not dissimilar to what Anzieu calls the skin ego. To offer but one example, Freud interprets the figure of God in Schreber's delirium as a displacement of Schreber's first doctor, Flechsig, who is in turn a displaced father figure. In other words, in order to 'make sense' of Schreber's psychosis, Freud Oedipalizes him, embroidering a point-for-point correspondence between the events of his life and the manifestations of his illness (Freud thus makes much of the early death of Schreber's father). But there exists, Foucault suggests, for those who follow this mode of interpretation "*without being taken in by it*, a different discourse", one that "no language could have expressed outside of the abyss that engulfs it" (Foucault 1998b, 7, emphasis added). For Foucault, there *is* a connection between the work and the person that produced it, but this connection appears as a rupture, a space of non-correspondence or nonidentity, and is not ultimately accessible via the biographical facts of that person's life. Nor is it reducible to them. It is not that the father's absence creates a psychosis out of which language emerges, Foucault argues, but that the father was never there in the first place, making language the bearer of a finitude that cannot be endured (Foucault 1998b, 16).

Canetti also rejects the psychoanalytic approach. For him, Freud's focus on paranoia as a result of repressed homosexuality is the greatest mistake made within studies of Schreber (Canetti 1973, 522). For Canetti, "the central point of his system was the attack on his reason" (Canetti 1973, 522–3). Schreber's anxiety over being turned into a woman equates here not with repressed homosexual desire but with loss of reason. As a result, Canetti is able to see Schreber's paranoid relationship to God as indicative of that wider cultural paranoia which culminated in National Socialism. In a similar manner, Santner reads the *Memoirs* as a precursor for Hitler's *Mein Kampf*, teasing out the similarities in both texts: their delusions of a calling to a higher purpose and their obsessions with decomposition and rot. He describes Schreber's text as "a work drawing on the very phantasms that would, after the traumas of war, revolution, and the end of empire, coalesce into the core elements of National Socialist ideology" (Santner 1998, ix).

Furthermore, Canetti's analysis also recognizes the role played by penetration in Schreber's paranoia, something not discussed by Freud. For Canetti, Schreber's penetrability is crucial, in that it brings together the various points of his delusional system: "they all have to do with the *penetration* of his body", he writes (Canetti 1973, 536, original emphasis). He further argues that as a consequence:

> The principle of impenetrability of matter no longer applies. Just as he himself wants to extend and penetrate everywhere, even right through the earth, so, in the same way, everything penetrates through him and plays tricks *in* him as well as on him. He often speaks of himself as though he were a celestial body, but he is not even sure of his ordinary human body. The period of his extension, the very time in which he was asserting his claims, seems also to

> have been the period of his penetrability. For him
> *greatness* and *persecution* are intimately connected,
> and both are expressed through his body. (Canetti
> 1973, 536, original emphasis)

The more Schreber's body is penetrated, then, the less sure he is of its existence, its status – the more celestial or immaterial it becomes. As this penetration is resulting in a transformation into a woman, we can say that it results in a heightened femininity within Schreber. Equally, argues Canetti, however, the more Schreber is persecuted through such penetration the *greater* he imagines he has become through the effort of enduring it. There is in Schreber's *Memoirs* a clear and vital ambiguity around penetration, a kind of masochistic thrill at overcoming its threat. It is not unlike the ambiguity around bodily penetration found in the writings of the German *Freikorps* which Klaus Theweleit analysed in his two-volume work *Male Fantasies*. A brief look at Theweleit's work will help clarify this relation being traced between masculinity, the symbolic order and a fear of (an always already perpetrated) penetration.

MALE FANTASIES

The *Freikorps* were a group of self-appointed vigilante soldiers in Wilhelmine Germany, who, refusing to abdicate their military status at the end of World War I, went around suppressing workers' revolts in the brutal manner of a war. Through close readings of these soldiers' private and public writings, Theweleit has identified certain recurring attitudes towards women, bodies, masses – attitudes of disgust, fear and murderous hatred. That such feelings cannot be neatly restricted to the geographical and historical specificities of Theweleit's primary texts has been noted by at least one reviewer: in the *New York Times Book Review*, Paul Robinson remarks that they are, rather, "the common property of bourgeois males – and perhaps non-bourgeois males as well" (cited in Benjamin and Rabinach 1989, xiv). Similarly, Barbara Ehrenreich argues in her foreword to volume one, that

> Theweleit refuses to draw a line between the fantasies of the Freikorpsmen and the psychic ramblings of the 'normal' man: and I think here of the man who feels a 'normal' level of violence toward women (as in, 'I'd like to fuck her to death') ... the man who has a 'normal' distaste for sticky, unseen 'feminine functions' ... the man who loves women, as 'normal' men do, but sees a castrating horror in every expression of female anger ... or that entirely normal, middle-class citizen who simply prefers that women be absent from the public life of work, decisions, war. Here Theweleit does not push, but he certainly leaves open the path from the 'inhuman impulse' of fascism to the most banal sexism. (1987, xv)

There is, in other words, a continuum established in Theweleit's argument between "ordinary male fantasy and its violent counterpart" (Benjamin and Rabinbach 1989, xiv). As Arthur W. Frank comments, Theweleit's text "both expands its concerns and decenters its specificity" (Frank 1996, 70). So what does Theweleit's analysis offer in terms of understanding that continuum and its workings within culture?

Theweleit demonstrates that the aspects of the body that are rendered fearful and thereby in need of control by the Freikorps are the flows of desire, the genitals, the anus and its flow of shit; all these threaten the impenetrably armoured body of the soldier, both within and without, with the result that

> The soldier male is forced to turn the periphery of his body into a cage for the beast within. In so doing, he deprives it of its function as a surface for social contact. His contact surface becomes an insulated shield, and he loses the capacity to perceive the social corpus within which his insulated body moves. (Theweleit 1989, 22)

The skin has become a shield, and social contact has been forfeited. This insulation is dangerous, for it removes the soldier from the social corpus. For the soldier, inhabiting the body is to remove it as an organ of the senses that can be opened up onto a reality that is shared with others. As Mary Douglas (1984) has shown, matter that flows from the body is often perceived as dangerous because of its transgression of boundaries. The bodily interior is experienced by the soldier as a dangerous mass that must be contained, just as the social mass becomes a threatening force that must be defeated, and both battles require exacting military strategies. Indeed, the two struggles are in reality one and the same battle, for "the terrain of their rage is always at the same time their own body" (Theweleit 1987, 233). Theweleit writes of the soldier: "the arena of war is first and foremost his own body; a body poised to penetrate other bodies and mangle them in its embrace" (1989, 191). A body, that is, incapable of acknowledging its own penetrability. A 'male' body.

BECOMING A MAN

The process begins early, in the military academy, where the young soldier's body is continuously on display during its reconstruction: "Withdrawal is impossible, since there is no place to retreat to" (Theweleit 1989, 144). Constant surveillance plays a crucial role in maintaining the vigilance of this bodily numbing. Punishment for a break in this vigilance is always oriented exclusively on the body, which is treated as something that must be broken before it can be made stronger. In order to survive, the young cadet inevitably develops a "thick skin" which Theweleit warns us not to read metaphorically.

> And little by little the body accepts these painful interventions along its periphery as responses to its longing for pleasure. It receives them as experiences of satisfaction. The body is estranged from the pleasure principle, drilled and reorganized into a

> body ruled by the 'pain principle': what is nice is what hurts ... (1989, 150)

A kind of masochism, then, is the consequence of such training, a channeling of the need for pleasure into a need for pain: a pain to be endured, overcome, transcended, as proof positive that the body can – indeed, must – be dominated. This is at the heart of becoming a soldier. The cadet found incapable of such transcendence is labelled a 'sissy', feminized through his inability to submit his body to the requirements of the military machine. In this environment, remaining within, and therefore at the mercy of, the body's innate vulnerability is a pejorative and feminine trait, with the result that the soldier "organizes his own struggle for survival as a direct onslaught on femininity" (Theweleit 1989, 279). As a consequence of this detachment from or erasure of the body, however, the capacity for pleasure is also purged. "Pleasure, with its hybridizing qualities, has the dissolving effect of a chemical enzyme on the armored body" (Theweleit 1989, 7). Pleasure itself becomes pejoratively feminine. Discipline is thus, as Foucault argues, an "anti-nomadic technique", primarily aimed at fixing, for "that which moves brings death, and one kills that which moves" (Foucault 1985, 205, 218).

The individual who emerges from this process is finely tuned to a certain corporeal and emotional anaesthesia – drilled to be part of a machine that is built to last, to succeed, to win (Theweleit 1989, 159). His only equals are those other components of the war machine, and "all others belong only 'under' him – never alongside, behind, or in front" (Theweleit 1989, 160). To become this 'man of steel', the soldier must construct an armour to protect him from his own flesh, from the flows of shit, urine, blood, sperm and desire that threaten to dissolve his boundaries. His most urgent task is "to pursue, to dam in, and to subdue any force that threatens to transform him back into the horribly disorganized jumble of flesh, hair, skin, bones, intestines, and feelings that calls itself human" (Theweleit 1989, 160).

Self-discipline thus becomes a relationship of dominance over one's own bodily flows predicated on the denial of their existence. All of the body's openings must be clammed shut against the threat of pleasure, but most significantly, it is the anus that becomes the site of greatest anxiety. Theweleit argues that

> the closing of the anus and the negativization of excrement play a crucial part in the damming-in of bodily flows in general. The anus, the ultimate sluice, remains persistently hidden. (Theweleit 1989, 312)

In other words, in order to function as a soldier-machine, the anus must become associated with what is hidden but must nevertheless be controlled; what lurks behind, unseen, but which still requires a certain vigilance. This will become more significant shortly, in the discussion of Lacan's quilting point. For now it is enough to note how quickly the anus and the closing down of the entire male body can become so intimately related.

In order to maintain control of this orifice, and thus, according to the logic being traced here, all of the body's flows, the whole of the soldier's body must become, Theweleit stresses, "*intensely absent*" (1987, 203, original emphasis). It must be "locked from itself, a terrible secret" (Theweleit 1989, 197); and "must not become familiar, 'known'; it must be an object and source of fear" (Theweleit 1987, 414). Fear of the body's openings leads the soldier male to abandon his body, and "his abandoned body becomes the burden he lays on the shoulders of his colonized victims" (Theweleit 1989, 418), and, once there, it is mercilessly persecuted. For to kill becomes the only pleasure permitted to the soldier, and Theweleit catalogues example after example of *Freikorps* accounts of the pleasure of killing, concluding from this that they "seem less to possess a sexuality than to persecute sexuality itself – one way or another" (1989, 61). They persecute sexual pleasure, *jouissance*, and the lack of control such a state threatens to produce, albeit through an act which brings, for them, its own form of pleasure: murder. The soldier, Theweleit writes, "desires to move beyond himself, bullet-like, toward an object that he penetrates" (1989, 179).

If sexuality is what is persecuted then, it is as the soldier's 'other', an external menace represented by the body of the other, an elsewhere that threatens the stability of the individual soldier. The soldier's own body is purged of sexuality, its erogenous zones cordoned off, deadened. For these men, the body individuates by a closure which renders it isolate and impenetrable.

Through what Santer calls 'corporeal mnemotechnics' the body becomes invested with a performative duty to stay on the right side of the Law by always and repeatedly remembering to do the right thing. That the 'right thing' for the male body to do is remain paranoically impenetrable is apparent not only in the Schreber case, where recognition of the body as a site of penetrability functions to erase its masculinity and construct instead a female body; but Theweleit's study identifies a similar logic in the writings of the *Freikorps*. The penetrated *male* body in each case becomes something unrepresentable, in excess of a logic within which it cannot register.

In order to understand more fully the notions of discipline, penetration and masculine embodiment being delineated here, the next section considers Schreber's early life. What kind of skin ego did he have, and what part did a disciplinary experience not dissimilar to that of the young cadet play in creating the conflict to which his psychosis bears witness?

SCHREBER'S CHILDHOOD

The chapter of the *Memoirs* in which Schreber provided an account of his early life was censored from the published text, and has never been found. William G. Niederland's research into the writings of Schreber's father, however, provide some evidence of what that early life must have been like. Schreber senior was a doctor, an orthopaedic specialist and a zealous pioneer of physical culture and health, whose books went through many reprints. To Schreber junior, his voice must have appeared like the word of God. Dr Schreber's work focused almost exclusively on childhood bodily discipline, from the age of only a few months. Niederland has traced some of Schreber's miracles directly to the experiences undergone in his childhood at the hands of his father, who placed both sons in contraptions aimed at preventing spinal and bodily deformities, obsessed as he was with correct posture. And whilst such point for point interpretation of the work via the life might be open to question, it is clear from Niederland's study that the two Schreber boys were forced "into a state of complete submission and passive surrender" by their father (Niederland 1984, 57). The psychosexual element of this submission is indicated, for Niederland, in the obsessive prevention of masturbation underlying Dr Schreber's disciplinary techniques (Niederland 1984, 73).

Given the widespread influence of Schreber senior's publications concerning the discipline of children, Schreber junior's response in adulthood to such discipline may only be an extreme version of the more general outcome of the surveillance of childhood sexuality, linking it with the procedures of power and technologies of health and pathology about which Foucault has written (Foucault 1990, 44, 47). This disciplining of the family is linked to a more general disciplining of society. Indeed, Niederland cites at least one commentator who has seen in Dr Schreber's beliefs a "sort of spiritual precursor of Nazism" (cited in Niederland 1984, 65). It is unsurprising, then, that the son's publication would provoke similar comments.

In the *Memoirs*, Schreber receives instructions from God's rays such as "do not think about certain parts of your body" (Schreber 1988, 141), pointing to a disciplinary strategy against which Schreber's mental illness can be seen as an extreme but perhaps inevitable response to the command for masculine disembodiment. For it was, significantly, a discipline spared the female offspring of Schreber senior, who, by all accounts, "apparently remained well" (Niederland 1984, 62). Given that Schreber's elder brother committed suicide and Schreber himself went mad and attempted suicide more than once, the efficacy of such discipline is highly questionable, to say the least.

The skin ego produced in such a climate of early bodily trauma will inevitably be one in which the skin's primary function to guard against penetration is seen as faulty. The skin becomes the site of a rupture rather than a barrier, the ego always already entered, submissive and passive. In such a climate, the body itself becomes a mode of collapse. Becoming female must have seemed to the young Schreber a means of escape from the tortures visited upon the male body. For both Schreber boys, eradicating the body – one literally, the other phantasmatically – was the only way out of an intolerable situation.

The young Schreber must have experienced his own skin as a battleground, as a highly invasive and fungible organ capable of registering both good and bad sensations. For as Niederland points out, Dr. Schreber insisted on the importance of performing his disciplinary techniques *"in a manner pleasurable and enjoyable to the child"* (Niederland 1984, 73, emphasis added). The skin's capacity to mediate or negotiate experience becomes highly unstable, and submission itself becomes dangerously pleasurable.

To cite only one example of the skin's ambiguity for Schreber, he refers to the softness of his skin as positive proof that he is becoming a woman (Schreber 1988, 94, 206). This perceived feminine status is contingent upon and mediated by the sensations of the skin, a multi-layered phenomenon by which the past (memory) is projected onto the future as the horizon or limit of all that can be. As Anzieu writes,

> The Skin Ego is the original parchment which preserves, like a palimpsest, the erased, scratched-out, written-over first outlines of an 'original' pre-verbal writing made up of traces upon the skin.
> (Anzieu 1989, 105)

For Schreber, those traces were ambiguous, both punitive and enjoyable. For him, the male body was a source of pleasurable sensations, a site of penetrability, that had to be forgotten in order to be represented – and it was represented, within his text as within discourse more generally, as both female and psychotic. He could not 'picture' his body – could not describe it – other than as a body being transformed into its apparent opposite. The skin as a surface open to both pleasure and rupture could not register as male for Schreber, nor for the culture in which his text 'makes sense', except as a moment of psychosis. If his body can only register as the 'other' of itself (i.e., female), then his language can only register as the 'other' of reason (i.e., madness). This registration or representation is a process of what Kristeva calls abjection, "a vortex of summons and repulsion" that "places the one haunted by it literally beside himself" (Kristeva 1982, 1). The abject is not an object, but a process, a movement by which fascination and terror become satellites of desire; it "simultaneously beseeches and pulverizes the subject" (Kristeva 1982, 5). Someone undergoing such a procedure, Kristeva argues, "presents himself with his own body and ego as the most precious non-objects; they are no longer seen in their own right but forfeited, abject" (Kristeva 1982, 5). Through this abjection, Schreber's body is "ejected beyond the scope of the possible, the tolerable, the thinkable" (Kristeva 1982, 1), and drawn "toward a place where meaning collapses" (Kristeva 1982, 2). The protocols of representation no longer hold true, co-ordinates become scrambled, and binary logic breaks down.

That Schreber's manhood was part and parcel of his reason, so that losing one meant losing the other, suggests that the gendered structurations of language are so inbuilt within the Western discourse of subjectivity that to refuse them or question them is to cease to be in any traditional sense 'rational' or 'reasonable' – i.e., to be no longer fully sane.

MADNESS AND THE BODY

Schreber's "rather pleasant" dream of passivity so poignantly figures for him the collapse of sexual difference that at the height of his psychosis, when he is assailed by talking rays from the sun, he is taunted with the phrase: "Fancy a person who was a *Senatspräsident* allowing himself to be f....d" (Schreber

1988, 148). This foregrounds, as Kaja Silverman points out, "the opposition between his sexuality and his professional position" (1993, 351). To Schreber's mind a passive sexuality does not bode well for an active public life. To be passive is not only to be powerless, but also to be unworthy of power. As suggested above, Schreber's body/text is the site of a radical conflict between the public and the private as they are embodied in specific gender categories. On another occasion the rays call him "Miss Schreber" (Schreber 1988, 119) – which appears in English in the original, suggesting to Marjorie Garber the absent phallus, what is soon to be *miss*ing (1992, 207). It is also suggestive, however, of the fact that in allowing himself to be "f....d" Schreber himself has gone missing, made himself absent. In addition, the unmarried status of *Miss* Schreber renders him/her even more invisible within a culture where a woman's status is contingent upon her legal attachment to a man. The sexual politics are clear enough: a position of public authority requires somebody (some 'body') incapable of penetrative submission, incapable even of contemplating it. To allow oneself to be "f....d" is to lose control, is to become 'Miss'-ing (unmarried, dispossessed, unregistered, unseen). Losing the job title loses him the phallus, that is, his reason. Being a man means having things (phallus, title, authority, knowledge, reason), not losing them.

It comes as no surprise, then, to find Schreber's vehemently distancing himself from such a position as that of the penetrated woman. After describing the above mentioned daydream, Schreber insists that the idea of playing the receptive role in sexual intercourse "was so *foreign* to my whole nature that I may say I would have rejected it with indignation if fully awake" (1988, 63, emphasis added). Instead, he attributes its occurrence upon "some external influences" which must have planted the idea in him (1988, 63), not recognizing that such a move is equally contingent upon his penetration from without. Elsewhere in the *Memoirs* he apologizes for having to touch on "issues of which as a man *I have to be* ashamed" (Schreber 1988, 206, emphasis added). By way of exoneration, he explains that the process of transformation into a woman – what he calls "unmanning" (*Entmannung*) – is God's will (Schreber 1988, 148).

This process of unmanning, Schreber explains,

> consisted in the (external) male genitals (penis and scrotum) being retracted into the body and the internal sexual organs being at the same time transformed into the corresponding female sexual organs. (Schreber 1988, 73)

It is a process he claims to have experienced himself. He writes: "several times (particularly in bed) there were marked indications of an actual retraction of the male organ" (Schreber 1988, 132). As the signifier of his social status recedes, his penetrability increases. It is also a process Schreber was clearly unhappy not only with experiencing but with recounting. "In order not to lose through such a confession the respect of other people whose opinion I value", writes Schreber, he must endeavour to *justify* the importance of talking about such things. He must *make sense* of his exposure to and experience of penetration. To this end he explains:

> Few people have been brought up according to such strict moral principles as I, and have throughout life practised such moderation especially in matters of sex, as I venture to claim for myself. Mere low sensuousness can therefore not be considered a motive in my case; were satisfaction of my manly pride still possible, I would naturally much prefer it; nor would I ever betray any sexual lust in contact with other people. But as soon as I am alone with God, if I may so express myself, I must continually or at least at certain times, strive to give divine rays the impression of a woman in the height of sexual delight, to achieve this I have to employ all possible means, and have to strain all my intellectual powers and foremost my imagination. (Schreber 1988, 208)

It thus becomes Schreber's moral duty to "imagine myself as man and woman in one person having intercourse with myself, or somehow have to achieve with myself a certain sexual excitement etc. – which perhaps under other circumstances might be considered immoral" (Schreber 1988, 208). To conform to God's wishes, he strives to make "absolute passivity [his] duty" (Schreber 1988, 145). There is thus not simply a reversal of gender in Schreber's new world, but a reversal of morality – indeed, gender and morality become almost interchangeable terms, such that gender itself becomes a form of morality: there are 'good' genders and 'bad' genders. With this reversal, what Schreber knows to be unacceptable or immoral behaviour according to his strict moral upbringing – i.e., "mere low sensuousness" – becomes not simply acceptable but obligatory. What had hitherto been the sign of "moral decay ('voluptuous excesses')" (Schreber 1988, 72) becomes instead the sign of moral duty. As Santner argues, "Schreber discovers that power not only prohibits, moderates, says 'no', but may also work to intensify and amplify the body and its sensations" (1996, 32). But in order to do so, Schreber must become a woman.

Schreber's acceptance of his role as 'God's whore', then, is by no means immediate. His initial response is one of resistance; he battles against this unmanning by which he is to be robbed not only of his masculinity but of his reason: "my whole sense of manliness and manly honour, my entire moral being, rose up against it", he writes (Schreber 1988, 76). For Schreber, to become unmanned – to become a woman – is coterminous with losing one's Reason (Schreber 1988, 78–9, 99). Within the late nineteenth century discourse on sexuality and gender (Showalter 1987), Schreber's experience of his body as 'female' could only be subsumed by and occasion madness, because within its mutually exclusive terms *having* a (male) body was always contingent on *losing* one's mind. Excessive sensual pleasure in either men or women, is considered socially unacceptable but in women it is less often deemed 'abnormal' because 'woman' is always already 'man's' Other, always already 'body', 'unconscious', 'nature', 'sexuality'. In men, however, excessive physical pleasure tends to carry with it the danger of placing the body above the mind, and such sexualization, being, at heart, a 'feminization', inevitably cancels out reason – the one thing that supposedly gives men their superiority over nature/woman/body. As Victor Seidler argues: "*masculine superiority is constructed against sexuality*" (Seidler 1995, 177, emphasis added). The battle identified by Theweleit as raging within the soldier is here applied to all men: a battle against sexuality. As the cultural default position, white masculine heterosexuality turns out to be no sexuality at all.

This becomes clearer when one considers that Schreber's unmanning is intimately connected to – and signified by – an extreme bodily jouissance, or what Schreber himself calls 'voluptuousness', a feeling of intense pleasure he tells us is usually only attainable after death, when a "state of blessedness" is bestowed upon the disembodied soul (Schreber 1988, 50–2). Voluptuousness, in turn, is connected to the nerve language through which God's rays speak to Schreber by penetrating him and causing his body to be experienced as the site of sensuality. This nerve-language or 'basic language' is described by Schreber as "a somewhat antiquated but nevertheless powerful German, characterized particularly by a wealth of euphemisms" (Schreber 1988, 50). These euphemisms reverse the meanings of words, and the implications of this semantic inversion will be explored more fully later in this chapter. Important here is the sexual difference Schreber ascribes to these nerves of voluptuousness, for, Schreber argues, whilst they occupy the *whole* of a woman's body, in a man's body they remain solely in the genitals. He writes:

> my whole body is filled with nerves of voluptuousness from the top of my head to the soles of my feet, such as is the case only in the adult female body, whereas in the case of a man, as far as I know, nerves of voluptuousness are only found in and immediately around the sexual organs. (Schreber 1988, 204)

At the heart of Schreber's psychosis, then, is a certain pleasure or *jouissance* he considers to be specific to female flesh, which makes answering Lacan's question *Am I a man or am I a woman?* particularly difficult – indeed, Schreber's inability to answer it with any certainty contributes to and defines his breakdown. Gender ambiguity and the penetrated male body often appear at the same time, femininity being one of its major tropes. Concern over this voluptuousness causes Schreber to appeal to the authority of one of his doctors. In response to Schreber's letter, Professor Weber, in Schreber's words, "did not dispute the fact that the feeling of sensual pleasure – whatever its physiological basis – occurs in the female to a higher degree than in the male" and, moreover, "involves the whole body" (1988, 205). The doctor's silence ("did not dispute") confirms for Schreber the truth of his claim, and this silence itself becomes the only response to the witnessing of an 'impossibility' such as that experienced by Schreber. It is a forgetting of the forgotten, a discreet silence which passes over that which must not be remembered: the *jouissance* of the male body.

Submitting to such *jouissance*, Schreber was well aware, "would render man unfit to fulfil his other obligations; it would prevent him from ever rising to higher mental and moral perfection" (Schreber 1988, 208), because thought and sensation are seemingly incommensurable. Thought is deemed to be disembodied, reason considered external and objective, untainted by the vagaries of the flesh. It is a clear dichotomization of the 'public' and the 'private', mapped, as so many other dyads, onto the 'masculine' and the 'feminine'. Excessive pleasure is at odds with civic duty, that traditionally masculine and public domain, and must be avoided if one is to remain within its (in)secure parameters. By contrast, women's 'domain' has been not only the private as in the domestic, but, more implicitly, the private world of the body and its 'unspeakable' pleasures. In many ways 'woman' came to represent 'pleasure', came to stand in for the body and its inherent penetrability.

The Madness of the Penetrated Body | 53

THE DISCOURSE ON PLEASURE

That physical pleasure was, for a long time, deemed 'unspeakable' by much public discourse is apparent from the fact that it was one of the last subjects to be scrutinized by the light of reason. Not until the middle period of the nineteenth century did a significant discourse on sexuality emerge, what Foucault called a *scientia sexualis*, and then it appeared under the aegis of medical science and criminology – that is, as a modern strategy for surveillance and control. This late appearance alone speaks volumes about its dubious and scandalous status as something unfit for the rarefied scientific inquiry that lay at the heart of Enlightenment reason; an unseemly topic for cultured minds. Those doctors who did turn their medical attention to sex did so reluctantly and apologetically. One example will suffice here. In 1857, the French sexologist Auguste Tardieu wrote: "the darkness that envelops these facts, the shame and disgust they inspire, have always repelled the observer's gaze ... For a long time I hesitated to introduce the loathsome picture into this study" (cited in Foucault 1990, 24). Schreber's own discomfort at having to touch on such matters is analogous to this professional unease at expending thought on something deemed so inappropriate for intellectual consideration. The irony is, of course, that scientific discourse denied these pleasures even as it sought them out, and provided a space for them to appear in the interests of public health (Bremmer 1989; Weeks 1981); what Foucault called a "reverse discourse" (Foucault 1990, 101).

In Volume One of *History of Sexuality*, Foucault argues that the body in Western discourse has become appropriated for a *scientia sexualis*, whilst in the Orient an *ars erotica* provided a cultural discourse on the body and its relationship with pleasure. In the West, the body is harnessed to an armory of scientific terminology by which it becomes objective, disciplined and docile, the mystery of pleasure elided by taxonomic procedures that categorize and explain, proscribe and control. Sexuality thus becomes viewed as the essential, though often hidden, 'truth' at the core of subjectivity – a move which gave birth to an identity politics from which we have yet to escape. As a consequence of the nineteenth-century *scientia sexualis*, the unspoken norm of masculine disembodiment has been bypassed through a prioritization of the pathological. It is only those male bodies deemed sick or abnormal that become visible (the homosexual, the pervert, the criminally insane); bodies proscribed at the expense of a more truthful account which would address the unspoken norm of the male body, which remains invisible, tenaciously resistant to a discursive appearance that would undermine its authority. That is, it is only those bodies that betray the masculine ideal which appear, their visibility contributing to the invisibility of that masculine ideal and their excommunication from it.

Schreber's conviction that only women possess the ability to experience pleasure beyond the phallus, a kind of 'supra-genital' *jouissance*, means that his own body's capacity for such pleasure marks it out as something other than 'male'. There is, in Lacan's words, "an extremely obvious discrepancy between the symbolic function and what is perceived by the subject in the sphere of experience" (cited in Brenkman 1993, 53). It is a discrepancy that, at its weakest ideological or symbolic stress points, becomes a profound conflict or rupture. The next section tries to locate the point of this rupture, to outline the contours of a gap, to locate the edges of an excess, in terms of the penetrated male body. It does this in order to begin formulating a relationship between the anus as a site of discursive rupture and Lacan's '*point de capiton*' or quilting point as that which names the process by which meaning is made to stick. The crisis of the body in Schreber is shown to be fundamentally a crisis in language perpetrated by the body – its status as abject, surrendered, passive and inherently, dangerously, penetrable.

THE RIDDLE OF THE SPHINCTER

Much has been made of Schreber's *Grundsprache*, or basic language – the language in which God addresses him. For

Freud, it is the language of the unconscious, containing residues of the symbolic relations as found in dream analysis (Freud 1974, 201). One thing is clearly certain – and that is that the basic language Schreber talks about is inherently ambivalent about the meaning of words, rendering meaning unstable. Schreber writes that it is "especially characterised by its great wealth of euphemisms" (Schreber 1988, 13). This 'ground-speak' proves vertiginously ungrounded, or groundless. Whilst it constitutes a system – what Schreber calls the 'writing-down-system' – it remains nevertheless

> extraordinarily difficult to explain to other people even vaguely. That it exists is overwhelmingly proved to me day after day; yet it belongs even for me to the realm of the unfathomable because the objective it pursues must be recognised by all who know human nature as something in itself unattainable. It is obviously a stop-gap measure and it is difficult to decide whether it arises from a wrong (that is contrary to the Order of the World) intent or from faulty reasoning. (Schreber 1988, 119)

Wrong intent or faulty reasoning – these are the proposed origins of Schreber's basic language. As a consequence, Schreber claims that whatever is said in this basic language, the reverse meaning is intended. For example, Schreber tells us that "souls which had not yet undergone the process of purification were not, as one would expect, called 'non-tested souls', but the exact reverse, namely 'tested souls'" (1988, 50). Such a reversal of meaning indicates not only a violent breach between signifier and signified, but also an about-face, which, for Jean-François Rabain, constitutes a sodomizing of language, language flipped over onto its belly and taken from behind. Rabain renders *Grundsprache* in the French (*langue fondamentale*) to make explicit its anality, its connection to the fundament (see also Niederland 1984, 43).

Such reversibility places the ambiguous quality of language close to the sexual ambiguity acting itself out on Schreber's body (Rabain 1988, 63, 65). "The basic language", writes

Rabain, "questions the value of the sign, its annulment, and its function of reversibility by allowing the free play of ambivalence and *the transformation into the contrary*" (Rabain 1988, 68, emphasis added). In this sense, Schreber's fundamental language, or language of the fundament, has much in common with Derrida's project of prising language open and rendering meaning undecidable. For the deconstructionist, as for Schreber, this is, according to Christopher Norris, "an activity of thought which cannot be consistently acted on" without risking "madness" (Norris 1988, xii).

Schreber's transformation into a woman is coterminous, then, with a breakdown in meaning, his equivocal flesh mirroring his equivocal language, and *vice versa*. As Lecercle points out, for Schreber,

> language is directly connected with the body; nerve speech, as its name indicates, is language embodied ... as it is also the cause of voluptuous sensations, there is a concordance between grammar and physical pleasure ... the persecution of which he is a victim takes the form of a dereliction of grammar. (1985, 126)

Not only did Schreber believe that the 'basic-language' used by the rays came from outside, but the "writing-down-system" by which Schreber's experiences are recorded is equally a phenomenon of exteriority: "I cannot say with certainty who does the writing down", he confesses (Schreber 1988, 119). The sovereignty of the unified, identifiable subject is replaced here by a multiple personality. These multiple personas which inhabit Schreber – and which include "an Alsatian girl who had defended her honour against a victorious French officer", and a "Hyperborian woman" (Schreber 1988, 93) – all aid in the writing-down-system. As such, they undermine the position of author(ity): there is no 'I' from which the text springs, only a collaborative plague of voices. As Derrida writes, "we must be several in order to write" (1978, 226); and as Lecercle notes, such "proliferation is always a threat to order" (1985, 95).

This proliferation reaches a point for Screber at which "the writing-down-material has increased to such an extent that it now includes almost all the words used in the human language" (Schreber 1988, 222). Stretched across the supposedly stable language structure of reason, Schreber places, like a veil, a parallel language, the meaning of which is, word for word, the exact opposite of its corresponding homonym. All language, for Schreber, is homonymic, each word harbouring its chaotic twin, its opposite meaning, within its seemingly self-evident appearance.

How might this reversal of meaning within Schreber's world connect with the reversal of gender he claims to have undergone? And what role does the anus play in both scenarios? What is most profoundly anal about Schreber's loss of reason and his loss of manhood? How did the anus come to function as a site of both bodily and discursive rupture in his text and in some of its interpretations?

In *Anti-Oedipus*, Deleuze and Guattari develop a radical theory of subjectivity which posits the subject as a residue of the processes of coding and overcoding by which the flows and multiplicities of the social body are mapped and restrained. The chaotic unravelling of these restraints – as in cases of psychosis, such as Schreber's – they call decoding. They argue that in advanced societies such as ours, decoding and coding are almost indistinguishable processes. That is, the high levels of complexity found in modern life necessitate an understanding of the subject as always already fractured, or 'schizo'. In short, fragmentation at the level of the ego is the inevitable outcome of modern overcoding. Because of this, their form of 'schizo-analysis' regards the psychotic as having something fundamentally profound to say about the nature of the processes of overcoding by which the body is repressed. Furthermore, they link these processes to the original privatization of the anus – the first erogenous zone that the infant learns to repudiate, repressing its possibilities for pleasure. They adopt the Freudian notion of the anus as "the symbol of everything that is to be repudiated and excluded from life" (Freud 1977, 104n). It is a process, however, that, due to the close proximity of the anus with the genitals, remains profoundly contradictory and unstable. For Freud, anal eroticism is never fully repressed.

Deleuze and Guattari argue that the anus was "the first organ to suffer privatization, removal from the social field" (Deleuze and Guattari 1983, 143); as a consequence "the entire history of primitive coding, of despotic overcoding, and of the decoding of private man" is founded on "the model and memory of the disgraced anus" (Deleuze and Guattari 1983, 211). They argue that the process of language acquisition is not only governed by the primacy of the phallus as the master signifier, as Lacan proposes, but also that the acts of separation and rejection characteristic of defecation prefigure the differentiation techniques of signification. In other words, language is not only acquired through the removal of the anus from any social function, but also through the displacement of the processes of shitting onto the systematic use and application of language structures. (Significantly, Schreber's writing-down-system is activated by the *posterior* or lower god, Ariman, linking, once again, anality and language.[12])

Kristeva makes a similar claim in *Revolution in Poetic Language*, when she writes that

> Language acquisition implies the suppression of anality; in other words, it represents the acquisition of a capacity for symbolization through the definitive detachment of the rejected object, through its repression under the sign. (1984, 152)

For Kristeva, poetic language retains a certain aspect of anality – a point the book will return to in Chapter Four in greater detail.

---

[12] For other accounts of anality's link to language, see Lee Edelman, *Homographesis* (New York and London: Routledge, 1994), 173–91; Avital Ronell, "The Sujet Suppositaire: Freud, And/Or, the Obsessional Neurotic Style (Maybe)", in *Finitude's Score: Essays for the End of the Millenium* (Lincoln and London: University of Nebraska Press, 1994), 105–28. Both writers link the anality of language to ambiguity or reversal of meaning: that is, to the instability of discourse.

Deleuze and Guattari argue that the privatization or overcoding by which the public self is consolidated and its desires held in check takes as its model the sublimation of anality. According to this, learning when to shit and when not to shit are coterminous with learning what to say and what not to say. Both are a form of discipline. Bodily regulation of flows and discursive decorum go hand in hand. It has already been shown how difficult Schreber considered it to speak of that which he speaks, and how this finds a parallel in the professional unease with which doctors first approached the issue of human sexuality. Entry into the symbolic order would seem to foreclose the possibility of certain, more open (and therefore dangerous) experiences of desire, except perhaps in the realm of the imaginary, a realm whose co-ordinates become structured by the very unspeakability in which desire is held. For this reason, Deleuze and Guattari insist that desire in its least restrained and most chaotic form is inherently revolutionary. Through the experience and articulation of what is in excess of the overcoding's strictures, the inherent fallability of those strictures is exposed.

This idea can be further clarified through a consideration of what Lacan terms the *point de capiton*, or quilting point.

LACAN'S *POINT DE CAPITON*

In his seminar on the psychoses, Lacan suggests that meaning is established by the fixing, the pinning down, of a signifier to the flow of signifieds. Such stasis gives a false sense of uniformity or universality to any signifier when in reality, "the relationship between the signified and the signifier always appears fluid, always ready to come undone" (Lacan 1993, 261). Meaning thus constitutes a nodal point that attempts to isolate what is essentially non-isolatable: the signifier. Lacan calls this nodal point a *point de capiton*, a quilting point, a stitching together of signifier and signified resembling the buttons which pin down the upholstery fabric on furniture to the stuffing within. This quilting point compresses the field of signification to a single location and thereby "polarizes it, structures it, and brings it into existence" (Lacan 1993, 260). In doing so, this quilting point creates creases which fan out from its centre, like the folds of fabric encircling an upholstery button, and, like an upholstery button, it is always in danger of being undone, becoming unfixed, resulting in the chaos of psychosis. Psychosis is, then, a hole in the symbolic order through which meaning vanishes, becoming unanchored and floating off on a sea of nonsense. Lecercle calls it a hiatus (1985, 136) – a word one meaning of which is 'a natural opening or aperture'. It is also a now obscure term for 'vulva'.

Is it no more than coincidence, however, given what is here being addressed – namely, the loss of reason associated with the penetration of the male body – that this quilting point, with its aureole of folds and its central cavity, resembles the privatized anus, that hidden hole the penetration of which dislodges meaning from its moorings and produces madness, that portal through which Reason's other passes? "But who", as Guy Hocquenghem asks, "would think of interpreting Schreber's sun, not as the father-phallus, but as a cosmic anus?" (1993a, 100). Who indeed, but Deleuze and Guattari, via Bataille.[13] In *Anti-Oedipus*, they write

> Judge Schreber has sunbeams in his ass. *A solar anus.* And rest assured that it works: Judge Schreber feels something, produces something, and is capable of explaining the process theoretically. (Deleuze and Guattari 1983, 2)

---

[13] Georges Bataille, "Solar Anus", in *Visions of Excess: Selected Writings 1927-1939* (Minneapolis: University of Minnesota Press, 1985), 5–9. For Bataille, too, this opening is intimately associated with language. "Ever since sentences started to *circulate* in brains devoted to reflection, an effort at total identification has been made, because with the aid of a *copula* each sentence ties one thing to another" (5, original emphasis). This copula, states Bataille, "is no less irritating than the *copulation* of bodies … because the verb *to be* is the vehicle of amorous frenzy" (*ibid*). On Bataille's 'excremental philosophy', see Sue Golding, "Solar Clitoris", *Parallax* 3, no. 1 (1997): 137–49.

Like Lacan, Deleuze and Guattari want to know what Schreber can teach us, rather than seeing him simply as 'mad', his position outside of 'normality' lending his story critical weight; heuristics rather than hermeneutics. Unlike Lacan, however, they refuse to locate Schreber's breakdown within the framework of the triadic Oedipal unit, even in the broader form of Freud's formulation offered by Lacan in the shape of the symbolic order. Deleuze and Guattari prefer to locate Schreber's psychosis within a politico-cultural context which interprets his witnessing as a reaction to, and movement against, the totalizing forces of capitalist and psychoanalytic normativity. And they associate his experiences with the privatization of the body by discourse, its colonization by language. Furthermore, they place Schreber's anus at the centre of his psychosis, as the primary point of his miraculous body,[14] a zone of intensity as productive as it is destructive (Deleuze and Guattari 1983, 11). They isolate the anus and its status as the original taboo in order to propose a less structured theory of desire which may account for the bodily flows so feared by the Friekorps, and by fascist thinking in general.[15]

Schreber's backside is certainly the source of both great anxiety and great pleasure throughout the *Memoirs*. He refers to a process of "picturing ... female buttocks on my body ... whenever I bend down" (Schreber 1988, 181) – as if his body were a *tabula rasa* – anticipating God's penetration, anticipating, even inviting, an "intimacy with the gods without seeing their faces" (Lyotard 1988, 15). He demonstrates an enthusiastic preoccupation with the scatological (a word which, surely, literally, means the science, the logic, of shit). "Like everything else in my body", writes Schreber, "the need to empty myself is also called forth by miracles" (Schreber 1988, 177). Therefore, his struggle to hold onto his shit is a

---

[14] Mira*cul*ous (*miraculeux*) because within the phonetics of the word itself lurks the *cul* (French slang for 'arse'). This point is developed further in Chapter Three in relation to Genet's work.

[15] In his preface, Foucault calls *Anti-Oedipus* "an *Introduction to the Non-Fascist Life*" (Minneapolis: University of Minnesota Press, 1983), xiii.

struggle for supremacy against Divine omnipotence, a classic Freudian characteristic of the infant's anal phase (Freud 1977, 205–15). However, this act of rebellion is used against him, and he is made to feel too stupid to shit, making the act itself a defiant one (Schreber 1988, 178). Stupidity leads to God's withdrawal, and God's withdrawal results in pain being inflicted on Schreber. Therefore, he is caught between holding onto his faeces in order to retain his sense of reason, and the urge to empty his bowels because doing so always results in "a very strong development of soul-voluptuousness" (Schreber 1988, 178) and soul-voluptuousness attracts God, who then re-enters him. In short, like Freud's infant, Schreber enjoys defecating. The fact that the divine miracle rays induce in Schreber the need to defecate "every day at least several dozen times" (Schreber 1988, 177) indicates a highly charged – indeed, vertiginous – anal eroticism. "The President's arse will pass into solar incandescence", as Lyotard comments (Lyotard 1993, 59).

Interestingly, Deleuze, Guattari and Lyotard choose to focus their readings of the *Memoirs* on the anal, linking this with their respective projects of opening up the body. Schreber himself never indicates that the penetration he undergoes is an anal one – indeed, it is not focused on any one part of the body but occurs all over. Why, then, this attention on the anus as the site of bodily disintegration, and what is the relevance of their insights for the production of meaning? How can the site of rupture/lack/castration – i.e., the anus – also constitute the site of (or seat of) identity, and the form of reasoning identity implies? In the following section, certain parallels between Lacan's notion of lack and Foucault's notion of rupture are explored to make clearer this duality and its significance for this book.

THE FOREIGN BODY

For Lacan, the body takes place – registers, carries (sexual) meaning – only within the symbolic order, that is, within language. As Bruce Fink remarks, the Lacanian body is "written with signifiers", a process that renders it "at the mercy of the symbolic order" (Fink 1995, 12, 11). Because of this, recognition of one's body is always *misrecognition* (*meconnaisance*), always giving a false impression of unity to something that is essentially fragmented or disunified. The unified structure of the body is implanted within the subject by its entry into the symbolic order. This symbolic order is the structure of the Other, making the symbolic body the property of the Other. This Other, however, is not an actual person, but the very structure in which one appropriates one's body. And one appropriates it as always already male or female. One bodies within a field of signification which marinates the flesh in an inescapable language: "the body is overwritten/over-ridden by language" (Fink 1995, 12). This is not unlike Deleuze and Guattari's notion of overcoding.

That the language in which the body takes place is inherently heterosexist in its assumptions of meaning, its structuring of reason and its construction of the body is one of the central claims of this book. Language seeks to restrict the male body and its pleasures within syntactical, logical and conceptual formations which constitute a discourse of prohibition.[16] The violence of this restriction presses against, leaves an impression upon, the bodies that do not 'fit in', that 'fail' or break down. The value of Lacan's work is that such breakdown – as it is for Deleuze and Guattari, too – is fundamentally what grounds *all* subjectivity. In short, there is no distinction, for Lacan, between psychotic and non-psychotic states of mind, only degrees to which one succumbs to breakdown.

Within the Lacanian economy of sexual differentiation, of course, the role of master signifier is filled by the phallus, that absent leader to which we are all expected to defer in order

---

[16] For Schreber physical pleasure and pain are intimately connected to the correct use of language: "whenever expressed in a grammatically complete sentence, the rays would be led straight to me, and entering my body (though capable of withdrawing) temporarily increase its soul-voluptuous-ness": Daniel Paul Schreber, *Memoirs of My Nervous Illness*, trans. Ida MacAlpine and Richard Hunter (Cambridge and London: Harvard University Press, 1988), 173.

to make sense of and register within the symbolic order. For a man, therefore, to rebel against the master signifier is to lose the privileges obtained through being a 'member' of the group marked 'male', a membership contingent upon having the phallus. To abdicate the phallus is thus to submit to a masochism marked by a loss of masculinity, through castration; to have one's membership rescinded: one becomes a symbolic 'woman'. To submit to that leader, however, is no less masochistic, for it places the male subject in a threateningly homosexual and, within such an economy, feminizing subject position. The male body must submit to the Phallus in order to become male. Paradoxically, that is, the male body must be penetrable in order to enter a symbolic order which will subsequently disavow such penetrability, providing that body with a phallus that acts as a guarantee against it, for within the symbolic order only those without the phallus (i.e., 'women') can be penetrated.

For Lacan, this dilemma is made more troublesome still by the fact that the ego, as such, does not exist, except as an alter ego, as the Other, through which the 'I' emerges within a linguistic command directed at the Other. For this reason, "reality is *at the outset* marked by symbolic nihilation" (Lacan 1993, 148), making the body, and the skin ego, inherently fragmented. The ego sabotages unity rather than supplying it. And if the ego, as we have seen, is the source – or mediator – of all knowledge of the body, the psychic map of an essentially psychotic flesh, then the body is always already ripped, dismembered, a site of rupture. Indeed, Schreber informs his readers that his body has "become increasingly grotesque" (Schreber 1988, 78-9).[17]

The ego and the superego are mediated by speech for Lacan, the 'I' making sense only as a source of the 'you' which is a signifier for the superego, the Law. This 'you', then, which makes possible an 'I', is, Lacan emphasizes, a foreign body (Lacan 1993, 276). The body is elsewhere, as it was for Theweleit's *Freikorps*. These men possessed no ego but were

---

[17] The notion of the 'grotesque body' as developed by Mikhail Bahktin will be explored in Chapter Four in relation to Joyce's *Ulysses*.

kept 'sane' by an externalization process which gave them a body in the form of their collective 'superiority' to the mass (Theweleit 1989, 164). By cathecting pain into pleasure, they survived as a function within their closed group, shoring up an identity against everything that they were not, which thus became negativized. By a similar process – though one marked by a more culturally apparent psychosis – Schreber turned the pain of God's penetration into a pleasure to which he willingly submitted: "If I can get a little sensuous pleasure in this process, I feel I am entitled to it as a small compensation for the excess of suffering and privation that has been mine for many years past" (Schreber 1988, 209).

For Schreber and the *Freikorps* the pain of submission becomes a pleasure, and in this way "the internal map of space, the body and the mind, and external map of space, the body and the social order are resolved one in the other" (Pile 1996, 205). This solution, however, as already stated, itself produces an excess which remains irresolvable, indissoluble. And in both cases that excess is the penetrable body. Whereas for the soldier, however, it is a body disavowed and externalized, resulting in the penetration and mangling of other bodies, for Schreber, for the psychotic, it is his own body that is penetrated and mangled. If the bodily ego/skin ego can be likened to Deleuze and Guattari's 'body without organs', then Schreber is the *Ur*-body without organs. Consider this extract from the medical officer's report:

> He maintains that in the earlier years of his illness he suffered destruction of individual organs of his body, of a kind which would have brought death to every other human being, that he lived for a long time without stomach, without intestines, bladder, almost without lungs, with smashed ribs, torn gullet, that he had at times eaten part of his own larynx with his food, etc. (Schreber 1988, 272)

This body, ripped and open, empty and fragmented, figures as a site of rupture, the rupture between discourse and the flesh. I have already said that the hole in signification which constitutes psychosis is a 'hiatus', that almost vulval aperture. In "The Father's 'No'", Foucault charges this hiatus with "the vitality of a rupture" (Foucault 1998b, 5), claiming that "the dissolution of a work in madness, this void to which poetic speech is drawn as to its self-destruction, is what authorizes the text of a language common to both" (Foucault 1998b, 18).

The Foucauldian body, often misunderstood as a discursive body constructed through language, is being understood here as a ruptured body, a hole or hiatus within language – a language that is common to both lyricism and madness, both meaning and dissolution of meaning. The text/body, for Foucault, is authorized by a rupture. The body is held – albeit in the most fractured state – within a multiplicity of discourses like a fish in water, but these discourses are also in the body like water passing through the fish: discourse sustains the body even as it dissolves it. The ambiguous status of Schreber's text frames and focuses this ambiguous status of representative language *per se*, and attaches that rupture to the particular hiatus of the penetrated male body.

Whilst it may be problematic to link Lacan with Foucault in this way, given Lacan's status as errant psychoanalyst and Foucault's critical engagement with psychoanalysis, it is nevertheless clear that both writers open a space for thinking the 'outside', that which doesn't – and cannot – register within language. Lacan's concept of lack is identifying something which Foucault, in his turn, has termed an excess. How can Lacan's lack be equated with Foucault's excess? It is important to keep in mind that for Lacan the lack is on the side of the symbolic order, it is something the symbolic order lacks, not something lacking in the subject him/herself. Lacan calls it the Real, something in excess of the symbolic order, something unreachable, impenetrable, unknowable. It exceeds the symbolic order's ability to grasp it. In this sense, it is like Foucault's excess, or what in 'The Father's "No"' he calls a "fundamental gap in the signifier, that transforms ... lyricism into delirium ... work into the absence of work" (Foucault 1998b, 17). It is, then, a rupture in the fundament, bringing us back to the question of Schreber's solar anus and its importance here. The Foucauldian body is closer to Deleuze and Guattari's body without organs – a patchwork of fragments, a multiplicity that is residual within discourse and characteristic of everything that discourse articulates. In his study of Foucault, Deleuze usefully identifies the process of "visual assemblage" by which 'Panopticism' operates, highlighting not only the role played by surveillance and discipline in the registering of the body, but also the fragmented and multiple nature of the body that results from this registration: its status as an assemblage (Deleuze 1986, 32).

For Gilles Deleuze and Claire Parnet, the assemblage is "the minimum real unit" (1987, 51). As such, it renders all meaning inherently and immediately multiple. Through what Deleuze terms a 'sympathy' or symbiosis, the assemblage allows for "the penetration of bodies" (Deleuze 1987, 52) within fields of force that generate representation. Within an assemblage "bodies interpenetrate, mix together, transmit affects to one another" (Deleuze 1987, 70). This fundamental gap, then, which Foucault and Deleuze have identified as the thing which makes possible the multiplicity and fragmentation of bodies and texts, is that through which such (inter)penetration occurs. The gap/hole/lack – what I am calling the behind – is therefore primary in that it contours the field of representation whilst remaining stubbornly resistant to representation.

THE PRIMACY OF THE HOLE

So far, through noting the productive anxiety surrounding penetration as a cause of madness, or loss of reason/phallus/manhood, the ruptures of discourse have been rendered coterminous with the anus as a hole or route into the male body. Penetration and madness are somehow considered mutually productive. At the same time, however, it has been seen how the notion of a rupture or gap functions in the thinking of Lacan, Foucault and Deleuze and Guattari, as that which exceeds representation whilst nevertheless contributing greatly to its structure. It has been stressed that the quilting point by which meaning is stitched down constitutes such a rupture – and one which, in its conglomeration of folds outlining a central hollow, more closely approximates the anus as the primary signifier than the phallus. It is, perhaps somewhat ironic, then, that it is Lacan's text on Schreber – a text which tries to show how psychosis replaces the lost father, that is, the lost phallus – which provides the tools necessary to reinforce the link between the *point de capiton* and the (a)signifying anus. There Lacan writes:

> If something in nature is designed to suggest certain of the properties of a ring (*anneau*) to us, it is restricted to what language has dedicated the term *anus* to, which in Latin is spelt with one *n*, and which in their modesty ancient dictionaries designated as the ring that can be found behind. (Lacan 1993, 316)

For Lacan, the property of the ring is to bind or hold together (Lacan 1993, 319) – that is, to give meaning. Its role, then, is not dissimilar to that of the quilting point. "A ring isn't a hole with something around it ... A ring above all has a signifying value" (Lacan 1993, 317). As *the ring that can be found behind,* the anus is occluded, out of sight (privatized), and must be actively sought out, and perhaps here can be found the penumbrated etymological origins of the term *anal*ysis, that project of sniffing out hidden things that lurk behind. Lacan himself makes no direct link between the ring and the quilting point, but their functions are clearly of a similar nature – to secure, bind and fix meaning to a specific referent. Meaning is always concentrated around a rupture.

Schreber's text demonstrates the relationship between the body and language, the origin of language in the sexual body. While one end of the alimentary canal talks, the other shits, or receives God's rays. Just as Schreber's language turns meaning on its head, so the nerves of voluptuousness spin his body upside down, till it is waste (nonsense) that spills from his mouth, and his anus becomes the seat of identity. One orifice takes the place of the other. Schreber is a latterday Oedipus condemned to solve the riddle not of the Sphinx, but of the Sphincter, that orifice which, as Avital Ronell notes, is "determinable neither as masculine nor strictly speaking as feminine", but which "nonetheless constitutes a sexuality, a shared space that is often vaginized" (Ronell 1994, 108). I would suggest that it is the fact of this vaginization of the anus that renders its use so problematic when it comes to conceptualizing the male body. As such, it is never a "shared space". For within the terms of the symbolic order, the male body is not entered, it enters. Pleasurable use of this sphincter on the male body therefore maps a hermaphroditic pairing of oxymoronic flesh (Rabain 1988, 63), which threatens to corrode or disrupt the boundary of sexual difference. That it doesn't fulfil the promise of this threat is due in no small part to the fact that it is "often vaginized". For this book argues that such vaginization is the inevitable outcome of the gendered chain of equivalences whereby body=penetrability=female. Schreber's *jouissance* was thus recuperated for a logic that disavowed it, or avowed it as psychosis. The axiom of male=mind/female=body is reinscribed upon his very flesh as he succumbs to God's penetration, thereby reinstalling the "harmony" (Schreber 1988, 252) its initial occurrence destroyed. The male body is lost in the war against it, and breaking the code of masculinity leaves one at sea, exiled from reason. To break the code is to break the law, and in that rupture the male body appears penetrated, open and radically exposed as its other, as female, and thus *dis*appearing at the same time. The hiatus/rupture/hole/gap that this movement or oscillation constitutes has been in this chapter linked to the hole in the symbolic that creates psychosis, and that hole in turn has been linked to the male anus. The next chapter expands the analysis to consider three texts in which the male body is penetrated in other ways: through the eyes, the mouth and the ear. A prose poem by Baudelaire and novels by J-K Huysmans and Wilde will be used to demonstrate the ways in which the male body is opened up to a constant threat from penetration in every orifice. This opening up of the male body continues the work of the rupture, making it the impossible condition of that body's emergence.

Chapter Two

The Limits of the Body

> "We must remember that even the simplest words,
> the word 'man' for instance, have a history"
> - Neil Bartlett, *Who Was That Man?*

> "…impenetrability is intelligible only as a mode of resistance"
> - Samuel Taylor Coleridge, *Biographia Literaria*

> "'To define is to limit'"
> - Oscar Wilde, *A Picture of Dorian Gray*

So far, this book has demonstrated that penetration of the male body is a limit-experience that threatens the masculine subject with dissolution. Because the concept of 'the body' is so closely bound to the concept of 'woman', the act of penetration – by making the male body more present – serves to destabilize the notion of a unified 'male' subject. Yet, paradoxically, as this chapter works further to demonstrate, such destabilization also occasions the emergence of the masculine subject. As such, 'femininity', far from being the conceptual opposite of 'masculinity', becomes the very condition of 'masculinity's' possibility. Penetration, and the submission it entails, will be seen to be something fascinating, pleasurable and, what is more, necessary to the emergence of a new masculine subject.

The impenetrability that has been identified with masculine embodiment is thus revealed, as Coleridge suggests above, as intelligible only as a mode of resistance.

The three modes of penetrating the male body explored in this chapter occur in literary texts from the second half of the nineteenth century, a time of particularly high-pitched anxiety over the mutability of gender roles (Showalter 1992). First, Charles Baudelaire's prose poem "Miss Scalpel" and its formulation of an 'ocular penetration'[18] will be employed to critique the concept of a strictly male gaze and demonstrate how the eye functions for Baudelaire as the site of a terrifying yet ultimately fascinating penetration. Next, a scene of oral penetration from Joris-Karl Huysmans' *A rebours* will show how such an event instigates an inversion not simply of gender, but of the bodily orifices themselves. Like Schreber, Huysmans' penetrated male body inverts not only the positions of anus and mouth, but of gender itself. Finally, in Oscar Wilde's *A Picture of Dorian Gray*, an aural or olfactory penetration is shown to be central to the submission to discourse itself, the interiorization of an 'other's' words which constitutes the possibility of a self, rendering that self always already subjected, or submissive: always already penetrated.

That these three modes of penetration occur within texts which themselves interpenetrate – Huysmans echoing Baudelaire, Wilde echoing Huysmans[19] – suggests a

---

[18] The phrase 'ocular penetration' appears in Berkeley Kaite's "The Pornographic Body Double: Transgression is the Law", in Arthur Kroker and Marilouise Kroker (eds), *Body Invaders: Sexuality and the Postmodern Condition* (Basingstoke: MacMillan, 1988), 150–68. Kaite's overview of a certain "contradictory and oscillating" gaze within pornography is similar to my own conclusions regarding Baudelaire and the gaze.

[19] In *A rebours*, Huysmans' (anti)hero, Des Esseintes, is an avid reader of Baudelaire. In Wilde's *A Picture of Dorian Gray*, Lord Henry Wotton gives Huysmans' novel to Dorian to read (although it is never mentioned by name, Wilde identified it as such in the trials, see H. Montgomery Hyde, *Famous Trials 7: Oscar Wilde* (Harmondsworth: Penguin, 1962), 114.

genealogical or rhizomatic non-originary origin to the act of penetration itself: a textual, not simply sexual, penetration. The body of the text, as well as the male body appearing within it, is shot through with holes out of which or into which things move.

Furthermore, that the modes of penetration explored in this chapter are not immediately of the male anus is important for understanding the breadth of the claim this book is making. Penetration is not being presented as a specifically sexual or specifically anal, or even specifically homosexual, act – although it may, simultaneously, be all those things. Instead, it is to be understood as what might be called an 'existential' penetration or psychosomatic vulnerability the perpetration of which is experienced as a violation of the inviolate masculinity to which masculine subjectivity is (supposedly) heir. The focus here is on those moments when the masculine subject feels himself disintegrating as a result of being penetrated, even though (or perhaps especially when) that penetration has been the source of a certain fascination and even erotic pleasure. At this moment the body falls short of the masculine ideal of *dis*embodiment or impenetrability and becomes an object of shame as much as of pleasure.

Within the standard logic of gender dimorphism, such shameful penetrability invariably feminizes, and thereby erases, the male body. It is as if the limits of representation themselves were being pierced and punctured, suffering a rupture the very infliction of which – by creating a hole, gap or abyss – is experienced as a passivity which can only be acknowledged by that body becoming its conceptual opposite: female. As if the horror of such an event can be made bearable by the magic trick of representation, conjuring a female form to take the place of that penetrated male. Or, perhaps, as if the penetration itself had infected the male body with a contagious femininity, suggesting a terrifying 'permeability' between the feminine and the masculine (Miller 1986, 107). Or even as if the impossibility of representing such an act must remain impossible, and the security of absolute gender difference imposed the moment it threatens to occur. For when does the skin stop being on the outside and start being on the inside, if not at those edges, those orifices where the threat of penetration lurks most insidiously? Those zones where what is internal can suddenly be rendered external, what is interior invaded, and the safety of distinction and difference between them left vertiginously unstable.[20]

Having said as much, however, in each case it will become clear how, above and beyond any generalized 'existential penetration', each orifice – eye, mouth, ear – can (perhaps, must) be reduced to a symbolic anus. As if, for the male, to experience submission to another male is always already coterminous with 'getting fucked' – an expression which in itself indicates the slippage between the sexual and the metaphorical registers of speech (see Rancour-Laferriere 1979, 58–9).

DECADENT GENDER

Firstly, in order to provide a context for the texts to be discussed, there follows a brief outline of the decadent period's flirtation with sexual ambiguity and gender inversion, and the anxiety it produced. Such anxiety was contemporaneous with the relatively recent division of human sexuality into homo- or heterosexual categories (Sedgwick 1993, 1; Halperin 1990, 43). According to Foucault, around 1870 'the sodomite' became 'the homosexual' and a physical act became compacted into a pathologized personality type (Foucault 1990, 43) predominantly identifiable by atypical gender behaviour (Bristow 1995; Sinfield 1994). It was a rapid change, which perhaps helps explain the enormous anxiety it generated. For example, in 1860, in *Les Paradis artificiel*, Baudelaire could refer to the ways in which an immersion in "the soft atmosphere of women ... gives birth to the superior geniuses" (cited in Pia 1961, 36–9) with relative impunity. Thirty-five years later, such intimate

---

[20] See, for example, the opening pages of Lyotard's *Libidinal Economy*, where he invites us to "open the so-called body and spread out all its surfaces", trans. Iain Hamilton Grant (London: Athlone Press, 1993), 1–2.

knowledge of female *accoutréments*, far from signalling masculine genius, would instead render one's sexuality – and virility – highly suspect. Even the man of letters was no longer exempt from the general suspicion that knowing too much about the 'mysterious domain of women' somehow feminized or emasculated him. The turning point was the Wilde trials, after which, according to Rupert Croft-Brooke:

> it was all right to like to see a woman well turned out – to know anything about her clothes was poisonous. In art galleries you might 'know what you liked' but any other knowledge of art was suspect. A man could smoke a pipe, large and heavy if possible, but cigarettes were for boys and effeminates. Perhaps the unhealthiest thing of all was to know anything about decor in the home – a healthy man left that sort of fal-lal to the wife. (Croft-Brooke 1967, 287)[21]

Such paranoid self-policing of the masculine subject is linked to Eve Kosofsky-Sedgwick's homosocial formulation: "For a man to be a man's man is separated only by an invisible, carefully blurred, always-already-crossed line from being 'interested in men'" (Sedgwick 1985, 89). To be a 'lady's man' is to admire how she looked, but not to pay so much attention that one seems to covet her wardrobe. The social and sexual implications of an interest in women and their milieu had become so overwrought as to provide unmistakable signs of homosexuality. Yet, such a reading can only make sense within a cross-sex matrix so contradictory as to be almost nonsensical. An interest in women's clothes, etc., suggests an interest in wearing them, which suggests a desire to be a woman, which suggests a desire for sex with men. The acts of displacement necessary for such a reading distance the desire from its origin to such an extent that it becomes itself originless – or, rather, the sexual desire itself is read as the origin.

---

[21] The date of Croft-Brooke's book – 1967 – was the year that homosexual conduct between consenting adults and in private was made legal in Britain.

Baudelaire was able to wax lyrical about the trappings(!) of femininity without implicating himself as a homosexual (indeed, the word would not exist for another nine years[22]). Half a century later, that interest would lead Proust to assume Baudelaire was a homosexual.[23] There occurred in the interim a clear shift in the meanings given to a man's interest in femininity from a desire for women to a woman's desire.

Such anxiety over gender roles and sexual ambiguity marked the emerging bourgeois culture of the late nineteenth century, resulting in an increased polarization of the sexes (Cohen 1993; Showalter 1992; Gay 1986; Weeks 1981). Femininity had the power – even as women themselves remained politically powerless – to penetrate the masculine citadel and contaminate it, render it impure. In an attempt to reduce that threat, gender became a mutually exclusive paradigm. As such, with the rise of sexology and the emergence of a discourse intent on policing sexual behaviours and reifying gender polarities, effeminacy became a spectre haunting masculinity – it became masculinity's other (Cohen 1996), with the consequence that sexual inversion was most often read as gender inversion (Hekma 1994). As Alan Sinfield remarks, whilst effeminacy is rarely addressed explicitly in theories of masculinity, "it defines, crucially, the generally

---

[22] The word 'homosexual' was invented by a novelist, Karl Maria Kertbeny, in 1862. Not until 1869 did he use the term 'heterosexual' to designate people whose primary erotic orientation was directed at members of the opposite sex. See Frederic Silverstolpe, "Benkert Was Not a Doctor: On the Nonmedical Origins of the Homosexual Category in the Nineteenth Century" (unpublished conference paper, Amsterdam Free University, 1987). The English homosexual writer Edward Carpenter called it a 'bastard word' mixing Greek (*homos*) and Latin (*sexualis*), preferring his own term, 'homogenic'. Carpenter, *The Intermediate Sex*, (London: George Allen & Unwin, 1908), 40n.

[23] In his *Journals*, Andre Gide writes of a visit to Proust during which Proust outlines his theory about Baudelaire's homosexuality: "The way he speaks of Lesbos, and the mere need of speaking of it, would be enough to convince me", *Journals 1889-1949*, trans. Justin O'Brien, (London: Penguin, 1967), 329–30.

acceptable limits of gender and sexual expression" (Sinfield 1994, 4). Sinfield usefully traces the history of effeminacy in order to locate its specific historical association with same-sex desire; namely, the Wilde trials. The unacceptability of effeminacy as an expression of anything other than the absolute opposite of masculinity became more marked with the rise of bourgeois masculinity in the second half of the nineteenth century, and effeminacy's association with homosexuality can be traced to this period. As a definite 'homosexual body' appears, characterized by a salient and pejorative femininity, the *absence* of effeminacy – that nineteenth century bourgeois obsession – defines normative heterosexual masculinity as the unmarked term. "Effeminacy is not banished by manliness", Sinfield observes, "it is its necessary corollary, present continually as the danger that manliness has to dispel" (Sinfield 1995, 62). Perceived and vilified as bearers of a terrifying effeminacy, homosexuals were excluded from the definition of masculinity that was established by that very exclusion. In such a climate, gender ambiguity could only become more and more intolerable as the consolidation of gender polarity became an ideological imperative.

CELEBRATING THE ABJECT

Yet, whilst the dominant culture – science in particular – recoiled in horror at the sight of gender ambiguity, seeing in it a breakdown of order, a threat to the *status quo*, and a degeneration of morals, many writers and artists of the time eagerly embraced it, often for the selfsame reasons. The Androgyne was the jewel in the crown of Decadent art, what Mario Praz in his study of the literature of the period calls "the artistic sex *par excellence*" (Praz 1962, 354). Novel after novel, poem after poem, spoke of the terror and the beauty of a being whose body gestures towards both sexes. In the words of the Decadent novelist Joséphin Péladan,

> The number of women who feel themselves to be men grows daily, and the masculine instinct leads them

> to violent actions, in the same proportion as that in which the number of men who feel themselves to be women abdicate their sex and, becoming passive, pass virtually on to a negative plane. (Cited in Praz 1962, 354)

'Femininity' and 'masculinity' are constructed to correspond with particular arrangements of genitalia; gender becomes the *telos* of biological sex. It is gender *behaviours* rather than specific sexual *acts* which are being policed. The most primitive anxieties about natural order are aggravated by the existence of women who act like men and men who act like women, and they inspire the most Draconian responses – responses noted as particularly typical of the *fin de siècle*: "in periods of cultural insecurity, when there are fears of regression and degeneration, the longing for strict border controls around the definition of gender ... becomes especially intense" (Showalter 1992, 4).

These gender anxieties were further exacerbated by the unclassifiable nature of creative imagination and the male artist in particular found himself caught in a cultural double bind: "neither pure artist nor fully masculine" (Weir 1995, 18). Any work of art that did not reflect and consolidate the strict polarity of the sexes was immediately suspect: the male artist must be as plain and as resolutely masculine as the men who read him. After all, Péladan's words testify to a more fierce denigration of men who display female characteristics. Such men, through their passivity, 'pass virtually on to a negative plane', becoming invisible, exiles of their sex. For men to adopt so-called 'female' behaviours invokes a greater punitive response than *vice versa*, because misogyny, denigration of the feminine, is governing their interpretation. (It was more understandable – though no less 'unnatural' – that within patriarchy, women should aspire to masculinity.) In that move towards the feminine, the masculine body disappears, and gender difference is reinstated. Such a transformation, however, suggests an ability to metamorphose from one sex to another which immediately problematizes their supposedly natural opposition, leaving corporeality even more unstable, and rendering gender dimorphism a central problematic of all representational protocols. For even those writers for whom gender ambiguity or reversal provided fruitful subject matter, there is nevertheless an investment in the polarity with which they play. As the remainder of this chapter will demonstrate, penetration becomes the point around which this play of anxiety and fascination gathers.

Deleuze extends the concept of decadence to incorporate a notion of 'the intolerable'. By this process, elements which lie beyond or in excess of the protocols of representation can be revealed. In order to do so, Deleuze writes, "it is necessary to make holes, to introduce voids and white spaces"; it is necessary "to make emptiness in order to find the whole again" (Deleuze 2000, 20). It was this sense of making holes (or ruptures) in order to reveal something else that characterized the anus in the last chapter. In the following discussion, certain points of entry upon the male body are considered in the same light. It is, in Deleuze's study of cinema, precisely the visual field which is being punctured in this way, precisely the eyes which function as a site of penetration. And it is to the eyes that the next section turns in its reading of some of Baudelaire's prose poems.

BAUDELAIRE'S WILL TO OTHERNESS

Baudelaire remains an ambiguous figure in that he challenges the dominant image of mid-nineteenth-century bourgeois masculinity whilst at the same time – being the son of a governmental administrator and stepson of an army general – so profoundly inhabiting it. Thus, in becoming a poet, Baudelaire was rejecting all that was expected of him and his familial rebellion is well-documented: the squandering of inheritance, the prostitutes, the dyed green hair, the experiments with drugs and drink. In his life as much as in his work, then, a kind of 'will to otherness' is more than apparent. In his work, this will to otherness manifested itself primarily in an attitude to art that can only be called 'modern', for in it lurks a critique and rejection of all that is traditional.

Indeed, in Foucault's reflections on modernity as an attitude rather than a specific historical epoch, Baudelaire is cited as "an almost-indispensable example" (Foucault 1998a, 310). For Baudelaire, modernity is not simply found in the fashionable, "the transient, the fleeting, the contingent" (Baudelaire 1972, 403) – this is only "one half of art". The other half is to be found in extracting from fashion "the poetry that resides in its historical envelope, to distill the eternal from the transitory" (Baudelaire 1972, 402). It is, in other words, a grasp at the present that remains only too aware of its status as nothing more than a grasp. For this reason, as Walter Benjamin claims, Baudelaire's work "cannot merely be categorized as historical, like anyone else's, but it intended to be so and understood itself as such" (Benjamin 1973, 164). Baudelaire's self-conscious modernity is thus an attitude, a pose, a willful knowing. In Foucault's terms, it is a heroization of the present that constitutes an ironic relation with the self – a relation which takes the self *as* a work of art. To quote from Baudelaire's journals, the Dandy "should live and sleep in front of a mirror" (Baudelaire 1989, 26). And such self-consciousness, such vanity, was considered to be the absolute antithesis of nineteenth-century masculinity. It brought with it, as shall be seen, an entire conceptual armature which, whilst its aim might be said to be the reinstatement of consolidated gender norms, turns out nevertheless to undermine them radically.

For Baudelaire, this relation to the self upon which modernity as an attitude is contingent centres on an openness or penetrability at odds with the impenetrability of traditional masculine subjectivity. Walter Benjamin places such penetration/loss-of-self "at the very centre of [Baudelaire's] work" and characterizes it as a conflict which is named "the creative process itself" (Benjamin 1973, 165). For Baudelaire, the poet must maintain a constant attitude of combat against docile conformity (Baudelaire 1989, 39), and revel in that state of flux in which the self is always an ambiguous and fragile entity: "for in the grandeur of reverie, the sense of self soon fades"

(Baudelaire 1991, 33). As such, the poet must remain *open* to all sensations in order to be a poet at all, yet it is this very state of openness that most threatens to dissolve his (masculine) subjectivity. According to Baudelaire, the impenetrability of masculinity must be overcome, or broken down, if poetry is ever to occur, making the male poet an inherently ambiguous figure within patriarchal systems of thought.

AMBIGUITY AND METONYMY

Such ambiguity is most self-consciously evident in Baudelaire's prose poems, where linear narrative and linear history are rejected in favour of a more haphazard conglomeration. One is free to choose the order in which the pieces are read, and such textual freedom is coterminous with the freedom to choose, in the Modernist moment, between an endless series of possible selves. Deleuze and Guattari might be referring to Baudelaire's prose poems when they claim that a book is all the more total for being fragmented (Deleuze and Guattari 1992, 6). Like their *A Thousand Plateaus*, Baudelaire's prose poems "can be read starting anywhere and can be related to any other [plateau]" (Deleuze and Guattari 1992, 22).

In *Baudelaire and Schizoanalysis*, Eugene W. Holland's Deleuzoguattarian study of the poet, this fragmented form of writing is related to what Holland calls a metonymic poetics, which he contrast with the more traditional poetics of metaphor. Holland's distinction between metonymy and metaphor is developed – as is that employed by Barthes in the introduction to this book – from the linguist Roman Jakobson. It turns on a differentiation between the distance or displacement effected by metaphor and the contiguity effected by metonymy. For, whilst metaphor functions through similarity and identity, concealing the gap between signifier and signified, metonymy opts to play with this gap, revealing as a consequence difference and fragmentation. Jakobson further asserts that whilst metaphor is concerned with metaphysics, that is, with establishing a fixed meaning through similarity, metonymy aligns itself with, in Holland's words, "a heroic acknowledgment of contingency and flux" which renders meaning "undecidable" (1993, 39).

Through metonymy, Holland argues, language functions not as a mediating representative attempt to grasp at a distant 'real', but is itself – and presents itself as - part of that real. With metonymy, words are not substitutes for the signified but are instead themselves a slice of the signification procedure. As such, metonymy is more suited to the registering of historical inscription, seeing it as an (impossible) history of the present. In Holland's words:

> History provokes responses in writing: writing registers effects of history: they are recto and verso of the same process of registration. History is thus always related metonymically to a text in two *different* ways: both as its context (producing effects) and as its referent (produced in response) rather than just one or the other. (1993, 262)

Holland finds in Baudelaire's prose poems a metonymic poetics characterized by an ironic attitude to metaphor, by which "metonymy *tends* to undermine metaphor" (Holland 1993, 75); that is, contingency and flux undermine fixed meaning. According to Holland, moreover, this undermining of the metaphor is achieved not only through focusing on instability and undecidability, but also – within the same move – by recognizing the role of the body. For whereas metaphors function by replacement or substitution of the object represented, metonyms retain an intimate connection to it, moving, he claims, "from cerebral to more corporeal sensations" (Holland 1993, 78). Metonymy thereby subverts the intellectual rule of the metaphor. In this move towards corporeality we find a masochism not dissimilar to that outlined by Theweleit in the previous chapter, an economy in which

> suffering is valued ... as a source of pure intra-psychic intensity, which arises from the exact coincidence between what is desired and what is condemned

> as evil by the laws of the socio-symbolic order.
> (Holland 1993, 18)

Within the metonymic move towards the body, that is, pain and pleasure become indistinguishable as that which is disavowed by the socio-symbolic order becomes indistinguishable from – or, rather, more recognizable as – that which is desired. In short, suffering is desired. In Baudelaire's prose poems such suffering is, moreover, intimately connected to a penetration of the male body. Yet for Holland this penetration reveals the modern masculine subject to be one "that virtually disappears between the pulsions of desire and the sanctions prohibiting them" (1993, 29). However, whilst it remains true that, for Baudelaire, the poet is of necessity an inherently penetrable being, thus rendering his claim to masculine subjectivity problematic by marking his distance from its cultural requirements, it will be seen that the body that does emerge from this virtual disappearance of the masculine subject is the penetrated male body. Its appearance, furthermore, provokes both fear and fascination. Indeed, fascination will be shown to attend the appearance of all three of the penetrated male bodies found in this chapter. And it will be seen that, as with many of its prefigurations of decadent art, Baudelaire's cosmology is one in which gender reversals are standard poetic fare. Not only that, but they appear most insidiously around the penetrated male body, marking out its challenge/threat to gender norms.

POETRY AND PENETRATION

It is clear that gender reversal provided potent imagery for Baudelaire's poetry, in which women often act as penetrators, the poet submitting willingly to being penetrated in order to be a poet at all, that is, in order to trace the event in language. In this sense, penetration is essential for Baudelaire in order to conceive and give birth to his poetry. Consider this, as an example, from "The Artists' *Confiteor*":

> How penetrating is the close of day in autumn! Oh!
> Penetrating to the very point of pain, for there are
> certain delicious sensations, which, while imprecise,
> are not without intensity; and no blade has a keener
> tip than that of Infinity. (Baudelaire 1991, 32–3)

Or this, from "The Crowds", where Baudelaire explicitly contrasts the necessary penetrability of the poet to the more habitually closed nature of the average man:

> He who finds it easy to espouse the crowds knows
> feverish pleasures which will be eternally denied to
> the selfish man, who is as tightly sealed as a strong
> box, or the lazy man, who is as self-contained as a
> mollusc. (Baudelaire 1991, 44)

The poet has to be open to that penetration, to those feverish pleasures which will inspire his poetry, and for Baudelaire such penetrability is a "holy prostitution of the soul which gives itself entirely" (Baudelaire 1991, 44). Other men, their bodies and their selves clammed shut, know nothing of this process. And poetry is denied them. For the poet, therefore, the act of being penetrated, whilst marking him as different from other men, remains nevertheless a necessary undertaking. Yet, while it feeds his art, it also contains an attendant fear of losing one's self. The poet, it would seem, is in this sense masculinity's other.

Similarly, in 'The Desire to Paint', Baudelaire writes: "Unhappy may be the man, but happy the artist pierced by passion!" (Baudelaire 1991, 87). Normative masculinity is at risk in the process of becoming a poet. And the key concept in such risk is penetrability and its attendant gender reversal. For, as Leo Bersani states in his Freudian reading of Baudelaire's poetry, "psychic penetrability is fantasised as sexual penetrability", and this always carries with it the danger that it "may change him into a woman" (Bersani 1977, 12).

However, as Margery A. Evans points out, this instability functions in the prose poems as a desire to suffer coupled with a desire to penetrate and dominate the poetic object; that is, a desire to be both passive *and* active (Evans 1993, 47). For if love, for Baudelaire, "resembles an application of torture or a surgical operation", then the apotheosis of pleasure consists in being "alternately victim and executioner" (Baudelaire 1989, 4, 24), that is, in inhabiting an unstable position of undecidability: neither male nor female, but more of a movement between, or gesture towards, both. Such conceptual instability hinges, for Baudelaire, on the dualistic movement of looking and being looked at; that is, on the eye as something both penetrating and penetrated. As such, the gaze becomes the site of intensely erotic physical sensations. Indeed, as Enid Starkie remarks in her biography of the poet, "the most intense physical sensations he ever received were through the organ of sight, sensations amounting almost to orgasm" (Starkie 1988, 93).

VISIONS OF ACCESS

This indeterminacy or undecidability of the gaze is most clearly evident in the prose poem "Miss Scalpel" (*Mademoiselle Bistouri*), in which the poet-narrator is mistaken for a doctor by a prostitute obsessed with incision. Miss Scalpel takes the poet home to show him her collection of portraits of doctors, one of whom is said to look "like a young lady" (Baudelaire 1991, 100). Not that the anonymity of this encounter is the first thing to be noticed – "[a] rendering oneself vulnerable to the risk of the stranger" (Haver 1997, xiv) – nor the resemblance between the doctor and a 'young lady'; but also, and above all, that Miss Scalpel is the dominant figure, orchestrating an erasure of the poet's self through her insistence on his being a doctor. She seems to penetrate the poet through this authorial gesture, to look into his eyes and see a void there to be filled with her own fantasy. Not for nothing is she named after a blade, a tool of penetration. As Evans writes, during this encounter between Miss Scalpel and the poet:

> The surgical blade initially intended for the penetration of 'Nature', the artist's model, is turned against the artist/surgeon himself, and the poet's initial

> movement to dissect the external world ... becomes a
> means of self-penetration. (Evans 1993, 49)

Significantly, several gender inversions attend this (self) penetration. From the outset, the young woman is presented in terms that draw on the masculine. She is tall and robust, she smokes cigars, and, in a period noted for its restriction on feminine mobility, this young woman proudly declares: "Oh, I go everywhere" (Baudelaire 1991, 99). At the same time, almost as if to redress the gender imbalance, she also employs distinctly feminizing terms of endearment towards the poet such as "my dear", "kitten" and "darling".

But this is not the only conceptual hierarchy to be inverted. Miss Scalpel recounts her visits to doctors, even though she isn't sick, and expresses her fantasy that one young surgeon, "pretty as an angel", visit her decked out in his operating robe, "even if there was a bit of blood on it" (Baudelaire 1991, 101). This fantasy inverts the authority of medicine as her desire for the narrator's portrait, and her insistence that he is a doctor, inverts the poet's desire to penetrate her personality by fixing it in words (Evans 1993, 48). At the same time, she quotes one doctor describing the appearance of another as "'That monster who wears on his face the blackness of his soul!'", setting up a correspondence between physiognomy and personality which the mistaken identity of the narrator contradicts.

Furthermore, the poet's initial assertion – "I am a passionate lover of mysteries because I continually hope to solve them" – is frustrated by his inability to understand the reason for the existence of such a monster. Likewise, his statement towards the end of the poem, "What bizarre things we find in a big city, when we know how to stroll about looking!" (Baudelaire 1991, 101), is contradicted by the earlier reference to Miss Scalpel as "this unlooked-for enigma" (Baudelaire 1991, 99). The poet allows himself "to be pulled along by this companion", to be embroiled in this mystery, because he hopes to solve it, penetrate it, know it. That his hopes are dashed and his anxieties heightened leads him to confirm the existence of something beyond, something in excess of, Pure Reason, something monstrous – like madness – the function of which perhaps only God can truly know. The poet's own attempt to impose reason upon this woman's obsession with doctors by asking, "Can you remember the moment and the occasion when this special passion was born in you?" is frustrated by her reply: "I don't know … I can't remember". Her inability to recall the cause of her obsession gives the lie to medical etiology. The poet cries to God: "you who are full of reasons and causes, and who have perhaps put into my mind a taste for horror in order to convert my heart, as a cure at the tip of a blade" (Baudelaire 1991, 101). Here, penetration is a cure as well as a wound, acting – like Derrida's *pharmakon* – as both poison and remedy. Indeed, in "Plato's Pharmacy", Derrida demonstrates how it is precisely through an act of "maleficent penetration" in the form of writing (1991, 135), that the *pharmakon*

> breaks into the very thing [memory] that would have liked to do without it yet lets itself at once be breached, roughed up, fulfilled, and replaced, completed by the very trace through which the present increases itself in the act of disappearing. (1991, 135)

Derrida's terminology bears witness to the violent register in which such an act takes place: the subject is "breached" and "roughed up" by discourse. Writing makes a hole in the subject and pours into that wound a drug which, whilst dissolving the recipient, also – paradoxically – increases its presence. In outliving the event, the written word both supplements it and replaces it, whilst retaining that metonymic link discussed above through a tracing of the body.

In Derrida and Baudelaire, then, writing acts as a means of administering the lethal dose *and* procuring the vaccine, this double-edged quality dissolving binary oppositions by creating something else, some space in which the neither/nor oscillates. Rather than dialectical synthesis, the *pharmakon* provides a proximity of absence and presence, toxin and antidote, death and restorative located upon the same site, a kind of interpenetration which produces or represents an excess of meaning that refutes binary logic, a something other that prevents any definitive decidability taking place. For the poet in "Miss Scalpel", what is cured is his curiosity. His initial fascination with this 'innocent monster' is likened to the tip of a blade, yet the penetration he endures/enjoys evades or dissolves any absolute meaning. And as will be shown next, the multiplicity or ambiguity of meaning provided by this experience provides, for Baudelaire, the curiosity which lies at the heart not only of modernity, but of the poetic gesture itself; a curiosity predicated on the opening up of the body's penetrability.

FASCINATION AND CURIOSITY

Andrew Benjamin has drawn out the complex of themes central to Baudelaire's aesthetic: curiosity, fascination, time and speed, and their close relationship to a project intent on securing the status of the unknown. For Benjamin, the gaze, once disassociated from a will to know, to master, as it is in Baudelaire's poetics, opens up as "a possibility of entry". Such ocular penetration is characterized by "the joy of abandoning oneself – giving up myself – to another form of knowledge" (Benjamin 1997, 4) and from this joy, Baudelaire's poetic proceeds. As shown above, for Baudelaire the eye is a site of penetration that provides a highly erotic charge. As such, for Baudelaire's poet this ocular penetration opens out the penetrated male body as an example of the unknown. Baudelaire's metonymic poetic allows this body both to appear and to provide the necessary means of apprehending its meaning. The act of submission, in other words, is linked to the very process by which knowledge is acquired.

In the prose poem "The Desire to Paint", for example, Baudelaire presents a woman whose most salient characteristic is said to be "the love of prey", and whose look awakens the desire "of dying slowly under her gaze" (Baudelaire 1991, 88). Knowledge is thus acquired through submission to the unknown, and this submission, for Baudelaire, goes by the name of fascination. Fascination – a bondage of the gaze – carries with it both the charge of an intense eroticism in

Baudelaire, and the uncertainty of (sexual) meaning that such knowledge implies. As Baudrillard argues, "fascination moves towards the neuter, towards an indeterminate chasm, a mobile, diffuse sexuality" (Baudrillard 1990, 27). Seduction lies on the other side of structured sexuality, in a parallel universe where gender polarities have no definite purchase, in the realm of the abject.

Indeed, for Andrew Benjamin, "part of the complexity at work within fascination is its link to the abject" (Benjamin 1997, 5). And this abjection is ambiguous, according to Kristeva, precisely because the abject figure casts "within himself *the scalpel* that carries out his separations" (Kristeva 1982, 8, emphasis added); separations, moreover, which supply him with a *jouissance* that maintains the perpetuation of his abjection (Kristeva 1982, 9). Like Miss Scalpel's obsession with portraits and photographs of doctors, the poet's curiosity is a morbid fascination in which alterity is complicated by the unsteady nature of the power of the gaze. The eye (the 'I') which looks is held by what it perceives, such that it no longer belongs unproblematically to the looker ("I let myself be pulled along"); it is as originless as Miss Scalpel's desire for doctors. Nor can he celebrate or claim that fascination as his own without unsettling the very sense of self from which such a claim might be said to originate. For, as Benjamin argues:

> The mark of the curious is the place of the unsettled, the unsettling, the aberrant, that which resists assimilation, what will endure as the curious. (1997, 6)

To say 'I am curious' is therefore not only to announce one's curiosity, but also to declare one's abjection as a *curio*, a freak, an innocent monster. It is to be – and at the same time – both looker and looked at, both voyeur and exhibit(ionist), roles which so often become reduced by a discursive or conceptual attachment to traditional genders by which the man looks at the woman. For the woman to look (back) thus has a domino effect on the concepts linking her to the role of object, which, when the object of her gaze happens to be a man, has the double impact of linking him to the conceptually feminine role and undermining the fixed determinations of this logic of the gaze. When this much power is so clearly at stake, the full strategy of the gaze takes on all the charge of erotic seduction, bringing with it a great deal of uncertainty.

SEDUCTION AS UNCERTAINTY

For Jean Baudrillard seduction is irreducibly feminine, though this femininity within seduction is neither the marked nor the unmarked term (Baudrillard 1990, 7), but is instead essentially uncertain; it is a play of uncertainty that uses the concept of "femininity" to represent something other than the female body. Instead, it is made to represent an "*erotic indetermination*" (Baudrillard 1990, 25, original emphasis) which, being linked to "the primitive seduction of language" (Baudrillard 1990, 54), pits itself, according to Baudrillard, against the mode of production that gender polarity serves: *se*duction versus *pro*duction. For this reason, femininity as seduction is, for Baudrillard, "on the same side as madness" (Baudrillard 1990, 17), as shown in Chapter One, where the more voluptuous Schreber became, the more God penetrated him, and the more God penetrated him, the more voluptuous he felt: a vicious circle inscribing psychosis. Yet, by using the concept of femininity to articulate this indetermination, Baudrillard ultimately reinforces – or at least relies upon – the chain of equivalences binding femininity and madness with penetration. To link femininity to uncertainty and seduction is to recapitulate the gender stereotypes by which meaning is consolidated.

Georges Bataille links seduction to the eye, and he goes on to locate this seduction "at the boundary of horror" (1985,17). As mentioned in the introduction, Barthes' reading of *Story of the Eye* finds in Bataille's poetic a metonymic register characteristic of modernity. This metonymy sets up a different chain of equivalences that trace a trajectory away from the more metaphysical equivalences found in metaphor. This eye, moreover, that "could be related to the cutting edge" (Bataille 1985, 17), invokes Miss Scalpel and the Baudelairean poet, presenting the eye not only as a site of rupture, but also as an instrument of incision, a blade of infinity with poison at its tip. That the incision it inflicts is also a penetration, a piercing, will inevitably increase the anxiety of the male body being thus entered – especially if one considers that for Bataille the eye is an anus, a bronze eye (Bataille 1985, 86–7). For Bataille, the penetration of one is always connected to and expressive of the penetration of the other.

Furthermore, the fact that man's "eyes continue to fetter him tightly to vulgar things" (Bataille 1985, 83) means that the looker is *bound* to look, *bound* to what he looks at, putting him in a submissive rather than dominant position in relation to what is exerting such fascination. There is thus no clear-cut distinction between the gaze and the object such that power can be said to reside on one side and not the other. The eye may have the power to look, to penetrate, but the object observed has the power to command attention, to inspire curiosity and, in the case of Miss Scalpel, to look back and inflict an equally severe penetration. Any attempt to gender this relationship, to talk of 'the male gaze', for example, therefore merely simplifies what is a continually shifting and mutually constituting power relationship. Instead, Baudelaire presents a shifting gaze, a multi-gendered gaze, as equally equipped within women as within men to penetrate, to dominate, as well as being ready to submit and to open up.

The politics of the gaze which genders the looker as male and the looked at as female is thus rendered imperfect, reversible and unstable by Baudelaire. Corrupt and corrupting, the penetrating female gaze enters the male body through the eye/anus and displaces his subjectivity, disrupts his equilibrium, robs him of his power by making him a visible object. Such visibility, however, being structurally problematic, means that the penetrated male body, in order to signify at all, immediately becomes dangerously ambiguous, its masculinity threatened with erasure by this abject status of ambiguity/femininity/passivity.

THE GENDER AMBIGUITY OF THE GAZE

More than this, however, as *both* male and feminine, both looker and looked at, the androgynous figure of the Poet in Baudelaire opens up a space of anxiety and production predicated on a concept of gender inversion which appears at or as the edges of knowledge itself. Opening himself up to the penetrating gaze and taxonomic enclosure of a woman, the poet in "Miss Scalpel" struggles to make himself understood ("*I had great difficulty making myself understood*") because to be in that position defies logic, evades understanding. It is to be, like Miss Scalpel herself, outside reason, in that wasteland of madness which, as Foucault remarks, "takes the false for the true, death for life, man for woman" (1989, 33).

Kaja Silverman suggests that differentiating *the gaze* from *the look* will overcome the association of looking with masculinity. She argues that a phallic divestiture surrounds this ambiguity of the gaze, a castrating ambivalence (1992, 125–30). Yet making the penis detachable does not so much alleviate the anxiety of feminization as heighten it, rendering masculinity unstable and removable. This instability, as can be seen in Baudelaire, arises from the double-edged function of the eye as both penetrator and penetrated. Theweleit characterizes the sexual ambiguity of the gaze as follows:

> If its beam is hard and active, it is phallic; its gleam represents the gleaming glans of the erect penis ... But the functions of the eye may also be receptive, melting or passive; even the male eye may take on the attributes of vaginal formations ... What is crucial is the eye's capacity for transformation; it is simultaneously able to perform both functions. The same eye may sometimes actively radiate (and thus be 'masculine') and at other times passively drink in light from elsewhere (and thus be 'feminine'). In conjunction with the gaze of another, it does both – it penetrates the other eye and receives its gaze. (1987, 134)

Theweleit and Baudelaire may disrupt the stability of the gendered gaze by making the male eye penetrable, but such penetrability remains, nevertheless, both conceptually represented by and associated with 'femininity', with "vaginal formations". Instability itself becomes a function of the 'feminine'. Far from rendering 'masculinity' more stable, however, this conceptual association of instability and femininity, as will be shown, serves to contaminate 'masculinity' by becoming the very condition for its emergence.

In what became known as 'the decadent Bible' – Joris-Karl Huysmans' novel *Against Nature* [*A rebours*] (1884) – this inversion of gender attendant upon the penetrated male body is figured as a more explicitly corporeal, though no less phantasmatic, phenomenon. The orifice penetrated this time is the mouth, the organ of speech. As such, discourse becomes more anxiously implicated in the maintenance of the masculine subject.

HUYSMANS' *A REBOURS*

Huysmans' *A rebours* tells the story of the wealthy aesthete, Jean Floressas des Esseintes, the last, childless male in the family line. Des Esseintes uses his wealth to implement a complete withdrawal from society into a world of his own devising. Selling up the family home in Paris, he buys a house on the outskirts of the city in which he locks himself away with only a couple of faithful servants. Bored and self-indulgent, Des Esseintes satisfies his refined taste for the extreme in a series of episodes that, like Baudelaire's prose poems (by which Huysmans was enormously influenced) can be read in almost any order. The novel is in no way linear in structure – there is no clear trajectory of beginning-middle-end – but rather unfolds in a series of spirals. The theme linking each one, however, is a savage attack upon nature/the natural. One episode describes a completely black meal Des Esseintes has prepared. Another recounts his attempts to create a unique visual stimulus by having a tortoise encrusted with jewels in order that he can watch it crawl across an elaborately patterned rug, only to find that the adornment of the creature's shell causes it to die. The one thing each episode has in common is a complete rejection of the natural world, a profoundly joyous pursuit of the artificial. As might be expected, a less than conventional approach to sexuality and gender comprises one facet of this assault against nature. Behind this love of artifice, however, lurks a very real terror of the penetrated male body, coupled with a fascination similar to that expressed by Baudelaire, though this time it is the mouth that is the site of this penetration – that orifice which, for Freud, is the first erotogenic zone of infancy. As such, the following analysis of Des Esseintes' experience of penetration through the mouth reinforces the claim made in the introduction of this book that adult masculinity is predicated on a repudiation of penetrability and its pleasures. Penetration of the adult male body is prohibited by penetration's association not only with femininity but also with infancy or stunted maturity.

THE OPEN MOUTH

As the sister orifice, or the 'other', of the anus – the opposite, unclean end of the alimentary canal – the mouth offends. Stuffed with food it will eject at the other end, it is a reminder of the body's capacity to be entered and as such, for men, is yet one more opening to be policed, clammed shut, and used selectively. This is no doubt not only due to the mouth's status as the child's first connection with its own sensuality, but also its status as the motor of speech: that is, its social or communicative function, which is inevitably foreclosed whilst the mouth is being entered. It is enough here to consider the childhood lesson that to speak with one's mouth full is to be lacking in manners. The lips, moreover, as Irigaray notes, recall the plurality of the female labia, rendering the mouth an inherently erotic orifice, ripe for penetration. As such, the mouth is problematic for the male, who possesses no such lower lips, unless one is to consider the anus as in some sense labial – a move which, as will be seen, severely disrupts the neat binaries of gender. But the glottal control mastered by speech also recalls the voluntary opening and closure of that other sphincter, the anus: man is, as Bataille succinctly notes, "a tube with two orifices" (Bataille 1985, 88). As stated in the last chapter, the acquisition of language is contingent upon the sublimation of the anus. The anus is removed from the social field at the precise moment of entry into that field, and as the primary condition of such entry. Initiation into the rites of the symbolic order – emergence into language, as such – is thus contingent upon controlling the openings of the body. Becoming a masculine subject is the result of closing off the body's chaos and submitting to order – both the order of language and the order of bodily cleanliness.

The mouth is thus a break in the surface of the body, a rupture of the skin, a gateway to be guarded with vigilance, under constant risk of violation. It is also, Kristeva argues, "the first organ of perception to develop and maintains the nursing infant's first contact with the outside but also with the *other*" (1984, 154). The child's instinct to engage with the world through inserting objects into its mouth is one of the first to be tamed. As such, the open mouth signifies curiosity, as much as hunger or speech, whilst closed it signifies not simply silence but control, repression, denial of speech. The urge to insert things in the mouth is replaced by the command to exert speech out of it, and what one may put into the mouth comes as much a matter of vigilance as what one may let come out. In terms of the masculine subject, as will be shown, the mouth becomes a dangerous reminder of the body's inherent penetrability.

PULLING TEETH

In Theweleit's analysis of life in a German military academy at the turn of the century, penetration of the open mouth and extraction of baby teeth is a rite of passage, a ritualistic removal of the vestiges of infancy and a bestowal of manhood through pain. For the young cadet, undergoing bodily penetration and overcoming physical pain are processes which instill masculinity. One former cadet was reassured by being informed that the tooth-pulling had replaced a more scatological procedure:

> As I stood bent over the bucket, spitting blood beneath the wicked smile of the tooth-flicker, Glasmacher consoled me by saying that it had formerly been customary to take the sacks [cadets] to the dispensary and fill them with the appropriate dose of castor oil to ensure they were purged internally and externally. (Cited in Theweleit 1989, 151)

The submissive positioning of the boy – bending over beneath the tooth-flicker – mirrors the obsolete ritual of laxation: the mouth replaces the anus as the site of masculine endowment, the penetration of the former replacing the evacuation of the latter.

Similarly, in Huysmans' novel a trip to the dentist dramatizes this dangerous and chaotic penetrability surrounding the open mouth. Suffering from toothache and unable to wait to see one of his usual "well-to-do business men" dentists, the anti-hero, Des Esseintes, resorts to "a common, lower-class tooth-doctor, one of those iron-fisted fellows" (Huysmans 1959, 60). The class position of this "strapping fellow dressed in a frock-coat and trousers that seemed carved in wood" (Huysmans 1959, 61) is contrasted to the refined and aristocratic Des Esseintes, the solid material presence of the working-class dentist counterpointing the first image of Des Esseintes presented earlier in the novel:

> a frail young man of thirty who was anaemic and highly strung, with hollow cheeks, cold eyes of steely blue, a nose which was turned up but straight, and thin, *papery* hands. (1959, 17, emphasis added)

The rawness and substance of wood in the description of the dentist contrasts with the fragility and refinement of the end product, paper, in the description of Des Esseintes. The lower class position of this "mechanic who called himself a dentist" (Huysmans 1959, 60) places him closer to nature, to the raw, whilst Des Esseintes' higher class position locates him closer to culture, the cooked – to the paper upon which civilization is inscribed. Des Esseintes' acculturation removes him from materiality, from the body, from the solid embodiment provided by a lower class association with nature. At the same time, his submission to the brute force of this lowly 'toothdoctor' renders his body all the more sentient, and salient, through pain. This provokes high levels of anxiety, not the least of which is due to the penetration of his body; a body made all the more visible, all the more substantial, through such violation. As Freud has remarked, physical pain plays an important part in our corporeal perception:

> the way in which we gain new knowledge of our organs during painful illnesses is perhaps a model of the way by which in general we arrive at the idea of our body. (1986, 451)

As such, pain signals a removal from the disembodiment of cultural consciousness, displacing the sovereignty of human subjectivity. In short, pain reminds us that we have a body, even if such certainty remains impossible to express in words. Whilst Elaine Scarry is correct to argue that "to have pain is to have *certainty*" (1985, 13), she fails to see that for men – as culturally enthroned arbiters of the mind – this reminder of the certainty of the body can exact a high price, the extraction of such corporeal knowledge as arduous and painful an operation as pulling teeth. Des Esseintes responds to such pain, for example, by "stamping his feet and squealing like a stuck pig" (Huysmans 1959, 62) whilst the dentist operates, signaling both a return to infancy and a regression to animality, an erasure of the adult human he purports to be. It is an example of what Deleuze and Guattari term 'becoming-animal' and is essential, according to them, not only to masochism, but also to the appearance of the body without organs (BwO). This BwO constitutes a different organization of the body, a *dis*organization, consisting of several strata, and "behind each stratum, encasted in it, there is always another stratum" (Deleuze and Guattari 1992, 159) – the BwO is a multiplicity. It thus constitutes a challenge to the conformity to which bodies are exposed, the command that "You will be organized, you will be an organism, you will articulate your body – otherwise you're just depraved" (Deleuze and Guattari 1992, 159). It is an erotic depravity that dissolves organization of the body's intensities, that loses control of its mastery over sensations. We are told that Des Esseintes "lost all control of himself and screamed at the top of his voice" (Huysmans 1959, 62). As with Schreber, the penetrated male body heralds the end of reason, the beginning of psychosis and the dissolution of masculinity.

That this loss of control, and its attendant resistance, is due to a fear of penetration is suggested by the image of Des Esseintes "fighting desperately against the man, who bore down on him again as if he wanted to plunge his arm into the depths of his belly" (Huysmans 1959, 62). The struggle to prevent the dentist's arm sliding into his gullet is a struggle of the disembodied subject, incapable of fighting against such enforced embodiment once robbed of its only weapon: language. The mouth is silenced, speechless, even while it has never been more open. As David Kunzle remarks,

> surgical intervention into a part of the body, the mouth, which is the source and instrument of vocal expression and resistance is a literal as well as metaphorical suppression and silencing. (1989, 31)

Deprived of the power of speech and reason, Des Esseintes can only fight, stamp his feet, and release muffled squeals, rendered powerless and speechless through the gagging effects of the dentist's iron fist. In a very real sense, the end of speech is the beginning of the body, suggesting not only the essentially non-discursive nature of corporeality, but also the transience of all discourse: in Foucault's words, "any possibility of language dries up in the transitivity of its execution" (1998b, 148). Yet this penetration, paradoxically, retains the power of fascination when, back out on the street, *sans* offending tooth, Des Esseintes feels "ten years younger", the experience having oddly rejuvenated him, the cessation of pain flooding him with waves of pleasurable relief. He remains haunted by the experience, desperate to "break the horrid *fascination* of this nightmare vision" (Huysmans 1959, 62, emphasis added). As with Baudelaire, penetration is presented here as an act with the power both to repel and attract.

What is more, if, as this book has been suggesting, impenetrability is an index of masculinity, opening up the male body renders masculinity increasingly fraught with tensions and dangers, risks and forbidden pleasures. Indeed, on the very first page of the novel the reader has been informed that Des Esseintes is the last in a long line of male descendents characterized as "progressively less manly" (Huysmans 1959, 17). More than merely articulating the discourse on degeneration which was central to the bourgeois response to decadence,[24] this imagined spectrum locates Des Esseintes upon a hinterland the other side of which is a terrain of ascending femininity: the male body is presented here at the point when it is evolving into its apparent opposite.

THE INVERTED BODY

In *A rebours*, this inversion of gender is attended, perhaps even facilitated by, an inversion of the body itself. The implied analogy between the mouth and the anus of the tooth-pulling scene is made yet more textually explicit when, towards the end of the novel, Des Esseintes orchestrates "the crowning

---

[24] Max Nordau (1896) writes, "decadence denotes a state of society which produces too great a number of individuals unfit for the labours of common life"; they are "enemies of all institutions which they do not understand, and to which they cannot adapt themselves": *Degeneration* (London: Heinemann), 301. Decadence, for Nordau, is the degeneration of society, the result of hereditary decline, and Des Esseintes is a typical specimen: "physically an anaemic and nervous man of weak constitution, the inheritor of all the vices and all the degeneracies of an exhausted race" (302). Nordau's book devotes an entire chapter to Oscar Wilde as exemplary of the degenerate artist.

achievement of the life he had planned for himself", namely, receiving his nourishment through peptone enemas. For him, this mode of ingestion is "the ultimate deviation from the norm" (Huysmans 1959, 208). Through the application of these enemas, the anus comes to function like a mouth, just as, during the encounter with the dentist, the mouth is fisted like an anus. The application of the enemas, after all, is necessary because Des Esseintes has become unable to ingest food through the mouth. Constant vomiting, evacuating food through the mouth rather than the anus, renders the mouth useless in its appointed task. The body has thus turned upside down, in a move that elevates what was lowly, and demeans what was on high. Such a "slap in the face for old Mother Nature" (Huysmans 1959, 208), moreover, delights Des Esseintes, and the experience of the enema – three times a day – brings a "faint smile" to his lips. The penetration of the anus is a pleasure registered by the mouth. One might also consider the vernacular expressions "verbal diarrhoea" and "talking through the arse" as indicative of a symbolic conflation or interchangeability of the anus and the mouth. Both expressions perpetrate an inversion of the body similar to that achieved by Des Esseintes.

This inversion is marked by a more insistent experience of the flesh, as the body replaces the mind as the primary mediating force between the self and the outer world. For the masculine protagonist, however, such acute and irrecusable corporeality makes subjectivity less, not more, substantial: it is a forceful and threatening connection to the world that seems to evacuate the male subject. As Christopher Lloyd remarks in his study of Huysmans' work, physiology always appears in his novels as a menacing force: "The body becomes a torture chamber", and "one cannot retreat from the body and ignore it" for "there is no escape from physical reality" (1990, 92, 93). Des Esseintes himself describes pain as a "useless, unjust, incomprehensible, and inept abomination" (Huysmans 1959, 92) – yet it is an abomination with which pleasure nevertheless remains connected. Recalling his affair with a schoolboy, Des Esseintes admits that "never had he submitted to more delightful or more stringent exploitation, never had he run such risks, yet never had he known such satisfaction mingled with distress" (Huysmans 1959, 116).

To concede to the finitude of the self through the recognition of the corporeal – be it through pleasure or pain – is thus always the defeat of an idealism that would place the self in a transcendent relationship to the body. But idealism's defeat is materialism's victory, and the decadent's relation to both is problematic. Baudelaire despised them equally, while the *decadisme* that succeeded him explored the limits of both, suggesting that the truth lay on neither side exclusively, but in the recognition of the contiguity of both. As Wilde will have his character Basil Hallward say of Dorian Gray, the young man represents "the harmony of soul and body – how much that is! We in our madness have separated the two, and have invented a realism that is vulgar, an ideality that is void!" (Wilde 1987, 24). Hallward suggests that acknowledgment of the inseparability of *both* elements – the body and the soul – will restore equilibrium. Shuttling between the extreme poles of both at vertiginous speed, rather than settling with one at the expense of the other, will reinstate harmony through paradox.

Once again, Derrida's *pharmakon* is useful here. For 'truth' to be established, Derrida argues, there is a necessary "neutralization of the citational play", a "blockage of the passage among opposing values" (1991, 127). The word is thereby turned "on its strange and invisible pivot" (Derrida 1991, 125) to present a single, reassuring meaning: only one of its poles is visible. There is a passage, Derrida suggests, that links opposing values, much like the passage linking the mouth to the anus, for example. Only through a blockage of this passage – through a kind of epistemological or etymological constipation – can uniform and universal meaning emerge. Similarly, the opposing values of 'masculinity' and 'femininity' remain linked by a passage the obstruction of which renders them separable and uni-dimensional. Gender ambiguity thus becomes a form of conceptual ambiguity, the mark and model of uncertainty.

GENDER AMBIGUITY AS CONCEPTUAL AMBIGUITY

To invoke the ineluctability of the flesh is thus not inevitably to appeal to some prolix materialism, some blood and guts 'reality' of the human body. It can and must be instead an imaginative engagement with the body, an act of *poiesis*, of fantasizing over its endless possibilities. And gender transformation is one such fantasy, the articulation of which succeeds in disrupting the clarity of any dominant ideology's claim that gender difference is insurmountable and absolute.

In *A rebours*, for example, the sight of the trapeze artiste, Miss Urania, a "strapping, handsome woman" with "muscles of steel, and arms of iron" (Huysmans 1959, 111, 110), causes Des Esseintes to feel himself undergoing a complimentary bodily transformation. The scene provides a perfect example of the cross-sex matrix of desire at work within the late nineteenth century model of sexuality:

> The more he admired her suppleness and strength, the more he thought he saw an artificial change of sex operating in her; her mincing movements and feminine affectations became ever less obtrusive, and in their place there developed the agile, vigorous charms of the male. In short, after being a woman to begin with, then hesitating in a condition verging on the androgynous, she seemed to have made up her mind and become an integral, unmistakable man ... By dint of considering his own physique and arguing from analogy, he got to the point of imagining that he for his part was turning female; and at this point he was seized by a definite desire to possess the woman, yearning for her just as a chlorotic girl will hanker after a clumsy brute whose embrace could squeeze the life out of her. (Huysmans 1959, 111)

Des Esseintes cannot succumb to the "charms of the male" and remain a man; he must become a woman, must conform to the logic of asymmetrical gender dimorphism. More than a male masochistic fantasy – he wants to dominate her, after all, even in his 'feminine' state – this corporeal role reversal dramatizes the impossible requirements of the 'desire as lack' model, which subjects same-sex desire to the logic of cross-sex normative heterosexuality, making homosexuality and transsexuality virtually interchangeable concepts. Des Esseintes clearly both dreads and desires to be treated to rough caresses, indicating the ambiguity attending the forgetting of "the man's part" – which is both the active role and the phallus which signifies it, constituting a binary opposition around active/passive and phallus/anus. To be passive is to forget the phallus, the man's part. That is – within the logic of Western gender dimorphism – to become a woman. To be a man, therefore, is to remember/*re*-member that part and adopt a role contingent upon repetition, mimesis, memory. It is an always tentative and unstable process, given the ambiguity of the mouth shown here: its status as the generative organ of discourse, as that out of which words come – expressing a 'self' – is constantly undermined by its equal status as that into which things can penetrate, thereby silencing or erasing that 'self'.

The *aerialiste* wavers in an androgynous state before 'making up her mind' to become an 'unmistakable man', which instigates Des Esseintes' transformation into a woman. For Huysmans, as for culture in general, gender can function only as an absolute, reassuring only in its unmistakable, non-ambiguous state. Once gender absolutism becomes unsettled, the world and the body turn upside down. In that wavering state between genders, nothing is clear. Bodies are on the move, but they can only be made sense of within the logic of non-contradiction by remaining stable opposites. The line about the 'clumsy brute' recalls the dentist who tries to squeeze the life out of Des Esseintes in the earlier scene, casting Des Esseintes in the role of the chlorotic girl longing for that fatal embrace. The extraction of the tooth becomes coterminous with castration, loss of the phallus, feminization, erasure of the masculine self. Penetration of the male body is suffered as a loss of inviolability, loss of status, the infliction of a wound. As Lee Edelman remarks in his reading of the psychoanalytic model of positional logic, men must "repudiate the pleasures of the anus because their fulfillment allegedly presupposes, and inflicts, the loss or 'wound' that serves as the very definition of the female's castration" (1994, 185).

And if, as has been suggested, the points of penetration on the (male) body can be read as displacements of the anus, a reversal of this interpretive manoeuvre allows for Edelman's comment to stand for Des Esseintes' penetration through the mouth. Yet the moment sexual difference imposes itself as the logic of non-contradiction, gender inversion occurs, providing the means by which sexual difference, paradoxically, becomes no difference at all, or at least a highly unstable one. The logic it tries to impose is undermined by its very imposition in the case of the penetrated male body.

The mouth thus serves a dual, indeed, contradictory, function – similar to Baudelaire's presentation of the eyes – in its ability both to penetrate (through speech) and be penetrated. The instability occasioned by such contradiction disrupts the gendered structuration of the body and calls into question the male ideal of corporeal impermeability. By calling on femininity to register the mouth's penetrability, gender thus functions as both a trope of exclusion and inclusion, undermining the very logic it is supposed to inscribe. In fact, it is through its imbrication with the opposed characteristics of activity and passivity that gender is used by Ernest Jones to encode the two functions of the mouth. Not unlike Theweleit's analysis of the 'bi-sexual' qualities of the eye cited earlier, Jones suggests:

> In anthropological, mythological and individual symbolism...the mouth has more frequently a female significance, being naturally adapted to represent a receptive organ. Its capacity, however, to emit fluids (saliva and breath), and the circumstances of its containing the tongue ... render it also suitable for portraying a male aperture. (1951, 273)

Amongst the examples of emissions from the "male aperture", Jones cites spitting as an act of displaced ejaculation, and one might be tempted to add the now antiquated use of the term 'ejaculation' for the emission of speech. Irigaray signals further the politics of this genderization of the mouth when she writes, "*either you are a woman or you speak-think*" (1993, 138, original emphasis). A man thus exposes himself to the threat of becoming a woman the minute he ceases to speak-think – when another man's fist is in his mouth, for example. But there also lurks in Jones' coy expression ('male aperture') a suggestion of the male anus, which becomes thereby not simply another hole for the emission of body fluids, but – as Des Esseintes' enemas confirm – another place to insert things, another site of penetration.

In contrast to the duality of the eyes and the mouth, however, the ear is only ever a receptive, that is, a 'feminine', organ and as such, as demonstrated in the final section, is a more anxiously problematic site of penetration for the male body. In the remainder of this chapter, a reading of Oscar Wilde's *A Picture of Dorian Gray* will provide an example of how the ear comes to function in this way, and how this submission to the discourse of another is constitutive of masculine subjectivity.

WILDE AND THE LAW OF SUBMISSION

Oscar Wilde's 1891 novel, *A Picture of Dorian Gray* charts the transformation of its eponymous 'hero' from innocence to corruption. When the novel opens, Dorian is the wide-eyed *naïf* posing for the painter, Basil Hallward. Sitting there watching, and pouring forth a diatribe of seductive ideas, is Lord Henry Wotton. On the painting's completion, Dorian makes a wish that he could remain as he looks in the portrait, whilst the portrait aged. His wish comes true, and as he descends into a maelstrom of unnamed sins, he retains his youthful appearance whilst the portrait registers the horrific appearance of his corrupt soul. Finally, in a state of anxiety, and having just murdered Hallward because he had discovered Dorian's secret, Dorian plunges a knife into the painting and at that point he himself dies. The novel's final image is of a grotesquely withered and deformed Dorian, only recognizable by the rings on his hands, lying below his portrait, which is as fresh as the day it was painted. Penetration (the knife entering the canvas) is once again characterized by a reversal (of Dorian's initial wish).

But what instigates this metamorphosis in Dorian is the penetration through his ear of Wotton's poisonous discourse. Equally powerful is the transformation instigated by Dorian's exposure to a poisonous book Wotton loans him – *A rebours*. Textuality and corporeality are intimately connected in this process of generating a new subjectivity, and the male body's submission to discourse is shown to be coterminous with a penetration of the body that is the very condition of the male subject's emergence.

THE UNCERTAIN SELF

Wilde's novel appeared at an historical juncture when homosexuality as currently understood was struggling for representation (Meyer 1994). For as much as *Dorian Gray* works toward *de*constructing the notion of a unified self (Brown 1997) – pitting itself against "the shallow psychology of those who conceive the Ego in a man as a thing simple, permanent, reliable, and of one essence" (Wilde 1987, 112) – it nevertheless also works self-consciously towards constructing the notion of a unified *homosexual* self, even in the absence of any recognizably homosexual activity or characters (Sinfield 1994). The novel thus immediately embodies a conflict between two different strategies, two opposed agendas, the outcome of which is not at all certain.

Such uncertainty, indeed, as will be shown, makes of the penetrated male body an event which refutes instrumental reason by insisting on the necessity of the experience of the flesh in the emergence of the masculine self. That self is thus always already submitting to a penetration through which it is constituted, yet which it must disavow as a consequence.

Moreover, such penetration is so deeply rooted within a feminine paradigm that the masculine self cannot be viewed as anything other than a paradox; for, in effect, the major outcome of this penetration is a masculine self that is so inseparable from the feminine self as to be anything but its conceptual other. And, as stated above, the orifice through which discourse enters the male body in this example is the ear. The ear thus becomes a channel for conception/conceptualization.

THE CONCEIVING EAR

In selecting the ear as the site of penetration, Wilde opts for an orifice which serves only one function: to receive. The ear cannot penetrate. Gone is the ambiguity of Baudelaire's eyes and Huysmans' mouth; here there is only one outcome: to submit, without resistance, if one is ever going to be certain of existing. Thus, whilst the concept of man may well be multiple and fragmented for Wilde – "a being with myriad lives and myriad sensations" (Wilde 1987, 112) – it is also, nevertheless, the result of a submission which for the male involved is as anxious as it is productive: a submission to discourse.

Whilst the central trope in the novel is the portrait of Dorian, this portrait figures as a displacement of Dorian's self, a distancing between the body and the soul which allows one to indulge in illicit pleasures whilst the other rots unseen in direct correlation to that indulgence. There is, however, another, less obvious trope, and it is this trope which allows for the penetrated male body to appear at all: that is, the trope of influence, of dissemination; constructing the self through the appropriation of the discourse of another. And it is charged with a profound and anxious eroticism – an eroticism of penetration by and surrender to that other's discourse.

Dorian Gray's attempts to understand who he is are initiated by a conversation with Lord Henry Wotton, and then further developed through reading a book loaned to him by Wotton; a book Wilde has identified as Huysmans' *A rebours*. Dorian Gray sees in its hero "a kind of pre-figuring type of himself"

(Wilde 1987, 102). In a phrase which reverses chronology and throws into question the certainty of origins, Wilde describes Dorian as discovering in Huysmans' novel "the story of his own life, written before he had lived it".[25]

Dorian feels an affinity not only with Des Esseintes but also with other fictional characters, his identification with these "ancestors in literature" suggesting a genealogy outside of, or against, nature; a non-teleological genealogy of *influence* which mirrors the lineage threaded through Baudelaire, Huysmans and Wilde. Not dissimilar to Derrida's definition of philosophy as "a fable transmitted from ear to ear" (1991, 114), it is a profound connection with past lives that gives the lie to any belief in a stable and essential singular self. Instead, Dorian finds in himself "strange legacies of thought and passion", finds his flesh "tainted with the monstrous maladies of the dead" (Wilde 1987, 112). Furthermore, at least one of these historical figures with which Dorian identifies is female, suggesting a process of identification that transcends or transgresses the limits of gender. Dorian's relationship with discourse is disclosed as a passionate identification above and beyond the mere mapping of knowledge.

Through this passionate engagement, the post-Enlightenment protocols which, according to Theodor Adorno and Max Horkheimer, demand that the body be "scorned and rejected as something inferior" are revealed as being also and at the same time a process of masking a body that as a consequence becomes "desired as something forbidden, objectified and alienated" (1972, 232). For Adorno and Horkheimer, the body is desired precisely because it is forbidden, but the process of outlawing the body has so far involved making it correspond in the conceptual economy with woman, and thus, by Western standards, a role demoted, subordinate and submissive. Adorno and Horkheimer argue that what has "made possible the supreme cultural achievements of Europe" is precisely, paradoxically, this discursive "love-hate relationship with the

---

[25] A similar prefiguration marked Wilde's own life, for Lord Alfred Douglas, often seen as the model for Dorian Gray, did not in fact enter Wilde's life until well *after* the novel was written.

body" (1972, 232). The event of the body becomes inseparable from the process that forecloses it, for it is a process made possible by the pulsional intensity it seeks to mask (Lyotard 1993, 6–12). Tracing this trope of influence makes discursive penetration of the (male) body central to the process of human thinking and cultural development.

DISCURSIVE PENETRATION

Wilde describes "a fantastic variation of Huysmans' over-realistic study of the artistic temperament in our unartistic age" (1962, 313). That Huysmans' novel – written in a prose style described by Léon Bloy as "continually dragging Mother Image by the hair or the feet down the wormeaten staircase of terrified Syntax" (cited in Baldick 1959, 14) – could ever be considered over-realistic is in itself fantastic, yet Wilde's comment nevertheless acknowledges a thematic genealogy underpinning the two texts. The word fantastic (strange, weird or fanciful in appearance; illusory; extravagantly fanciful; unrealistic) derives from the Greek *phantastikos*, meaning capable of producing images, via the Late Latin *phantazein*, meaning to make visible. The following reading will suggest that what Wilde makes visible within the pages of *Dorian Gray* is a penetrable male body which, whilst marked by femininity, nevertheless insists on such femininity as the condition of masculinity *per se*. To be masculine is only possible through a submission to discourse that marks one simultaneously feminine and consequently destabilizes the very gender norms it attempts to install/inscribe.

The novel opens in Basil Hallward's garden, late in the afternoon. Dorian Gray is taking a respite from modeling for Hallward, whilst Hallward's friend, Lord Henry Wotton, discourses on the transience of youth and beauty:

> Dorian Gray listened, open-eyed[26] and wondering. The spray of lilac fell from his hand upon the gravel. A furry bee came and buzzed round it for a moment. Then it began to scramble all over the oval stellated globe of the tiny blossoms. He watched it with that strange interest in trivial things that we try to develop when things of high import make us afraid, or when we are stirred by some new emotion for which we cannot find expression, or when some thought that terrifies us lays sudden siege to the brain and calls on us to yield. After a time the bee flew away. He saw it creeping into the stained trumpet of a Tyrian convolvulus. The flower seemed to quiver, and then swayed gently to and fro. (Wilde 1987, 32)

This undulation of the flower's "stained trumpet" – observed as a deliberate distraction from the desire to yield – echoes the "vibrating and throbbing to curious pulses" experienced by Dorian two pages earlier, when he feels as though the words he is hearing have come from himself, displacing their origin, confusing the neat distinction of inside/outside, speaker/listener. The flower and the ear mirror each other as vessels or modes of reception and penetration. Each in turn also echoes with the image of the anus.[27]

The pollination of the flower is suggestive of the dissemination undergone by Dorian, who discovers himself through or in the words of another, succumbing to an influence Lord Henry describes as "immoral" (Wilde 1987, 28). Immoral, perhaps, because it is a clearly penetrative pleasure, defined by Wotton later in the novel as the ability "to project one's soul into some gracious form, and let it tarry there a moment" (Wilde 1987, 41).

---

[26] The opening of the ear would seem to bring with it in this instance an equally widening ocular reaction. A circuit connecting each point of entry on the male body is emerging.

[27] The connection with the ear will be developed later in this chapter, whilst that with the flower is tackled in the following chapter, through a reading of Genet's work.

Something, moreover, about Wotton's "low, languid voice" is described as "absolutely fascinating" to Dorian. Once again, penetration carries with it the charge of fascination. That fascination, and its attendant threat of the unknown, makes Dorian fearful, and the fear shames him, because he knows that in the presence of another man he should not feel fear, however fascinating that man is (indeed, he may fear him all the more for knowing that one man should not be fascinated by another – even though the act of thinking is only possible through such fascination). To find something fascinating, as Dorian discovers after reading *A rebours*, is not the same thing as liking it, however; on the contrary, "There is a great difference" (Wilde 1987, 102). It is, rather, to fall under its influence, its spell, and thereby to lose control. Following the insemination perpetrated by Wotton's influence, Dorian's exposure to this poisonous yet fascinating book (Wilde 1987, 101)[28] changes him, literally splitting him in two. The process of Dorian's emergence creates an alter ego in the form of the portrait, and the two paths that his life subsequently takes – one of superficial purity, the other of profound corruption – will only reunite at the end of the novel, when both Dorians die. Like the *pharmakon*, Dorian's self is dualistic, ambiguous, existing in the in-between of undecidability, that uncontrollable state where nothing is certain. Once again, fascination is the mark of a maleficent penetration.

The loss of control attending this fascination, however, as shown in the readings of Baudelaire and Huysmans, is a double-edged sword: both a source of pleasure and a source of fear, marked by a vertiginous uncertainty. But Dorian's fascination is not, as with Baudelaire, contingent upon vision, nor, like in *A rebours*, upon the mouth, but upon discourse. It is a fascination with, as well as a fear of, words:

---

[28] *The Daily Chronicle* reviewer called *Dorian Gray* "a poisonous book". In his memoir of the artist, writer and poisoner Thomas Wainewright, Wilde calls poisoning an art form. Poison raises the question of an in-between, of an undecidable position, as Derrida's *pharmakon* demonstrates. It doesn't simply kill, therefore foreclosing the question, but corrupts, and as such opens up the question.

> Words! Mere words! How terrible they were! How clear, and vivid, and cruel! One could not escape from them. And yet what a subtle magic there was in them! They seemed to be able to give a plastic form to formless things, and to have a music of their own as sweet as that of viol or of lute. Mere words! Was there anything so real as words? (Wilde 1987, 30)

A fascination, then, with listening, with the spoken word, a submission to the voice, to the influence of another. Wotton's words *alter* Dorian Gray like no others he has ever heard. Wotton's discourse disseminates a monstrous version of Dorian (the suppurating portrait which must be hidden in the attic), an *alter ego* which rots with sin, pustulates with corruption and immorality. Furthermore, this fascination is also a process of self-recognition or self-construction: "Why", Dorian wonders, "had it been left for a stranger to reveal him to himself?" (Wilde 1987, 31). As with Miss Scalpel and the poet, as with Des Esseintes and the dentist, this fascinating, fearful penetration is an act between strangers. Exposure to the unknown comes through encounters with persons unknown, creating a chaos out of which some sense must be rendered.

To make clear the penetrative quality of discourse, Wilde compares Wotton's words to the trajectory of an arrow: "He was amazed at the sudden impression that his words had produced ... He had merely shot an arrow into the air. Had it hit the mark? How fascinating the lad was!" (Wilde 1987, 30). Like Saint Sebastian, Dorian is piniomed by arrows which, though discursive, are no less penetrating, no less violent, and no less effective for all that.

Although it is clearly a mutual fascination, then, it remains an unequal one, perhaps because for Wotton it is the *sight* of Dorian which fascinates, whilst for Dorian, it is Wotton's *words* that exert this dangerous fascination; words Wilde represents as an arrow shot in the air, penetrating the ear of the young man who hears them, as the bee penetrates the flower's trumpet in order to pollinate it.[29] This aural fertilization creates a monster in the text the very representation of which is as impossible as it is monstrous. It cannot be demonstrated, cannot be shown, except as and at the point of its own rupture, its own disappearance. When Dorian reveals the rank face of his soul rotting on the canvas, its presence cannot be tolerated or sustained, and he rips it to shreds with a knife, killing himself in the process. To adopt an image from one of Baudelaire's poems, he becomes like a vampire at its own veins (Baudelaire 1982, 80).

This ear, then, through which Wotton penetrates Dorian – like Baudelaire's eyes and Huysmans' mouth – appears as a site both of fascination and fear, pleasure and anxiety. Unlike the eyes or the mouth, however, the ear is not capable of penetrating, but can only remain passive, eternally listening to the Other. In her study of schizophrenia and telephonic communication, Avital Ronell identifies a *jouissance* of the ear by which the submission to discourse is likened to a form of addiction. The submission to discourse, she claims, means that "[t]he ear has been addicted, fascinated" (1989, 21), and will never be the same again. For Blanchot, "what fascinates us robs us of our power to give sense", that it is "both terrifying and tantalizing" (Blanchot 1982, 32). Fascination pulls one further away from reason, threatening to destabilize the world as something known. In this powerless state, one submits to what fascinates, as Dorian submits to Wotton's influence. One is addicted to – *fas*tened or attached to – the object of *fas*cination. In other words, meaning is not synonymous with reason. The ambiguity that surrounded the eyes and mouth in the readings of Baudelaire and Huysmans, here surrounds the concept of fascination. Fascination is both a spell and the breaking of a spell. When it attends something about which one should not be fascinated – such as, for a man, having one's

---

[29] A similar trope of a bee's pollination of a flower as figuring male-male intercourse can be found at the beginning of Proust's "Sodom and Gomorrha", in *In Search of Lost Time*, Volume 4, trans. C. K. Scott Moncrieff and Terence Kilmartin, rev. D. J. Enright (London: Chatto and Windus).

body penetrated – the ambiguity of that emotional response is all the more unsettling.

Furthermore, when that penetration becomes a necessary process in the emergence of a subject who must, subsequently, remain impenetrable, the instability and anxiety is increased. As the next section demonstrates, moreover, when the ear, through which such necessary penetration occurs, becomes readable as a displaced anus, a model of masculine subjectivity emerges that is highly unstable and profoundly at odds with more traditional gender concepts.

THE EAR AS DISPLACED ANUS

Like the eye and the mouth, the ear can also be read as a displaced anus, reaffirming the paranoia attending the male body, but also simultaneously delineating a network of concepts at work behind the representation of the penetrated male body. As openings upon the male body – that is, as sites of potential penetration – the eyes and the mouth function as displacements of the primary site of anxiety: the anus, and thereby they enter an economy of libidinal investment. Such displacement is not, however, the displacement effected by metaphor, which forecloses contiguity by establishing difference. It is, rather, the displacement effected by metonymy. Continuing on from Barthes' reading of Bataille, and Holland's reading of Baudelaire, this metonymy is being understood here as a process by which the body is more clearly attached to representation. This attachment refutes the intellectual rule of the differentiating metaphor by providing a channel of contiguity or flow. For example, the flower as anus, the anus as eye/mouth/ear/sun – all the attachments to the penetrated male body so far explored in this book – obtain their logic within a chain of equivalences radically different to the one which traditionally attaches that body to the concepts of passivity, femininity and submission. At the same time, however, by remaining within discourse – as its behind – this chain of equivalences nevertheless connects in some way to that metaphoric use of language which attempts to remove the penetrated male body and replace it with that of a woman. This connection between the two chains – the links between metaphor and metonymy – create a wavy or blurred meaning, as Barthes claims.

The anxiety over penetration centres on the anus in an attempt to define and reduce the entire body *at the same time* as moving beyond or behind it, connecting with all the body's holes, opening up the entire field of the male body to a more destabilizing discursive appearance. The ear as anus, however, as already stated, is more highly fraught with dangers because it can only ever receive. Permanently open, it is also the only organ of sense which can be used to detect activity behind the listener.

Like the Madonna, Dorian conceives through the ear, that orifice Ernest Jones claims is "best designed to receive thought" (Jones 1951, 349), and which Michel Leiris calls "the organ by means of which auditory sensations penetrate into us".[30] Making explicit the implicitly masculinist properties of discourse, Derrida adds that "speech is the sperm indispensable for insemination" (1982, xiv). (The silencing/castrating effects of the dentist's fist in Des Esseintes' mouth thus become clearer). The ear is the receptacle for this speech-sperm, and as such remains a terrifyingly permanent opening. In his essay on the Madonna's conception through the ear, Jones argues, furthermore, that the ear functions as a displaced anus, through a symbolic chain linking breath with flatulence (Jones 1951). This helps provide a clearer understanding of the fear attending its penetration. Derrida echoes this thought, taking it further by suggesting that all of philosophy might be characterized as "conception through the ear" (1982, xiv).

---

[30] Leiris' text runs in a narrow column alongside the main text of Derrida's essay "Tympan", in *Margins of Philosophy*, trans. Alan Bass (New York, London, Toronto, Sydney, Toyko and Singapore: Harvester Wheatsheaf, 1982), ix–xxix. The quotation here appears on page xv. Leiris' text, moreover, echoes Wilde's analogy of the flower and the ear, when he writes of "a connivance between that which could seem to be only a human voice and the rhythms of the fauna and flora" (xxiv–xxv).

But if the ear can be read as a displaced anus, and if thought occurs there via an act of penetration, what does this do to masculinist discourse intent on mastery and impenetrability? What does it say about the paranoia of the (im)penetrable male body if the generation of that discourse – that is, thinking itself – is contingent upon an act of penetration coterminous with sodomy? Is there a link between anality and human thought, and, if so, what is it?

In *Civilisation and its Discontents*, Freud argues that

> with the assumption of an erect posture by man and with the depreciation of his sense of smell, it was not only his anal eroticism which threatened to fall a victim to organic repression, but the whole of his sexuality, so that since this, the sexual function has been accompanied by a repugnance which cannot further be accounted for, and which prevents its complete satisfaction and forces it away from the sexual aim into sublimations and libidinal displacements … All neurotics, and many others besides, take exception to the fact that '*inter urinas et faeces nascimur* [we are born between urine and faeces]'.
> (1985, 296n)

This horror of anal eroticism is, moreover, explicitly linked for Freud to a gender ambiguity which is masked behind the reduction of masculinity to activity and femininity to passivity: "a view which is by no means universally confirmed in the animal kingdom" (Freud 1985, 295n). This suggests not only that the strictly maintained differences between men and women as, respectively, active and passive, is a response to and refusal of an innate bestiality, but also that such differentiation is above all a way of avoiding sexuality altogether. The division of the human species into two supposedly different sexes or genders, whilst discursively posited as a natural division, remains, for Freud, a paradox. Within this division, moreover, lurks the association of anality with passivity, femininity and neuroticism.

Georges Bataille similarly argues that the assumption of an erect posture lead to the repression of what he calls anal forces

(Bataille 1985, 88–9). No longer on permanent view, the anus lost its erotic significance and the energies it once expressed find an outlet at the other end of the alimentary canal – the mouth, or, more generally, the head. For Bataille, whilst the cultural and intellectual supremacy of humans over apes may well be at the expense of this anal energy, it nevertheless also remains as an expression – albeit diluted – of its original force.

In a similar vein, Deleuze and Guattari argue that the anus was "the first organ to suffer privatization, removal from the social field" (1983, 143). As already discussed, the private status of the anus is constituted by, and helps to constitute, the public status of the phallus.

It is clear that a residue of anality is retained despite these processes of sublimation, repression and privatization by which the anus is hidden. They all suggest some kind of original anality that is subsequently tamed or displaced by socialization, but which is never fully removed.

It is also clear how impossible it is to discuss the anus without discussing its function – that is, without discussing shit. This is perhaps the single most difficult issue when it comes to considering that particular orifice. As such, the focus is on its function as a point of exit, not a point of entry, and the issue of penetration is avoided. Consider this description of the desiring-machine, for example, from Deleuze and Guattari:

> Every machine, in the first place, is related to a continual material flow (*hyle*) that it cuts into ... the anus and the flow of shit it cuts off, for instance; the mouth that cuts off not only the flow of milk but also the flow of air and sound. (Deleuze and Guattari 1983, 36)

Whilst the mouth cuts off both the entry of nutrition and the exit of air and sound, the function of the anus is presented as one-way, only ever cutting off the flow outwards. Its association with the ear is therefore immediately problematical, given that the ear has an equally unidirectional purpose, but in the *opposite* direction, inwards; nothing comes out of the ear; it remains permanently receptive, incapable of 'closing' off, only ever a point of entry into the body.

As a displaced anus, the ear suggests an equally ungovernable and inexorable penetration of that other orifice, emphasizing the penetrability of that orifice it is displacing. It is, perhaps, only through this displacement that the penetrability of the anus can at all be considered. But as the next section will demonstrate, as the orifice through which subjectivity is instilled by a necessary penetration by discourse, the ear/anus renders masculine subjectivity a deeply submissive phenomenon.

SUBMISSION AND (MALE) SUBJECTIVITY

Wilde's *Dorian Gray* describes and reveals Dorian's gradual submission to a discourse of sin – that which James Joyce called "the pulse of Wilde's art" (1986, 59). Wilde writes:

> There are moments, psychologists tell us, when the passion for sin, or for what the world calls sin, so dominates a nature, that every fibre of the body, as every cell of the brain, seems to be instinct with fearful impulses. Men and women at such times lose the freedom of their will. They move to their terrible end as automatons move. Choice is taken from them, and conscience is either killed, or, if it lives at all, lives but to give rebellion its fascination, and disobedience its charm. For all sins, as theologians weary not of reminding us, are sins of disobedience. When that high spirit, that morning-star of evil, fell from heaven, it was as a rebel that he fell. (1987, 144)

Here, even rebellion is a submission to the will of another, disobedience to God an obedience to Satan. If Wilde is here associating disobedience with sin, in "The Soul of Man Under Socialism", he associates disobedience – and, therefore, sin – with progress: "disobedience, in the eyes of anyone who has read history, is man's original virtue. It is through disobedience that progress has been made" (Wilde 1987, 1020). In a transvaluation of values, Wilde claims sin as a virtue. Such disobedience, however, is always in direct conflict with a necessary obedience to a leader. Indeed, such conflict creates the subject, as shown in the previous chapter.

> There are three kinds of despots. There is the despot who tyrannises over the body. There is the despot who tyrannises over the soul. There is the despot who tyrannises over the soul and the body alike. The first is called the Prince. The second is called the Pope. The third is called the People. (Wilde 1987, 1038)

For Wilde subjectivity is constituted by a masochistic submission to the domination of another, be it Prince, Pope or People. Whilst Wilde makes no distinction between men and women in relation to this submission, Freud will go further and locate that masochistic moment at the heart of a specifically male subjectivity (1961). As David Savran observes, all Freud's examples of *feminine masochism* are men who fantasize about being in the woman's position; it is called feminine precisely because of this positioning *as a woman*. As such, "the masochistic scenario splits the subject and disrupts normative gender identifications" (Savran 1998, 27), thereby revealing "the deep-seated cultural logic that defines masculinity as a kind of submission" (Savran 1998, 319).

For Savran, this masochistic submission is "part of the very structure of male subjectivity as it was consolidated in Western Europe during the early modern period" (Savran 1998, 10). Furthermore, if the "new bourgeois must tirelessly police himself and his desires while calling this submission 'freedom'" (Savran 1998, 25), then subjectivity itself becomes a problematic of pleasure and bodies as they function in the strategies of its very emergence. The male body – the sensuality, openness and vulnerability of its highly charged corporeality – is locked within a masochistic moment that binds it inextricably to a profound association with femininity as the *sine qua non* of submission.

The paradox of masculine embodiment is that whether disembodied in its traditional form or intensely embodied in its feminized/penetrated form, it is, either way, a submissive phenomenon; and, as such, inseparable from cultural notions of femininity – though not as femininity's other, but its epiphenomenal condition.

From the outset, Dorian Gray is presented in terms which feminize him, described by Wotton as a "brainless, beautiful creature" (Wilde 1987, 19), removed from the realm of thought, his beauty indeed contingent on thought's absence. As an artist's model his primary role is visual, a role which, in art history, has been reserved almost predominantly for the female body (Walters 1978). As Eve Sedgwick has commented, whilst the renaissance of Greek thought and Hellenic ideals at the end of the nineteenth century, particularly among a homosexual elite, functioned to make the male body visible, it was charged with an anxious and prohibited eroticism. This eroticism challenged, whilst remaining essentially linked to, the Christian condensation of 'the flesh' as the *female* body (Sedgwick 1993, 136). The spectacularized male body refutes the dominance of the male gaze as much as it charges it with an illicit homoeroticism. Visibility of the male body defines a nexus of power centred upon a dynamics of domination and submission. Thus, whilst the late-nineteenth-century Hellenic renaissance attempted to open up this univocal interpretation, it had to contend with a tradition of art history and politics in which those assumptions had taken on hegemonic and seemingly irreversible gender binarics. By simply reversing those gendered terms, however, especially when the penetrated male body serves as the fulcrum of that reversal, the language of the dominant fiction is reinscribed, the tyranny of gender reconfigured in a different hue. By becoming feminized, the penetrated male body may give the lie to the stability of gender polarity, whilst at the same time revealing the implicit gender assumptions of language. Such assumptions problematize the presentation of the penetrated male body through a conceptual chain of equivalences linking penetrability with femininity and submissiveness.

But need this always be the case? Is the penetrated male body inevitably a feminized body, always destined to be represented as masculinity's Other? This chapter has demonstrated how far that representation masks the submissiveness at the core of masculinity. Yet it nevertheless remains true that the penetrated male body as female/feminized is the representational outcome of a binaric logic governing language and conceptual thought. The either/or of gender dimorphism both frames and focuses the either/or of traditional logic, so that disruptions in one cause disruptions in the other. The next chapter explores this link further in an attempt to demonstrate its relationship to the Law. This Law is understood not simply in judicial terms, but, above and beyond that, in symbolic terms, as a Law of Representation or Discourse. Focusing on the work of Jean Genet, a criminal and sexual outlaw, it will be shown how even when one is seemingly 'outside' of the law one is still inside it; indeed, that 'outside' is constituted by the inside and as such recapitulates the laws it claims to break.

Chapter Three

The Male Body and the Outside

> "Behind the permitted words, listen for the others!"
> - Jean Genet, introduction to *Soledad Brother*

> "Outside reigns terror"
> - Genet, *Our Lady of the Flowers*

> "The name is the glorious body of the thing named"
> - Jean-Paul Sartre, *Saint Genet*

> "Regard the holes if you can."
> - Jacques Derrida, *Glas*

So far, I have argued that the penetrated male body can be understood as indicative of the behind of discourse – that is, as circulating within the discursive economy as its most anxious or stressful blind spot. Such a manoeuvre allows the phenomenon of the penetrated male body to register a challenge to binary thinking, being neither one thing nor the other, but something else entirely. The behind, in other words, signals an excess or multiplicity within discourse that nevertheless remains essentially unrepresentable. Furthermore, this blind spot carries with it an erotic charge – or *jouissance* – that is beyond/behind the phallus and, as such, it becomes the source of an uncertainty which inspires both fascination and terror. At the same time, through its links to a metonymic poetics that destabilizes the concept of the male body as impenetrable, this behind is also a profoundly productive aspect of discourse, generating ways of opening up the male body. As such, two discursive mechanisms – or chains of equivalence – are being delineated. First, metaphor in its traditional register removes masculine corporeality by inflicting a kind of castration by which the penetrated male body becomes feminized. The second trajectory is outlined by the metonymic links which allow for a chain of equivalence that breaks from this metaphorical/metaphysical register and places the penetrated male body within an economy of flows that confuse and refuse such differentiated gender categories. Metonymy takes the traditional feminization of the penetrated male body as evidence of a destabilization of all epistemological categories. Metonymy thereby locates the erotic corporeality of the penetrated male body as necessarily inside discourse, as that part of discursive reality most resistant to the protocols of representation, and as a consequence capable of throwing them into greater relief.

This chapter reads the work of Jean Genet to explore the concept of the outside in terms of the male body, with the aim of clarifying the process or processes by which the penetrated male body, whilst traditionally remaining outside discourse, nevertheless appears within it as its most anxious blind spot or behind. It will be shown how Genet's outside remains at odds with the concept of the behind which also appears in his work. And whilst the struggle between metonymy and metaphor is the motor of his poetics, the body, as will be shown, nevertheless functions as a site of absence in his work, as something that lies beyond or behind representation. In Genet's writing, a conflictual dyad of language/body can be discerned which is reducible to a genderization that inverts yet retains/relies upon the *status quo*; Genet needs to maintain this *status quo* in order to transgress its terms. In his last novel, *Querelle of Brest* (1947), Genet buckles the metaphor of the penetrated male body as feminized in a move which brings into question the metaphoricity of language *per se*. However, such a move, as will be seen, merely reinscribes the terms of traditional gender categories, with the body – particularly when penetrated, as we will see – remaining very much within a feminine paradigm, whilst language – as an articulation of culture/consciousness – remains definitively masculine. Indeed, for Genet language reduces or erases the actual body and replaces it with an abstract concept, even as he works to represent the body in the most graphic and florid ways possible. Prefiguring Judith Butler, Genet's work insists on the performativity of gender. Yet whilst Genet's buckling of the metaphor throws into relief the inadequacies of language in terms of the body, by reinscribing the hierarchical terms by which the body is excluded from discourse, Genet leaves in place the dichotomy he has exposed.

Querelle of Brest is Genet's most novelistic fiction, in contrast to the more autobiographical tone of his other books. As with all his books, however, Genet's authorial presence is strong. He tells us at one point that "we must have recourse to the conventions of the novel" (1987, 232); at another, "this book has already occupied too many pages and is beginning to become a bore" (1987, 233). The constructed nature of the tale, and Genet's power as its constructor, are always making an appearance, undermining its reality by constantly referring to its status as fiction. This technique – which appears throughout Genet's work – allows him to reflect on the nature of his storytelling and what it is he is attempting. For example, in a passage from *The Thief's Journal*, he says of his characters, "I wanted them to have the right to the honours of the Name" (1982, 90). He wants to name the unnamed, investing pimps, queers, murderers and criminals with a discursive space. But he wants also, at the same time, to complain that the process of naming as such is reductive, inaccurate and fraudulent. In describing the character Lou Daybreak in *Miracle of the Rose*, Genet claims that:

> Lou's name was a vapour that enveloped his entire person, and when you pierced the softness and approached him, when you passed through his name, you scraped against thorns, against the sharp, cunning branches with which he bristled. (1975, 21–2)

The name does not hold together, but rather signifies a dispersion. In piercing it, a certain violence is encountered. The inadequacy of the name, then, is also for Genet an excess. This excess remains for him outside, no matter how much his words may sing.[31] Yet, as outside, it is never fully separate or other. As such, his work articulates what might be called a politics of abjection; it constitutes an attempt both to name this excess and to interrogate language's ability to do this. Whilst this politics of abjection requires that the *status quo* remain in order for its trangressive elements to function, it nevertheless values that transgression in terms which ultimately destabilize discourse, or reveal it as always already destabilized.

In her study of abjection, Kristeva establishes a radical inseparability of the experience of abjection and the subject undergoing it. The abject does not, in reality, lie outside the subject, as an object to be faced or denied, but is instead a "twisted braid of affects and thoughts" (Kristeva 1982, 1). Yet although the abject is a movement more than an object, it nevertheless shares one quality with the object: its inherent opposition to *I*. But whilst the object provides meaning and certainty, the abject provides, on the contrary, "the place where meaning collapses" (Kristeva 1982, 2). Abjection collapses the mastery of meaning. Moreover, "I abject *myself* within the same motion through which 'I' claim to establish *myself*" (Kristeva 1982, 3). Subjectivity itself, in other words, is established through abjection, whilst remaining forever challenged by it; even penetrated and contoured by it; much like Dorian was penetrated and contoured by Wotton's words. However much the subject may eject, "beyond the scope of the possible, the tolerable, the thinkable", all that threatens to undermine it, this impossible, intolerable and unthinkable something nonetheless remains there, "as tempting as it is condemned" (Kristeva 1982, 1). The politics of abjection, as such, is primarily characterized by a profound discursive instability by which one is tempted and condemned simultaneously.

---

[31] "Nothing will prevent me, neither close attention nor the desire to be exact, from writing words that sing": Genet, *Miracle of the Rose*, trans. Bernard Frechtman, Harmondsworth: Penguin, 1975, 17–8.

DISCURSIVE INSTABILITY

If Schreber's response to the call of desire represents a breakdown in the law from *within* its domain, Genet's response to that call can be said to represent a breakdown from *without*. As criminal and sexual outlaw, Genet's body is already abject, born of abjection: illegitimate. As much as Schreber's incarceration locks him inside the law's domain, Genet's willful transgression of its boundaries places him equally within its remit. The two men, in this sense, represent the two sides of the same coin, or two responses to the same command to have a body, but to keep that body invisible, unknowable, impenetrable. That is, they constitute an example of

> the complex and unstable process whereby discourse can be both an instrument and an effect of power, but also a hindrance, a stumbling-block, a point of resistance and a starting point for an opposing strategy.
> (Foucault 1990, 101)

For Foucault, as shown in Chapter One, power requires a body upon which it can act, and which it can remove from the social body as a punishment for transgressions. But it also requires that body to be placed in a secondary, subservient position to the mind as the primary site of subject formation. This in no way suggests a neat or self-evident division between mind and body, however, for each of these discursive requirements – to have a body, and to subsume that body – are so complex and unstable as to suggest not simply a two-tiered system whereby a dominant discourse controls an excluded one, but "a multiplicity of discursive elements that can come into play in various strategies" (Foucault 1990, 100). For Foucault, instability is the very condition of all discourse.

This chapter approaches the novels of Jean Genet as an exemplary moment of that discursive instability: the strategy of homosexual fiction as heterosexual critique; that is, as a self-conscious transgression of the modes of bourgeois sexual subjectivity which nevertheless require – and therefore reinscribe – those modes in order to function. With Genet, as with

Schreber, the penetrated male takes on the status of abject femininity, but with the former it does so in order to refute the law it reflects. In *Querelle*, the protocols of representation to which the penetrated male body conforms are turned on themselves to disarticulate the very terms of its representational acceptability.

As Kate Millet points out, Genet's presentation of the passive homosexual as female and inferior is a comment upon how "sex role is sex rank" (1972, 343). This critique functions both to uphold a radical division between masculinity and femininity within Genet's world, and to undermine the traditional view that these qualities adhere, respectively, only to men and women. Whilst passivity remains a characteristic of the feminine homosexual for Genet, there is nevertheless at work in his prose, as will be seen, an attempt to link masculinity to passivity. Central to this move is Genet's conception of the male anus as a flower, a move which opens the male body whilst retaining its masculinity. This anal flower appears on the bodies of the most masculine characters in Genet's prose, undermining the view that is it only the passive and feminine homosexual whose body can be opened and entered.

THAT FINAL FLOWER OPENING[32]

In *Glas* (1990), Derrida discusses the giving of a name, and the inevitable limitation that this process involves. Giving a name delimits, cuts off, and leaves a remainder which nevertheless speaks: "when a name comes, it immediately says more than the name: the other of the name and quite simply the other, whose irruption the name announces" (Derrida 1993, 89). Such a move is always, Derrida states, a crime, a betrayal: "To give a name is always, like any birth (certificate), to sublimate a singularity and to inform against it, to hand it over to the

---

[32] This phrase is taken from Paul Hallam's script for Constantine Giannaris' film *Caught Looking* (Maya Vision, 1991). In one scene, the penetrated male anus is described by the narrator as "that final flower opening".

police" (1990, 7). This sublimating of a singularity is effected by a process of exclusion or abjection by which the remainder – that which lies outside the name, noun, or concept – becomes the evacuated waste matter which nonetheless inhabits us, or allows us to inhabit our name; being named hands us over to the law. This is not unlike Kristeva's concept of abjection, and the way in which subjectivity, or the taking of a name, is constituted by the rejection of an outside which paradoxically allows the name or the subject to emerge. What remains from this process, Derrida states, is waste product, but it is no less a necessary component of the name for all that. Without this waste, the name is meaningless, just as without the name "there would be only excrement" (Derrida 1990, 4). There is a necessity to naming, then; however, it must not become the goal, must not suggest an identity at the expense of what lies behind or outside it. The name must acknowledge its debt to that waste the exclusion of which constitutes its most pressing claim to legitimacy.

This waste, these remains, once the name of male is branded upon a subject, is the body itself, the blood and shit and sperm of a body rendered static and impenetrable within the confines of an abstracting conceptualization. As the not-quite-removed, as the remainder, these flows haunt the name which betrays itself, folding back onto the concept which disavows them and consequently threatening the legitimacy of the name. These flows, which Derrida identifies in the writings of Genet – in the unfinished sentence "*je m'éc* …"[33] (which could be "'*je m'écoulais*', 'I was flowing' in my body, in the body of the other", or "'*je m'écrivais* [I was writing myself]"

---

[33] This phrase, which Derrida returns to again and again throughout *Glas*, is taken from Genet's essay on Rembrandt, "What Remains of a Rembrandt Torn into Four Equal Pieces and Flushed Down the Toilet", trans. B. Frechtman and R. Hough, (Madras and New York: Hanuman Books, 1988). The English translation of this Genet text does not reproduce the layout, in two irregular columns, of the original French version – a layout Derrida reproduces in *Glas*. The phrase "*je m'éc*" – which Derrida calls a "stump of writing" – is suspended, unfinished – undecided – in Derrida's text.

(1990, 43)) – dissolve the stability of the body named male. They are, Geoffrey H. Hartman argues in his study of *Glas*, "the sign of an internal discourse that has become lacunary, because censored or mutilated or converted into nonverbal symptoms" (1981, 58) – such as Schreber's psychosis, for example. The conflict experienced by a recognition of these flows – of desire, shit, and sperm – within a body disciplined to be static, rigid and immutable, always threatens to destroy the subject in whom they dwell, threatens to manifest itself in a dissolution which, if not released through a projection onto an abjected, externalized and negated Other, may well turn on its source with destructive force, as seen in the case of the *Freikorps*. In short, behind the seemingly static singularity of the name lurks a fluid multiplicity ready to undermine it.

For all Derrida's talk of names, however, there is one name that eludes his text, that is censored from it, evacuated from it, haunting it with its grotesque unnameability: the anus. Waste, shit, farts, all punctuate Derrida's text; the orifice from which they emerge is salient precisely by its absence. For Derrida, the flowers that Genet scatters throughout his writings are always phalli or vaginas, signifying either castration or virginity. He writes:

> Thus the flower (which equals castration, phallus, and so on) "signifies" – again! – at least overlaps virginity in general, the vagina, the clitoris, "feminine sexuality", matrilinear genealogy, the mother's *seing*,[34] the integral *seing*, that is, the Immaculate Conception. (1990, 47)

With its stem, the flower is phallic; with its bud, a clitoris; with its petals opening, a vagina, or, as *seing/sein* (see

---

[34] "'*Seing*' means 'signature' in English – or, more specifically, 'simple contract; private agreement'. To translate it here, however, would be to obvert its undecidable relation to that other word 'sein', which in French means 'breast' and the play of this undecidability throughout the text", thus writes Barbara Harlow, the translator of Derrida's *Spurs: Nietzsche's Styles* (Chicago: University of Chicago Press, 1979), 159.

footnote 34), the maternal breast. But never for Derrida does it signify an anus.

Hartman's reading of *Glas* comes closer to identifying that "the cloaca is still a *bottom* of a sort" (1981, 65, emphasis added), but even this – however much I may wish to retain its signifying power as *double entendre* – turns out to be "a false bottom" (1981, 66), and Genet is revealed (to Hartman, at least) as "trying to steal the womb itself", or steal *into* it (1981, 108). Immaculate Conception is, Hartman suggests, "perhaps the most persistent – obsessive – theme in *Glas*" (1981, 104). For Derrida wishes to question the concept of absolute (immaculate) knowledge (conception) by playing Hegel's paternal discourse against Genet's maternal one. In doing so, however, Derrida falls into the trap of traditional gender roles, for the paternal, for him, is always the property of the masculine, as the maternal is always the property of the feminine. As such, it's the opposite of Deleuze's immaculate-conception-as-philosophical-buggery, although it's still possible within Derrida's more traditional genderization to link the Virgin Mary with anal penetration.

As seen in the last chapter, Ernest Jones' reading of the Immaculate Conception figures the ear as a displaced anus (Jones 1951). In *Dorian Gray*, this ear-anus becomes the site through which language penetrates the body. Here, it allows us to connect the Immaculate Conception in Derrida's *Glas* with the anus of which that text does not speak. Derrida prefers to conflate the anus-flower of Genet's prose with the vagina, that is, with *female* sexuality. In discussing the appearance of a golden fleece around the neck of Harcamone, a murderer about to die in Genet's *Miracle of the Rose*, for example, Derrida writes:

> The golden fleece surrounds the neck, the cunt, the verge, the apparition or the appearance of a hole in erection, of a hole and an erection at once, of an erection in the hole or a hole in the erection: the fleece surrounds a volcano. (1990, 66)

For Georges Bataille (1985, 5–9) at least, the volcano is always an anus, a bronze eye,[35] an eflluvial orifice of great force. However, in Genet's *Funeral Rites*, the golden fleece is seen to surround the male anus. Genet writes:

> The veneration I feel for that part of the body and the great tenderness that I have bestowed on the children who have allowed me to enter it, the grace and sweetness of their gift, oblige me to speak of all this with respect. It is not profaning the most beloved of the dead to speak, in the guise of a poem whose tone is still unknowable, of the happiness he offered me when my face was buried in a fleece that was damp with my sweat and saliva and that stuck together in little locks of hair which dried after love-making and remained stiff. (1969, 21)

Elsewhere in the novel, Genet's narrator revels in eating bits of shit whilst devouring his lover's anus; the lover's waste is valued and consumed: venerated. As Bersani argues, in the act of rimming

> the other is momentarily reduced to an opening for waste and to the traces of waste. The foraging tongue inspires a dream of total penetration, of entering the lover through the anus and continuing to devour him at the very site of his production of waste. (1995, 158)

Genet links penetration of the male body with murder or death. Erotic use of the male anus would seem to foreclose or betray masculinity in a way that will be discussed soon in relation to a scene of buggery from *Querelle of Brest*.

Furthermore, it is only within "the guise of a poem whose tone is still unknowable" that this opening may appear: for Genet, the male anus and the unknowable are linked through poetry – that is, through words that sing, or through a baroque language described by Brigid Brophy as "the overblown,

---

[35] Genet also refers to the anus as a bronze eye. See *Funeral Rites*, trans. Bernard Frechtman (New York: Grove Press, 1969), 21.

peony-sized language of devotional flowers" (1979, 71). And whilst Genet himself insists his use of flowers is anything but symbolic, they do form a metonymic link with the male anus.

THE ANAL-FLOWER IN GENET

A clear example of Genet's linking of the flower with the male anus can be found in *The Thief's Journal*, when the character Roger sticks a flower between his buttocks (Genet 1982, 198). To the old man with whom Roger has gone home, who has likened Roger to a rambling rose-bush, Roger says with the flower protruding from his arse-cheeks: "'And you're going to ramble over this one!'" – making explicit the link between orifice and flower.

In *Funeral Rites*, a scene in which the narrator is rimming his lover culminates with the confession

> I saw the eye of Gabès[36] become adorned with flowers, with foliage, become a cool bower which I crawled to and entered with my entire body, to sleep on the moss there, in the shade, to die there. (Genet 1969, 253)

In one scene from *Miracle of the Rose*, Genet describes his realization that one of the Toughs he so admired was about to be buggered. Genet writes: "When I saw him go behind the laurels with his big shot, my heart sank at the thought that it was the visible form of a male – a male flower – that was going to be deflowered [*effleuré*]" (1975, 147). An earlier translator's note has already informed the reader that the noun *effleuré*, meaning, in argot, "one who is buggered", derives from the word *fleur* (flower) (Genet 1975, 137). Like Proust, to whom he is indebted, Genet forges a link between homosexuality and botany. But whereas Proust in *Sodom and Gomorrah* contrasts the fertilization of an orchid by a bee with the sterility of male-male intercourse, Genet insists on a fertile contiguity

---

[36] A translator's footnote informs that "*L'oeil de Gabès* ('the eye of Gabès') was African Batallion slang for the anus" (Genet 1969, 19).

between a flower and the male anus. That is, he insists that the penetrated male body is in some way fertilized, generating a kind of excess which will shortly be seen to be a lyricism or poetry which corrodes virility, fertilizing a florid bouquet of words.

The either/or symbolism of the flower as phallus or vagina in Derrida which conflates male penetrability with femininity is therefore clearly at odds with Genet's own insistence that the flower is a metonym for the male anus. Derrida thus reinstates sexual difference around an axis of corporeal passivity. But if the flower is also virginity, as in the final example from Genet above, losing the flower is a penetrability of the male body by which the flower becomes the (lost) anus, the anus as hymen, that Derridean concept which attempts to name the undecidable (Derrida 1992, 160–75). In French, hymen can mean both virginity *and* marriage, both the vaginal membrane *and* its rupture. By thus gesturing in two (opposite) directions at once, it is, like the pharmakon, inherently ambiguous, inherently critical of identity thinking.

Derrida's conflation of the male anus with the vagina thus performs, and conforms to, the binary logic it was his intention to question. For if the male anus is only ever a vagina, penetration inevitably feminizes the body attached to it, making penetrability an index of femininity. Yet if the threat of *male* penetrability is thereby diffused by this move, it remains a profoundly paradoxical one. In transgressing the boundaries by which sexual difference has been made to make sense, the absolutes of gender are revealed as anything but absolute. For in this move the male body *becomes* the Other against which it has defined itself, rendering such Otherness meaningless.

In *Miracle of the Rose* the penetration of the body of the condemned child-murderer Harcamone discloses a Mystical Rose where the heart should be. Four men enter Harcamone's suddenly Brobdingnagian body (two through the mouth, two through the ear). The ear and the mouth are linked to the displaced anus of the Madonna's insemination, which turns out to be a Mystical Rose. Derrida links this rose to the Immaculate Conception (1990, 72), that is, to a process of invagination, as discussed above. But it can equally be read – following Genet's own chain of equivalence – as the male anus. In Genet's words, this rose – this "red rose of monstrous size and beauty" – is "a kind of dark well" (1975, 274). Seized by vertigo, the four men stand "at the very edge of this pit, which was as murky and deep as an eye" (Genet 1975, 274) – a bronze eye, Bataille's volcano. Losing their balance, "they toppled into that deep gaze" (Genet 1975, 274): Harcamone is deflowered, and the Mystic Rose turns out to be a solar anus ("The rays of the rose dazzled them at first").

Such is the glare of this radiant orifice that Derrida turns away. He will not look directly at – will not contemplate – this shining flower which Genet places at the very centre, the very heart, of a character whom all the other inmates have consented is: "what I call a man!" (Genet 1975, 90). The miracle of the rose is the miracle of the male anus, mira*cul*ous[37] because it allows the impossible: through it, the impregnable male body is entered. Whether one begins in the mouth or the ear, all roads lead there.[38] It is linked to the golden fleece which halos Harcamone's neck by the fact that *cou* (neck) is a near-homophone for *cul* (arse). That *cul* is not only present within the Imma*cul*ate Conception, but also within what Hartman calls Genet's "thievish, maternal 'cal*cul*us'" (1981, 98).

The Immaculate Conception must be viewed in terms of Genet's Catholicism, for this not only provides Genet with his most sacrilegious imagery, but, as Brophy argues, this inevitably conjures the notion of an outside: "you must screw your eyes tight shut and *exclude* the outside world – that is, you must *induce* the images" (1979, 71). The use of the flower-as-anus in Genet moves beyond the vaginization recognized by Derrida, that is, beyond the phallic economy.

Every text, writes Derrida, contains an absent word, which one must encircle, thus "creating a void at the centre of the space reserved for it, without ever writing, ever pronouncing

---

[37] *Cul* is French slang for arse.
[38] Or, indeed, the eyes, as demonstrated in Chapter Two through the reading of Baudelaire.

what you are nevertheless constrained to understand" (1990, 128). In *Glas* that word, that void, might be anus, conspicuous by its absence in a commentary on a writer for whom a man's backside was a Station of the Cross, a Wayside Altar,[39] an object of beatific contemplation and a source of poetry: the "ultimate treasure" (Genet 1969, 22).

"The text", Derrida concludes, "therefore *presents itself* as the commentary on the absent word that it delimits, envelops, serves, surrounds with its care" (1990, 129, original emphasis). In this sense, *Glas* might be more usefully read as a commentary on the male anus, and the silence surrounding it in Derrida's text is therefore also a loving embrace of that orifice (it "surrounds it with care"). The text *presents itself*, offers itself like a proffered behind for analysis. And, as Derrida remarks elsewhere, analysis always comes from behind: "to turn one's back is the analytic position, no?" (Derrida 1987, 178).

Genet's concept of male anus-as-flower thus becomes an analytical tool for exploring this absence to which Derrida points. Why is the male anus absent or displaced within (his) discourse? What is it about the open male body that renders it unseemly, unsightly, and thus places it behind discourse?

LANGUAGE AND VIRILITY

In *Querelle of Brest*, the opening of this anal-flower is intimately linked with the death of the male subject. After murdering his friend Vic, seaman Georges Querelle submits to the brothel keeper Nono (Norbert) as a self-inflicted punishment – Genet writes "execution" (1987, 62) – an annihilation of the virility proven by the murder, as well as an expiation of or atonement for the crime. Vic's murder is provoked by his refusal to allow Querelle to fuck him; with Nono, Querelle adopts the role he wished Vic to perform. Only through murder, Genet seems to be saying, can such an act occur: murder not only of the object (Vic) but of the subject (Querelle). In submitting to

---

[39] The original French word, *reposoir*, is translated by Frechtman as 'Station of the cross', and by Derrida, in *Glas*, as 'Wayside Altar'.

Nono, Querelle ceases to be a man; he kills his virility, apparently confirming what Sartre claims in *Saint Genet*, that homosexuality and virility are mutually exclusive (Sartre 1964, 408). Yet Genet is doing something much more sly. His distrust of language propels him to open words up to alternative or multiple meanings, so that the word virility becomes something else entirely. In *Our Lady of the Flowers*, he writes: "When closed words, sealed, hermetic words, open up, their meanings escape in leaps and bounds that assault and leave us panting" (Genet 1966, 130).

Edmund White comes closer to Genet's understanding of virility when he states that it is "determined by the role one plays, not the gender of one's partner" (1993, 149). Ostensibly, a homosexual who remains active could retain his virility; one who is only ever passive, however, abdicates any claim to being virile. Genet is signaling the profound conflict at the heart of submission, the complex play of power at work in male-male desire. The answer to John Fletcher's question: "can a male be homosexual, combine with another male, without loss of virility?" (1993, 74), would seem to depend upon the role taken, for submission itself appears always haunted by the ever-present spectres of dishonour and femininity; or, to use Schreber's term, unmanning.

As Foucault points out in *The Use of Pleasure*, "the principle of isomorphism between sexual relations and social relations" at work in Ancient Greek culture was "always conceived in terms of the model act of penetration, assuming a polarity that opposed activity and passivity" (1992, 215). As a consequence, dishonour attended the indulgence in passivity of either form, be it sexual or social. A man's duty was to be active in both the social and the sexual sphere. Passivity of any kind was unacceptable. Whilst this ancient Greek model did not suggest a specific and discrete identity to those males who chose passivity – that identity (homosexual) would not appear until the nineteenth century – it did characterize them by effeminacy (Foucault 1992, 84–6; 190). These themes of dishonour, sexual passivity, effeminacy and social disqualification nevertheless came into play in the formation of a homosexual identity at the end of the nineteenth century.

And it is this notion of a homosexual identity that Genet problematizes, refusing the logic of such positionality by refusing altogether the ontology of *being* homosexual. He offers sexual acts rather than identities, performances rather than essences, thereby disrupting the existentialist tenet that to do is to be. Which is not to say, as Sartre does, that Genet is an essentialist, because Genet's understanding of homosexuality does not rely on essence, but on a rejection of *any* stable identity. For Genet, as for Baudelaire,[40] sexuality is bound to notions of evil, and part of that evil is the refusal of bourgeois subjectivity. *Querelle* is charged with homoerotic desire, yet the only character identified as *being* homosexual is, ironically, the only character whose desire for men is *not* acted upon: Lieutenant Seblon must resort to sentimental longings for Querelle, sublimated into the poetic yearnings of his journal entries. He never has sex with a man at any point in the novel, whereas the ostensibly heterosexual characters, such as the cop Mario, the brothel keeper Norbert and the mason Gil – and, indeed, Querelle himself – do. Paradoxically – and perversely – the acceptance of a homosexual identity would seem to foreclose the opportunity for sex with men; it is the self-proclaimed heterosexual males in Genet's novel who indulge in sex with other men.

This logic of non-identity is also found in Genet's approach to language; he rejects the notion that language can in any way capture the reality it claims to represent. His lyricism, his figurative use of language, exceeds any simple correspondence or identity between word and thing. Lyricism will be his vengeance not only on the logic of identity, however, but, as will be seen, it will also provide the tools for his vengeance upon masculinity. The lyricism of all the characters in *Querelle*

---

[40] For Brigid Brophy, the first thing to realize when considering Genet is that "Genet virtually is Baudelaire ... a Baudelaire of the twentieth-century": Brophy, "Our Lady of the Flowers", in Peter Brooks and Joseph Halpern (eds), *Genet: A Collection of Critical Essays* (New York: Prentice Hall, 1979), 68.

is, Genet states, something with which they are invested by the author, *apart from Seblon*: Seblon's lyricism is his own, and he alone "must be regarded as being solely responsible for the part he plays" (1987, 25). His is an autonomy predicated on his being (impossibly) outside the text; Genet insists that Seblon is not 'in' the novel at all. Could Seblon's lyricism, then, be linked to the fact that, despite being a "well-built" and "broad-shouldered" man, he, nonetheless, is "deeply conscious of the presence of something feminine in him" (Genet 1987, 26)? The following quotation from *Our Lady of the Flowers*, would seem to suggest so:

> The queens on high had their own special language. Slang was for men. It was the male tongue. Like the language of men among the Caribees, it became a secondary sexual attribute. It was like the coloured plumage of male birds, like the multicoloured silk garments which are the prerogative of the warriors of the tribe. It was the crest and spurs. Everyone could understand it, but the only ones who could speak it were the men who at birth received as a gift the gestures, the carriage of the hips, legs and arms, the eyes, the chest, with which one can speak it. (Genet 1966, 89)

Language thus demarcates gender difference within this world of unassailable sexual positioning/posturing. Yet, note how Genet gives the male tongue a flamboyant visibility ("coloured plumage" and "multicoloured silk"), such that it possesses its own lyricism. Seblon's lyricism is coterminous with the presence of something feminine in him. Yet if lyricism and virility are the poles of this sexual positioning, by investing all the characters in *Querelle* with lyricism, Genet is slyly robbing them *all* of their virility.

Anxiety about virility (and its potential loss) is indeed a central concern for all of the characters, especially for Seblon, who has his hair cropped short to gain the respect of his men, to be treated as one of the lads, unaware that it makes them shun him. Virility, Genet suggests, is a fragile entity, and, as such, is a source of anxiety for *all* men. A relentless and harsh self-policing is necessary for its maintenance. Inside the sailors' world of *Querelle*, men are brimming with it (Genet 1987, 19) – yet it is no less tentative for all that. Indeed, in an atmosphere of such all-pervasive virility, virility itself becomes all the more impossible to assert. Gender anxiety becomes something which, in Genet's all-male world, is experienced in response to other men, rather than the effect of a need to maintain an essential sexual difference between men and women.

In *The Thief's Journal*, Genet states that his own lyricism is a mode of heroization – as it was for Baudelaire – a way of making gold out of base metal via the alchemy of words. The presence of "wounded males" (Genet 1982, 224) bestows upon Genet a gift of something the world holds in contempt (and what is a wound if not a site or mark of penetration?). Making such broken creatures shine as heroes – and thus making a hero of himself – is the task of Genet's singing words. He names something unnameable whilst recognizing that the name leaves a remainder.

THE CITADEL OF INTEGRITY

In T. E. Lawrence's *Seven Pillars of Wisdom* – a book with which Genet was very familiar[41] – an account of male rape culminates with the statement: "that night the citadel of my integrity had been irrevocably lost" (1952, 456). Without wishing to downplay the horrors of Lawrence's ordeal, or, conversely, without considering how far he himself might have overplayed them,[42] it is nevertheless clear that the irrevocably

---

[41] See Edmund White, *Genet* (London: Chatto and Windus, 1993), 98–9. White claims that Genet was fascinated by Lawrence, although he doubted the truth of Lawrence's account of his life with the Arabs.

[42] See Jeffrey Meyers, *The Wounded Spirit: A Study of Seven Pillars of Wisdom* (London: Martin Brian and O'Keefe, 1973) for a discussion of the differing accounts Lawrence gave. Meyers cites a letter by Lawrence in which he admits his reluctance to include the passage, stating that it was a story he could not tell "face to face" with anyone (cited p.60).

lost object is his anal virginity – his flower. Lawrence's sense of wholeness – his integrity – is dependent upon remaining impenetrable. Being penetrated by another man/men costs Lawrence his manhood: it is a symbolic castration. The male body is likened to a citadel, an impregnable stronghold, a fortress the defending of which requires eternal vigilance. Masculinity is equated with impenetrability, and the loss of integrity experienced by losing one's flower becomes a *dis*integration. One is no longer integrated, either to oneself or within the social whole. In consequence, those who practice such an act – and thus who court such dissolution, such disappearance – become socially outlawed, marginal, outsiders. As Hans Mayer has written, Genet "establishes the maxim of non-integration" (1982, 265).

In *Miracle of the Rose*, for example, the tough guy Harcamone hooks two huge bunches of lilac to his cap – a gesture which would feminize anyone else, but the fact that "he was a true male", meant that "he alone could coyly adorn himself with flowers" (Genet 1975, 89). Genet concludes from this that Harcamone "must have been quite sure of his *integrity*" (1975, 89, emphasis added), that is, of his masculinity, which is intact, whole, and impermeable enough to carry off such a feminine gesture without loss of status.

To be sure of his integrity, a man must be sure to remain integral, whole, complete, bound by an unbroken and impenetable surface. He must be integrated within his skin and his sex, with both conceptualized along lines which anathematize the certainty of the flesh.[43] It is an anathematization, however, constantly plagued by uncertainty, an uncertainty ever-present as the *certainty* of the flesh, that undeniable though uncertain object. Harcamone, after all, is staking his masculinity through a display of femininity that is predicated, for Genet at least, on the metonymity of the male anus and the flowers with which Harcamone is bedecked.

---

[43] "…the flesh is … the most obvious means of certainty": Genet, *Miracle of the Rose*, trans. Bernard Frechtman (Harmondsworth: Penguin, 1975), 16.

The maintenance of an impenetrable male body, as a totality which disavows nonidentity or contradiction, becomes, in addition (as seen in Chapter One), a prerequisite for a fascistic model of society. The fascist body is a highly disciplined body that refutes the flows of desire and pleasure, abjecting them to an outside that is deemed immoral. As such, it promotes a morality that can only ever see the penetration of the male body as a sign of the breakdown of the moral code upheld and sustained by a seemingly impervious masculinity cherished within a seemingly impervious nationhood. As seen in Theweleit's study of the *Freikorps*, the individual bodies of men are integrated – that is, they vanish – into a body of men (a nation).

The multiple meanings of integrity thus gather in a constellation around the dark star of the closed male anus, delimiting a libidinal economy within the parameters of which the pleasurable use of that orifice must always cost one one's manhood. The credit of anal pleasure tallies with the debit of manhood. In *Querelle of Brest* it is figured as a debt to be paid. Before being penetrated, Querelle reflects: "'This is the moment that I pay off'" (Genet 1987, 70).

This abdication of manhood, however volitional, unsettles Querelle. We are told he "felt like weeping over his past self now sloughed off", forced to consider whether he wasn't "a proper brown-hatter" (Genet 1987, 70), a fear that attends the pleasure he takes in the act. The fact that Querelle "had not known how to restrain himself" is irrefutable "proof to Norbert that the matelot was not completely male" (Genet 1987, 70). Lack of restraint – or Schreberian voluptuousness – puts Querelle's manhood in question, renders it incomplete or compromised. Not only should a man not submit to such an act but, if forced, as Lawrence was, he certainly should not enjoy it but grieve the irrevocable loss of his integrity. At the same time, however, Genet has written elsewhere that it is false to believe that "a male that fucks another male is a double male" (Genet 1972, 226). In his world, neither position is any guarantee of virility or masculinity. The performance of gender is always unstable, always about to crumble, the mask of masculinity about to come off.

In language which resonates with that used by the *Freikorps*, Genet describes this past self which Querelle now sloughs off through the act of buggery in the following terms:

> His body was fitted with guns, iron-clad, armed with torpedoes, easy to manoeuvre though heavy enough in all conscience, bristling and bellicose. He was now LA QUERELLE, a huge destroyer, a greyhound of the ocean, a vast, intelligent, thrusting mass of metal.
> (Genet 1987, 33)

Here, Querelle himself is presented as a citadel – impenetrable, strong, heavy. But for all his armour, all his bulk, Querelle's body, Genet writes several pages later, "was an empty shell" (1987, 55). He is busy defending an unpopulated citadel, a hollow edifice. Like Theweleit's *Freikorps*, Querelle is protecting a lack, a void; the male body constitutes a vanishing point into the black hole down which subjectivity itself threatens to disappear: "Querelle was conspicuous by his absence" (Genet 1987, 17).

Foucault's work on the rise of the penal system demonstrates how the body was replaced by the mind as the site of punishment. The body is removed and incarcerated in order to establish a self-surveillance of the soul or mind in modern disciplinary societies. For Foucault, "the soul is the effect and instrument of a political anatomy; the soul is the prison of the body" (1985, 30). In our own secular age, the concept of the soul has been more or less replaced by the concept of identity, as a true inner nature. Identity, therefore, can be viewed in Foucauldian terms as a prison of the body. The body that is released from it through the act of penetration, however, for Genet takes on the female form, and the metaphor is buckled.

BUCKLING THE METAPHOR

White argues that *Querelle of Brest* signals a break from the insularity of Genet's earlier novels (White 1993, 336–7), in that the I becomes a we, suggesting a new, more complicit relationship with the reader. However, that relationship is by no means clear within the novel itself, and that lack of clarity is most tellingly present in Genet's presentation of the penetrated male body. His use of the metaphor of the penetrated male body as female both relies upon the traditional protocols of representation and undermines them. He buckles the metaphor and, with it, all of representational thinking. Describing the scene in Nono's bedroom, with Querelle awaiting his execution *a tergo*, Genet writes:

> Querelle was waiting, his head bowed and the blood mounting to his face. Nono looked at the sailor's arse; the parts were small and hard, round and smooth, covered with almost a fleece of light brown hairs which continued on round to his thighs and – but there more sparsely spread – up to the small of the back, where his striped vest was just peeping out from under his rucked-up jersey. (1987, 68)

Bent over before another man, he becomes red in the face – the blood rushing to his bowed head signifying shame. This position, moreover, places emphasis on the parts to be penetrated, and the fleece once again appears, but this is how Genet describes it:

> The shading on certain drawings of female backsides is achieved by a few incurving strokes of the pencil after the style of the different coloured circles on old-fashioned stockings, and it is desirable that the reader should thus imagine the bare parts of Querelle's thighs. (1987, 68)

The reader is invited to see the curly hairs on Querelle's haunches as stockings on a woman, his proffered behind an unmistakable (unavoidable) emblem of a feminine and feminizing passivity. Furthermore, this metaphorical feminization of Querelle at the point of penetration is itself a displacement, for it is not a real woman that the reader should bring to mind, but a pencil sketch, a representation, a pornographic image – something the very purpose of which is to provoke desire; something representative of nothing more than itself and its own power to arouse. Like Dorian Gray, Querelle is turned into a fascinating *object d'art*, and this process feminizes him. Moreover, what to make of this interpellated reader – for whom Querelle's bare backside should register as a woman's lingerie-clad hind quarters – when at the very start of the novel Genet has made it clear that "this story is addressed to inverts" (Genet 1987, 7–8)? Why would a story addressed to inverts ask its readers to imagine the proffered male behind as a bestockinged female behind? What game is Genet playing? Is he trying to conjure some desire for a male backside in the mind of a (unaddressed) heterosexual male reader, or a desire for a female backside in the mind of a homosexual reader? Or is he rather refusing to categorize the reader at all? Or perhaps conflating both male and female, hetero and homo, pointing instead to an instability, an undecidability, an ambivalence, inherent in representation, mimesis – even desire itself?

The tension created by these two statements of Genet's – the invitation to see Querelle's buttocks as female and the declaration that his novel is for inverts – constitutes a buckling of the metaphor of penetrated-male-as-female which has wider implications for the status of language *per se*. For whilst Genet's novels constitute a major exemplary corpus of the explosion into discourse of a homosexual fiction by, for and about homosexuals/homosexuality, at the same time they contain – and nowhere is this more apparent than in this scene from *Querelle* – the deconstruction of representation itself, a suspicion that our systems of expression themselves are warped or queer. In *Prisoner of Love*, for example, Genet asks:

> What if it were true that writing is a lie? What if it merely enabled us to conceal what was, and in any account is, only eyewash? Without actually saying

> the opposite of what was, writing presents only its visible, acceptable and, so to speak, silent face, because it is incapable of really showing the other one. (1986, 27)

Writing, for Genet, is two-faced, hypocritical, occurring within what Simon Critchley calls an economy of betrayal (1999, 41). In showing one face, another lurks behind. Paradoxically, language for Genet constitutes a form of silence. But whilst for Critchley it is only Genet's last and posthumous book, *Prisoner of Love*, that exemplifies this betrayal, this lack of direct correspondence between writing and the truth of an event, it can nevertheless be clearly seen as the arena in which all his work is acted out.[44]

By buckling the metaphor in this way, Genet is not only suggesting that all metaphors are ultimately useless, but, much more significantly, that all language is essentially metaphoric. That is, it operates through displacement, differentiation and substitution. By showing one face, it inevitably masks another. Genet claims in the above quotation that the visible, acceptable face is, ultimately, the silent face; writing is incapable of showing the other, non-silent, invisible and unacceptable face. As such, he is gesturing towards a surplus to writing whereby any attempt to represent the singular-multiplicity of here, now, the eventness of the body, for example, is bound to fail – bound here signifying not simply an unavoidability but also an irrefutable bondage to failure. Indeed, for Genet, failure is the very essence of writing. By representing anything at all, Genet is saying, writing has failed.

Bataille has commented on this failure of Genet's language. In *Literature and Evil* (1993), Bataille locates Genet's particular evil in his refusal to communicate, which, for Bataille, is a refusal of sovereignty. To be sovereign, Bataille argues, is to communicate a feeling of impenetrable common subjectivity. Genet's communication is "feeble" because it disavows such impenetrability. In a paradoxical move, Genet's closure

---

[44] Derrida makes reference to it, as shown earlier, in *Glas*, which was written long before Genet's last book emerged.

(refusal to communicate) is also an openness (avowal of penetrability), his invulnerability also vulnerability. As Derrida remarks in *Glas*, Bataille's condemnation of Genet misses the point completely because Genet's task has always been failure. He writes:

> 'Genet's Failure'. What a title. A magical, animalistic, scared denunciation. What is the sought-after effect? But hasn't Genet always calculated the 'failure'? He repeats it all the time; he wanted to make a success of the failure. (1990, 219)

This failure indicates a realm of nonconceptuality outside of representation, a surplus or remainder that is first and last material and erotic, because for Genet that failure is the body itself, located behind discourse, irreducible to language. By using the metaphor of femininity to represent the penetrated male body, therefore, Genet is not, with *Querelle*, suggesting an unassailable sexual difference, whereby penetrability must always and inevitably be the conceptual property of a female or feminized body. Instead, he is suggesting that in using *metaphor* (the trope of resemblance) to represent something else is always already to suggest the opposite: similarity or lack of sexual difference. By establishing a metaphoric or mimetic relation between Querelle's hairy backside and that of a woman in stockings, resemblance is replaced by equivalence. But in the logic of noncontradiction, such equivalence is meaningless: Metaphor, and perhaps therefore language *per se*, thus becomes catachresis.[45] Language is not to be trusted, and the flesh itself becomes the only certainty: ineluctable, unavoidable flesh. As William Haver has argued, "there is neither symbol nor metaphor in Genet, and if we miss that fact, we

---

[45] "Something monstrous lurks in the most innocent of catachreses: when one speaks of the legs of the table or the face of the mountain, catachresis is already turning into prosopopeia, and one begins to perceive a world of potential ghosts and monsters": Paul de Man, "The Epistemology of Metaphor", in *Aesthetic Ideology* (Minneapolis: University of Minnesota Press, 1996), 42.

miss entirely the intense eroticism of Genet's texts" (1999, 12). That intense eroticism is not symbolic or metaphoric – that is, does not signify or offer anything other than itself. This offering, moreover, suggests the offering of Derrida's anal-text as well as Querelle's behind; an offering suggestive not of what the object offered might mean or signify or mimetically represent – an offering not, that is, as sacrifice (of meaning, manhood, or Logos) – but an offering of something to be taken for its own sake, for pleasure's sake: erotically.

Take, for instance, Genet's recurrent use of flowers. Of this, Genet himself writes:

> Flowers amaze me because of the glamour with which
> I invest them in grave matters and, particularly,
> in grief over death. I do not think they symbolize
> anything. (1969, 166)

Rather than a simplistic regression into solipsism, however, such a move promotes a fragmentation of subjectivity, and generates a prismatic fracturing into an event-ness which words alone can never hope to capture. As Critchley points out, "a nonlinear accretion of images, anecdotes, snatches of dialogue, maxims and reflections is characteristic of Genet's earlier prose" (1999, 35). Fragmented prose is Genet's way of exploding the myth of a unified subject, whilst his subjective writing style aims at rejecting any so-called objectivity.

"We know", Genet writes – or we should do by now – "that our language is incapable of recalling even the pale reflection of those bygone foreign states" (1982, 58). That is, the here, now is lost irretrievably, and no amount of words can capture it. Fooling ourselves into thinking it can be captured will only lead, moreover, as Hartman points out, to a bloodless closure (1981, 149), or what Derrida calls an anaemic conceptualization or white mythology. All life is drained from the event once it has been translated into words. Genet would seem to be asking, then, along with Derrida: "Are not all metaphors, strictly speaking, concepts?" (Derrida 1982, 264). And further, are not all words metaphors? Do not be taken in by his words,

Genet warns, for the book you're reading is only a fragment of his life:

> This story may not always seem artificial, and in spite of me you may recognise in it the call of the blood: the reason is that within my night I shall have happened to strike my forehead at some door, freeing an anguished memory that had been haunting me since the world began. Forgive me for it. This book aims to be only a small fragment of my inner life. (1966, 59)

As pleasure is only a fragment, an event, of the body; just as the body is only a fragment, an event, of pleasure, so too is any writing only a fragment of life's so-called truth. The body occurs – is embodied – within a pleasure language bleeds dry in its attempt to capture or represent it. Put another way: the relationship between writing and the body is metonymic. For this reason, the absolutizing of the body within one gender is language's attempt to capture the state of the body, to fix it and retain that fixed state, when, in truth, no such fixity is possible. If gender is performative – constituted by and in language (understood as gesture as much as word) – then language's essential mutability and uncertainty surely make of gender something equally mutable and uncertain.

Nor, for Genet, is such fixity as language attempts in any way desirable. He writes: "my sensibility required that it be surrounded by a feminine order. It could do so inasmuch as it could avail itself of masculine qualities: hardness, cruelty, indifference" (Genet 1982, 58). In expressing a feminine sensibility through the adoption of masculine qualities, Genet radically separates gender from biological sex, placing gender in the domain of language at its most performative. In *Gender Trouble*, Judith Butler claims genders are constructed through the reiteration of gestures, behaviours and acts. It is a doing pretending to be a being. And as Genet relates the failure of representation to the certainty of the body, Butler relates the failure of gender to ideological imperatives to be a given gender: "The injunction *to be* a given gender produces necessary failures" (1991, 145). Those who, for Butler, necessarily fail – butch women and effeminate men – throw into relief the fact that everybody fails, that gender is a regulatory ideal forever unattainable. However, by locating gender's failure so specifically within atypical behaviours, Butler implicitly relies on a notion of success contained within the closer correspondence of the body and its expected performance: the further away from femininity a man can get, the more successful or complete his performance as a man will be. But what are the consequences of such a theory for the idea of the penetrated male body? Can performativity account for it other than in the standard pejorative terms of femininity and failure? Or does the penetrated male body enable the limits of performativity to be unveiled?

THE LIMITS OF PERFORMATIVITY

Long before Butler chose to adopt performativity as a theoretical model for gender, thinkers such as Deleuze and Guattari, Lyotard, Derrida and de Man were already criticizing performativity for its inability to account for the excess of meaning generated by any citation or discursive utterance, its refusal to see a surplus to representation. In *Allegories of Reading*, for example, de Man states, "any speech act produces an excess of cognition, but it can never hope to know the process of its own production" (de Man 1979, 300). This excess is not outside discourse, but produced behind it, as a blind spot in the field of vision accessible to knowledge, or as an uncertainty within the folds of discourse itself. And that blind spot is the site or location of the subject's inability to conceptualize its own objectivity without endangering its status as subject. In men, as this book is attempting to show, that blind spot is intimately connected with the body's penetrability – with what I am calling the behind.

By using a concept derived from speech-act theory, such as performativity, to deconstruct gender, Butler inevitably evokes this excess only to exile it to an outside of language from which it cannot speak or move. She thus constructs a dialectic of gender within which any contradiction can only ever be negative. The radical break between gender and (biological, anatomical) sex brought about by feminist critique has had the consequence, argues Butler, of making sex play the part of nature to gender's culture. Commenting on the feminist division of gender from sex, she comments

> when the constructed status of gender is theorized as radically independent of sex, gender itself becomes a free-floating artifice, with the consequence that *man* and *masculine* might just as easily signify a female body as a male one, and *woman* and *feminine* a male body as easily as a female one. (1990, 6)

Butler proposes to conflate the two terms and argue that *both* are culturally produced. To this end, she writes:

> Gender ought not to be conceived merely as the cultural inscription of meaning on a pregiven sex (a juridical concept); gender must also designate the very apparatus of production whereby the sexes themselves are established. As a result, gender is not to culture as sex is to nature; gender is also the discursive/cultural means by which 'sexed nature' or 'a natural sex' is produced and established as 'prediscursive', prior to culture, a politically neutral surface *on which* culture acts ... This production of sex as the prediscursive ought to be understood as the effect of the apparatus of cultural construction designated by *gender*. (1991, 7, original emphasis)

Butler argues for the constructed status of both gender *and* sex. For her, there is no prediscursive origin upon which gender is constructed, except on the phantasmatic and idealized level: there is no *male* or *female* body at all without the discursive configurations through which each body achieves the status of intelligibility in our gender dimorphic system. Within the matrix of gender, therefore, the penetrated male body is an abject or failed body and as such does not matter/materialize.

In *Bodies That Matter*, Butler claims that "bodies which fail to materialize provide the necessary 'outside', if not the necessary support, for the bodies which, in materializing the norm, qualify as bodies that matter" (1993, 16).

Similarly, in Genet's cosmogony, the demarcation of gender is predicated not on anatomy but on gesture. The queens achieve a transsexual alchemy by adopting the gestures of the female, just as the toughs perform a swagger which marks them as masculine.

> Genet's poetic world is an indefinite exchange of forms and gestures, a crisscross of transmutations, because everything has been reduced to the gesture and because the inner substance of the gesture is the gaze of others. (Sartre 1963, 324)

For Butler and Genet, gender is constructed and maintained by the gestural, the superficial, by words, acts, performances, which have no bearing on any ontological essence or irrefutable truth about sex. For example, in *Our Lady of the Flowers*, Genet writes: "I shall speak to you about Divine, mixing the masculine with the feminine as my mood dictates" (1966, 72), refuting any direct and obvious correspondence between anatomy and its gendered categorizations.

However, as much as Genet subverts the violent hierarchy of active/passive by elevating the queen to the status of saint – as he does with Divine in *Our Lady of the Flowers* – he can only do so by remaining within a binary logic that reasserts itself as hierarchical. In this sense, performativity remains stuck within what Derrida claims is the first phase of deconstruction, where "the hierarchy of dual oppositions always reestablishes itself" (1981, 42). Genet might amuse himself at its expense but he doesn't displace it, because he needs it. Performativity merely reproduces the binary logic of language by reconfiguring the mind/body split as a language/body split, and locating the body outside of language, in excess of language, and leaving it there.

By claiming that gender performativity functions through making some bodies materialize at the expense of those that remain outside and immaterial, the performative reinscribes the very terms it claims to challenge. The metaphysical assumptions of inside/outside, success/failure, material/immaterial, draw a deep line of demarcation the transgression of which relies on its remaining in place no less than does its acceptance.

Genet's transgression of the norms of mid-twentieth century French bourgeois society equally required that those norms remain unchanged. He didn't want to alter the world because that would undermine his own position of being *against* the world. In this sense, transgression feeds on normativity, requires it, as much as normativity requires transgression. For Genet, transgression requires the maintenance of an outside, the transgressor's outlaw status contingent upon the *status quo*.

TRANSGRESSION AND THE OUTSIDE

Foucault argues for a different understanding of transgression, one that is unrelated "to the limit as black to white, the prohibited to the lawful, the outside to the inside" (1998b, 73–4). He insists instead on a non-dialectical transgression that "contains nothing negative", but which exists by virtue of a "nonpositive affirmation" achieved through a "testing of the limit" (1998b, 74). Foucault's notion of transgression is more of a continual play or fold between excess and limit which might be said to constitute the critical element of discourse. Writing is such a limit-experience for Foucault, as exemplified by the work of such writers as Bataille, Sade, Pierre Klossowski and Maurice Blanchot. Moreover, by exploring "this language which is neither complete nor fully in control of itself" (Foucault 1998b, 76), such limit-experiences perpetrate an "*actual penetration* of philosophical experience in language" (Foucault 1998b, 86, emphasis added) – an act which unhinges the certainties of philosophy.

For Foucault, there is no outside to language because it is *within language itself* that what cannot be said *is* said, must be said. For if thought can think the outside, then it is no longer outside. The task then becomes to find a language adequate enough to articulate this outside without closing it off within a dialectical negativity. It is not, Foucault warns, an easy task. In "The Thought from Outside" he writes:

> It is extremely difficult to find a language faithful to this thought. Any purely reflexive discourse runs the risk of leading the experience of the outside back to the dimension of interiority; reflection tends irresistibly to repatriate it to the side of consciousness and to develop it into a description of living that depicts the 'outside' as the experience of the body, space, the limits of the will, and the ineffaceable presence of the other. (1998b, 152)

Like Genet, Foucault considers language to be unfaithful – it betrays what it seeks to communicate. Unlike Genet, however, Foucault believes a language *can* be found that is faithful to thought and does not betray the vagaries of truth. It is a language which tests the limit, a language tracing the discontinuities of discourse, and as such always challenges the *status quo*. It is the language of a certain type of literature, says Foucault; an open literature – open to an outside it explores and describes. According to Foucault, the writings of Sade, Klossowski, Blanchot and Bataille form a "discourse on the nondiscourse of all language" (1998b, 154), a thought of the outside which stops itself from sliding into interiority and thus reinforcing the barrier between subject and object by remaining within ruptures, by articulating excess, by inhabiting limits. Yet it might be argued that Genet equally volunteers a "language about the outside of all language, speech about the invisible side of words" (Foucault 1998b, 154) when he asks in *Funeral Rites*:

> was it true that philosophers doubted the existence of things that were in back of them? How could one detect the secret of the disappearance of things? By turning around very fast? No. But faster? Faster than anything? (1969, 48)

Such spinning produces a vertigo that leaves Genet dizzy with words, disillusioned with discourse and no nearer to attaining "the secret of the disappearance of things" – a dog chasing its tail. Genet's reference to "things that were in back of them" (behind them) not only links thought to the visual, but names that blind spot mentioned earlier: it is (the) behind. The body lurks behind knowledge, its existence doubted; a doubt that could only be overcome by turning around fast enough to see what lurks behind. As such, the outside and the behind appear coterminous. For Genet, words themselves are responsible for the disappearance of the body:

> I was quite certain that a time would come when that wonderful language which was drawn from him would diminish his body, as a ball of yarn is diminished as it is used up, would wear it down to the point of transparency, down to a speck of light. It taught me the secret of the matter that makes up the star which emits it, and that the shit amassed in Jean's intestine, his slow, heavy blood, his sperm, his tears, his mud, were not your shit, your blood, your sperm. (1969, 62)

The singularity of the loved one's body is destroyed by the necessity of expressing it in a communal language. If language is always public, always shared, then in that commonality of words all individuality of the body is erased. The same words apply to parts of the body which, being loved or not loved, known or not known, are as distant from one another as two stars. *Your sperm is not his sperm.*

Faced with this, Genet holds onto the one thing he does know, that there *is* an outside, and he is in it, as the negative, the other, the abject, the feminine, the outlaw. It is worth considering here the ambiguity of the concept of an outside in Genet. As a homosexual convict he is *in* the outside – outside acceptable society, outside the law – and yet, at the same time, his status as a prisoner makes him one for whom the concept of an outside was formulated through incarceration, for whom the outside was at a remove, unreachable and constitutive of a world with which he felt at odds and by which he felt persecuted. In *Our Lady of the Flowers*, he writes that "the world of the living is never too remote from me. I remove it as far as I can with all the means at my disposal" (Genet 1966, 176). His work can be seen as one long mourning of the loss this removal inflicts.

The outside was something that, from the confines of his cell – in which he wrote much of his fiction – must have been for Genet both a source of threat and a source of (be)longing, both torturous and comforting. In many of his plays, for example, the outside is constantly alluded to, a world beyond the confines of the stage in which a significant part of the play is being acted out off-scene. For this reason, windows appear in many of his plays, and the action that is taking place beyond the parameters of the represented space plays a significant part in the action onstage. In *Our Lady*, Divine's garret looks out onto Monmartre cemetery. Genet's maintenance of and investment in an outside becomes clearer. The outside is, for him, the imagined elsewhere that cannot be represented, for it is both invisible and abject.

However, through such a move he abandons himself to a dialectic similar to Butler's, and recapitulates to the logic by which such terms make sense. For both Butler and Genet, language is a constitutive act of violence inflicted *upon* the body from without. Butler writes that the "figuration of masculine reason as disembodied body is one whose imaginary morphology is crafted through the exclusion of other possible bodies" (1993, 49). But for her this act of exclusion is perpetrated by language, not bodies – as if language circulated free from the bodies in which it originates, and upon whom it acts. The relationship between language and bodies, however, might be better conceived as a circuit rather than a divide, as will be demonstrated in the following chapter through a reading of Joyce's *Ulysses*. In this way the subject's status as always already object might be better understood and the full multi-dimensionality of discourse more clearly perceived.

THE BETRAYAL OF LANGUAGE

Time and again, Genet stresses the ineptitude of words and how it renders the body incommunicable. Each word cuts out, cuts off, a part of the thing he wishes it to express; that is, language leaves a remainder, something inexpressible and nonconceptual, but somehow still there, inhabiting a negative space, an invisible domain which, nevertheless, functions as the crucible in which his writing is forged: "I keep within me a charnel house for which poetry may be responsible" (Genet 1969, 214).

For Genet, words do not recall or recapture the past, but serve as an inevitably distorting lens through which it may be viewed, constituting a new moment, a new present:

> It is not a quest of time gone by, but a work of art whose pretext-subject is my former life. It will be a present fixed with the help of the past, and not vice versa. Let the reader therefore understand that the facts were what I say they were, but the interpretation that I give them is what I am – now. (Genet 1982, 58)

Language, for Genet, simplifies the complexity of the body, generalizes its singularity, its specificity, erasing its difference in the quest for identity. In *Funeral Rites* he states: "My book will serve perhaps to simplify me" (1969, 178), though it is a simplicity that, if he must endure, he prefers to figure in a visual rather than a textual manner: "I want to make myself simple, that is, to be like a diagram, and my being will have to gain the qualities of crystal, which exists only by virtue of the objects that can be seen through it" (1969, 178). As in his presentation of Querelle's behind, a diagram, an artwork, functions in the place of a metaphor, and it functions as a prism – not a prison – for the body. Writing, Genet states, is a "prismatic decomposition" (1969, 22), placing an emphasis on the visual and the material rather than the linguistic or discursive. There is a gap between words and things, and in this space of nonidentity the object breathes. As Blanchot states, "languages do not have the reality they express, for they are foreign to the reality of things" (1982, 40n). Language functions through an illusion of immediacy, and it is within this space of literature, within, that is, a certain *poiesis*, that this power of language is most clearly shown to fail. In literature, language is a forgery, a betrayal, a ruse. But it is an endlessly productive failure.

How is this possible? How is language's failure to be counted as the body's successful interruption of discourse? The answer lies, as already suggested, in Genet's use of a pencil sketch to describe Querelle's bare and hairy haunches. In this appeal to a non-linguistic form of representation, Genet exposes the male body as an object; more, as a specifically sexual object; a pornographic image. Every subject, as Adorno claims, is also always an object. Such objectification has been refused almost universally when it comes to the human subject. The objectification of the human body, in pornography, for example, or in art, is criticized as a violation or degradation – more so in Anglo-American countries, as Hartman points out, than in France, where what he calls "pornosophy" has flourished (1981, 97). To view the human body as an object is traditionally considered as robbing it of what makes it human. To refuse to acknowledge our object-ness, however, as Adorno warns, will only ever result in the idealized reification of subjectivity as the beginning and end of knowledge, of truth, of reality: an ontologization of the ontical. A totality will thus establish itself around this reified subjectivity, and the body as object will be relegated to the negative realm of nonidentity (Adorno 1996, 22, 119, 180–6). The body is what remains outside once reified subjectivity has taken hold. This objecthood of the body – within the traditional Western metaphysical division of the object and the subject – makes it eternally other to the subject, and this otherness prevents a foreclosure of the subject into a self-referential totality or tautology.

The metonymic presentation of Querelle's backside through the imagery of a pencil sketch of a woman's backside serves to highlight the body as object, for in a drawing the body can only ever be an object, however much the artist may strive to capture the subject's personality. The problem, however, remains that in claiming that language excludes the body,

Genet presents a dialectic between the body and language that cannot be synthesized in language because language will only ever represent one side of this dialectic. This is clearly a very restricted conception of language, a restriction made tighter still by Genet's insistence upon the diagrammatic as somehow closer to the body than language. In the brothel scene with Nono, Querelle's hind quarters are likened to a *picture* of a woman; that is, to an artwork. Expressed differently: the body functions, in this instance, as a work of art. A channel or a passage is established which runs between art and the body.

WHAT REMAINS...

In his essay "What Remains of a Rembrandt Torn into Four Pieces and Flushed Down the Toilet" (1988), Genet explores this passage between art and the body. He places great emphasis on the presence of the flesh, focusing on the bodies beneath the clothes in Rembrandt's paintings, claiming even to be able to smell them. This flesh, these bodies, are, Genet claims, presented as objects, nothing more than meat. In order to achieve this, Genet argues,

> Rembrandt had to recognize himself as a man of flesh – of flesh? – rather of meat, of hash, of blood, of tears, of sweat, of shit, of intelligence and tenderness, of other things, too, ad infinitum, but none of them denying the others, in fact each welcoming the others. (1988, 48–9)

Likewise, Genet's own work turns on a recognition of himself as, in Haver's words, "a man of skin, flesh, blood, bones, shit, cum, spit, and all the rest of it" (1999, 19). All these properties place the body, or make the body *take place*. For Haver, as for Genet, flesh is bound to place, to an impossible certainty unavowable within a language plagued by equivocality. Flesh is bound to place and "without *this* impossible thought of place – as here, now, this – there can be no thought of the essential mortality and therefore pleasure of flesh"

(Haver 1999, 18, original emphasis). And the place to which flesh is bound is inarticulable, uncodifiable, nonverbal, which is why Genet places emphasis on the visual – the sketch of the woman's behind, Rembrandt's paintings and, elsewhere, cinema and the work of Giacometti – not because the eye can be trusted (reading is, after all, for most of us most of the time, a visual process) but because of the non-linguistic properties of these mediums. It is words of which he is most wary. For Genet words are the universal, flesh the particular. If all language functions through a metaphoricity which differentiates and substitutes words for things – as it does for Genet – then the particularity of the body is replaced by a universally accessible language. To locate the subject within language is thus to make it conform; individuality – and especially erotic specificity – is for him located in the flesh (*His sperm is not your sperm*). The flesh is what remains: the blood, the skin, the sperm, all remain as remains, or remainder. It remains *as* remains, and also remains to be grasped, conceptualized, thought. What remains is indissoluble: it won't go away or dissolve; it cannot be cleansed but remains as a trace (Adorno 1996, 135). The body is a stain upon the fabric of discourse.

In this sense, Genet argues for the inability for a certain something (which is for him, always erotic or libidinal) to be represented: either the representation is meaningless or, if meaningful, has excluded an essential component of what it claims to represent:

> any novel, poem, painting or musical composition that does not destroy itself – by which I mean, that is not constructed as a blood sport with its own head on the chopping block – is a fraud. (Genet 1993, 176)

Such self-destruction, for Genet, is contingent upon the existence of two opposing interpretations – the recognition of which is greeted with joy because "all the remains are in shreds" (Genet 1993, 175). This shredding of truth that comes from art's presentation of two opposing interpretations renders critique itself undecidable, if not impossible. If language is to be something other than a vehicle for communication, it must do so by becoming, or striving to become, as particular and individual as embodiment. Language must become something other than mere identity or representation, must remove itself from its source, in order to stand alone, as art, that is, as representative only of itself.

In the light of such a claim, critique can no longer sustain itself on the belief that art is representative of the artist's unconscious, and therefore open to interpretation, if the code can be cracked. Art in and of itself refuses such a code, by containing contradictory or conflicting codes and thereby presenting a multi-dimensionality which traditional thinking refuses or ignores.

For Genet, this destructive dimension remains a negative space. Querelle's desire to murder Vic, for example, comes upon him slowly, "rather like the mounting of amorous emotion, and almost, it would seem, through the same channel, or rather through *the negative of that channel*" (Genet 1987, 54, original emphasis). In this sense, Genet's thinking is closer to Derrida's in "White Mythology", where he also locates the self-destruction of the concept of metaphor within the same system as its conceptual triumph, as sublated positivity. For Derrida, as for Genet, the self-destruction within conceptual thinking appears as a negative form of this structure: "The metaphorization of metaphor, its bottomless over-determinability, seems to be inscribed in the structure of metaphor, but as its negativity" (1982, 243). For Derrida and Genet, there can be no concept of an entity because there will always be an element of that entity – an indissoluble something – remaindered by the very process of conceptualization. Characterized by Adorno as negative, or non-identical, this contradictory excess both 'is' and 'is not' at the same time. As such, the task of any thinking which refuses to console itself in a self-enclosed and self-evident system of totalized concepts is to acknowledge this, not as a simple reversal or negative theology, but as an ambivalence at the very heart of meaning. But does Genet's art do this?

The meeting of two forces – language/body, desire/murder – is always coded for Genet within a dialectic of positive/negative, and this, in turn, always reinscribes the gendered structurations of logic itself. Genet's understanding of gender as essentially oppositional thus retains the traditional logic he wants to displace, remaining – as stated earlier – at the first stage of the deconstructive move which has as its goal a revaluation of the binary terms along non-hierarchical lines. For example, when discussing sexual relationships between men in *Querelle*, Genet writes that the very absence of women obliges "the two men to discover whatever feminine streak there may be in their make-up, to invent the woman in them" (1987, 112). A binary logic thus reasserts itself as a natural law. He continues,

> It is not necessarily the weaker or younger, or the more gentle of the two, who succeeds the better; but the more experienced, who may often be the stronger or the older man.[46] They are united by a mutual complex; but since it arises from the absence of a woman it has the power to evoke and sustain the idea of a woman who, by the very fact of her not being there, acts as a link uniting them. (1987, 112)

Even in its absence, then, femininity remains, for Genet, the governing principle, the unifying link: femininity remains in or as an outside which nevertheless contours what is present/presented. As such, it is not really an outside at all, or is a very strange outside indeed. By tracing the metonymic links that explore the limits of the male body – those that gather together the bodily orifices of the mouth/eyes/ear/anus within a decidedly non-phallic economy – this book has suggested that this outside constitutes a behind of discourse. The behind – as erotic site and discursive blind spot – has been seen as the governing principle of a discourse that refutes it. It appears within discourse as a rupture or gap, a hole through which *jouissance* passes and affects what is represented within

---

[46] According to White, Genet was disappointed by his own inability to cross over from passive to active as he got older. See *Genet* (London: Chatto & Windus, 1993), 261. This disappointment coincided with the writing of *Querelle of Brest*.

discourse. Discourse is the embodiment of (erotic) thought, and it is an embodiment that occurs along a continuum – from the most explicit to the most covert – marked by an absence of the (erotic) body. Yet even in its absence, I would argue, it is nevertheless somehow still present. Discourse is manifested *jouissance*, contoured by its kinetic charge:

> In cracking the socio-symbolic order, splitting it open, changing vocabulary, syntax, the word itself, and releasing beneath them the drives borne by vocalic or kinetic differences, jouissance works its way into the social and symbolic. ... [P]oetry shows us that language lends itself to the *penetration of the socio-symbolic by jouissance.* (Kristeva 1984, 79–80, emphasis added)

Signification always registers the flows of *jouissance*: it cannot do otherwise. If poetry or literature is, for Kristeva, in a very real sense revolutionary, it is because "literature has always been the most explicit realization of the signifying subject's condition" (Kristeva 1984, 82) – and that condition is marked by a rupture between what Kristeva calls the semiotic and the symbolic. That is, between the dehiscent flows of the erotic body and the signification process by which that body is denied or repressed even as it struggles to represent. Through symbolic language – and that is the only language we have, according to Kristeva – the semiotic speaks. Whilst Kristeva restricts the field of the semiotic to the relationship with the maternal body, through this *jouissance* that is the semiotic – a jouissance that penetrates the socio-symbolic order – it is possible to expand that field to incorporate the penetrated male body, or the behind, as it is being delineated here. As such, the penetrated male body is equally capable of exploding language, of shattering the symbolic. And it is through a reading of James Joyce – one of Kristeva's representatives of this literature of violence and revolution – that the next chapter will explore this process. It will be shown to be a process by which the body's multiplicity is channelled into a force capable of disrupting the chains of equivalence binding the penetrated male body to an essential femininity.

If Genet buckles that metaphor, Joyce will be seen to tear it pieces.

Chapter Four

Writing the Behind

> "The English language allows very little
> independence to the organs of the body"
> - Derek Attridge, *Peculiar Language*

> "The evidence of the body reveals
> a tremendous multiplicity"
> - Nietzsche, *The Will to Power*

> "Too little importance has been attached
> to the use of this word 'multiplicity'"
> - Gilles Deleuze, *Bergsonism*

> "We haven't been taught, nor allowed, to express
> multiplicity. To do that is to speak improperly"
> - Luce Irigaray, *This Sex Which is Not One*

James Joyce's *Ulysses* reveals a very different representation of the penetrated male body than so far encountered in this book – one which allows for that body's entry into discourse in a way that does not conform to the protocols of representation. The essentially binaric form taken by those procotols, it has been shown, often shackles representations of the penetrated male body with an inescapable femininity. What follows here is an attempt to demonstrate how Joyce's text manages to break the chain of equivalences that binds the concept of the penetrated male body to the concept of femininity. Instead, *Ulysses* works towards a multiplicity of the body which refuses the traditionally neat, binaric distinctions of gender in favour of a multi-gendered subjectivity. For Joyce, masculinity is not reducible to the either/or logic of gender dimorphism without a certain loss. This loss is the loss experienced by Odysseus when bound to the mast, the loss of the sensual, physical body in the struggle against desire, which in Joyce is presented as the struggle against representation. Odysseus cannot respond to the call of desire expressed in the song of the sirens – his body is bound, immobile, removed – yet at the same time, as the only one on board the ship whose ears are not plugged, he is nevertheless bound to hear it, nevertheless exposed to its unavoidable and minatory *jouissance*. As with Wilde's *Dorian Gray*, the ear and desire exist in a state of tension. Or, put another way, discourse is that state of tension. Understood as such, discourse can be seen to express that tension in curious ways. One way, as this book has argued, is to treat as waste certain discursive appearances. How that waste is treated takes many forms. One form, which I have been calling poetic, strives to counteract the more dominant form of denial and repudiation. The treatment of the penetrated male body as waste – that is, the understanding of *jouissance* as in excess of representation – has been shown to centre upon the male anus as a site of rupture within discourse. Representations of the penetrated male body – by unhinging the logic of gender dimorphism – have been shown both to consolidate and destabilize gender norms, and to do so through a language marked by the poetic figurations of metaphor and metonymy. As such, the exposure of this *behind* of discourse – as both the site of anxiety over penetration and as blind spot – has been understood as modernity's acknowledgement of the production of meaning. This replaces the more classical understanding of knowledge as the painstaking discovery of a pre-given reality.

The behind recognizes no such reality, only its partial – that is, both biased and fragmentary – construction. Joyce goes further still in suggesting that, in linking the behind of discourse with the anus, all art is ultimately anal, and that, moreover, this not only makes binaric logic illogical, but replaces that dualism with a multiplicity that shatters language. The penetrated male body as presented by Joyce is capable of not only exposing the gendered structuration of language, but of destroying the entire structure and using the pieces to build something else entirely: a form of representation more grounded in the shifting realities of flux and sensation, more geared towards registering the intensities of material bodies. For Joyce, the anus is revolutionary.

In the seventeenth chapter of *Ulysses* ("Ithaca"), Leopold Bloom finds in a drawer the prospectus for the Wonderworker, a curious device for "insuring instant relief in discharge of gases" (Joyce 1992, 850). Note that the Wonderworker itself does not appear. We are merely offered "the textual terms in which the prospectus claimed advantages for this thaumaturgic remedy" (Joyce 1992, 850). That is, the prospectus serves as a metaphor for the device itself, and as a metonym of the orifice the Wonderwork is designed to police. But what does the Wonderworker do? It functions as a kind of fart catheter, discreetly releasing intestinal gas without the embarrassment of sound or smell. But, more importantly for what will follow here, it brings together the several themes of this chapter: it is – like the anus – non-gender specific ("Ladies find Wonderworker especially useful"); it links anality and language ("Recommend it to your lady and gentlemen friends"); it highlights the grotesqueness and anti-sociality of the open(ed) body; and it functions through a penetration of the body ("Insert long round end"). It also serves to highlight a further theme of Joyce's novel – one not covered here – namely, the absurdity or excess of commodity capitalism in late modernity, and Bloom's status as gullible consumer. The excessive claims of the prospectus ("making a new man of you and life worth living") accentuate the pejorative attitude towards bodily functions, whilst the sweetness of its language ("a pleasant surprise when they note delightful result like a cool drink of fresh spring water on a sultry summer's day") attests to the pleasure to be had in using it.

Mikhail Bakhtin's work on the grotesque can help to clarify Joyce's use of the open, sensual, excessive body in the throes of *jouissance*, which can be wrestled from the pejorative tones of the grotesque only by pursuing their most demanding claims. For Joyce, consciousness is always *bodily* consciousness and if that consciousness is a multiplicity, as it is for him, so too is the body. Deleuze and Guattari's notion of the rhizome will be employed to develop this point. It will be shown how Joyce folds male and female, one into another, refusing to categorize the penetrated male body as female, instead presenting a more multiple body contoured by *jouissance*. Using Deleuze's *The Fold*, this approach to embodiment will be discussed in terms of a certain peristaltic movement that links language and the body to the behind. Clearer insights into Joyce's insistence on the scatological aspects of the body can thus be gained from understanding how those aspects function for him in relation to writing itself. If discourse is to be capable of registering the body's multiplicity, it is only through a discourse ruptured and indecent that this will happen. Only by filthy writing – writing, that is, that recognizes the behind – can the body's multiplicity be even remotely suggested.

Joyce's text writes the behind, presenting it in all its ambiguity. Not simply the homographic ambiguity by which that word signifies both the most anxious site of the male body and the blind spot or rupture within discourse; but, further, the behind here also signifies the process by which consciousness is constituted and marked by that ambiguity. The process of consciousness, that is, occurs behind the subject, as the subject's impossible heterogeneity, its absence of unity or totality, its absence of clear cut gender identity.

WHAT ODYSSEUS LEFT BEHIND

In *Dialectic of Enlightenment*, Theodor Adorno and Max Horkheimer read Odysseus' encounter with the Sirens as allegorical of this unknowability. They consider it to be characteristic of the dialectic of Enlightenment: a dialectic of myth and anti-myth, or instrumental reason. They argue that the Enlightenment's project of disenchantment through "the dissolution of myths and the substitution of knowledge for fancy" (Adorno and Horkheimer 1972, 3) is inherently patriarchal. "What men want to learn from nature", they write, "is how to use it in order wholly to dominate it and other men" (1972, 4). This domination of nature and other men, which for the latter becomes conformity "to the rule of computation and utility" (1972, 6) takes two forms: ignorance or denial. Both are dramatized in the Homeric tale.

In order that Odysseus' men not succumb to the temptations of the Sirens' song, he has their ears plugged with wax; yet in order that he himself not succumb, he has himself bound to the mast, his own ears unplugged. Thus restrained, submission to the call of desire, to the temptations offered by the Sirens, becomes impossible and the safe passage of Odysseus and his men is assured. But this overcoming of temptation, Adorno and Horkheimer argue, is itself a submission – to the primacy of labour and the efficacy of restraint. It is a submission that, moreover, recognizes the power of desire, the force of nature, even as it resists and overcomes it. Odysseus is bound to the mast because succumbing to the temptations offered by the sirens would be inevitable without such restraint. Yet whilst Odysseus' men row on in silence, knowing "only the song's danger but nothing of its beauty", Odysseus knows its beauty – but only as "a mere object of contemplation"; that is, only as art devoid of practical application and thus neutralized (Adorno and Horkheimer 1972, 34). Adorno and Horkheimer's premise, then, could be said to be an example of what Foucault calls the repressive hypothesis (1990). The Frankfurt School saw modern capitalism as responsible for the negation of eros (see Marcuse 1987). But they also saw that negation as marking something unsayable within discourse. This unsayable something – this behind – will be shown to be the meeting place of the body and language.

The dominant form of thinking that Adorno and Horkheimer are criticizing – what they call instrumental reason – is predicated on a denial of nature as myth which is itself a reaction to the dangerous and powerful force of nature. Instrumental reason presents itself as a process of disenchantment by which nature is dominated, its forces controlled. This domination and control, aimed at promoting the idea of nature as nothing more than mythical, also serves to highlight the status of instrumental reason itself as equally mythic. For Adorno and Horkheimer, the denial of myth is itself a myth, the domination of nature itself an expression of nature. In this way, the dialectic of Enlightenment moves. For,

> Just as the capacity of representation is the measure of domination, and domination is the most powerful thing that can be represented in most performances, so the capacity of representation is the vehicle of progress and regression *at one and the same time.* (Adorno and Horkheimer 1972, 34-5, emphasis added)

Just as the terms of this dialectic oscillate almost indiscernibly, then – from domination to representation, from progress to regression, from enlightenment to myth – so too does the claim to absolute truth shift its location from one site to another, its appeal to stability denied. Impotent in the face of desire, yet convinced such bondage constitutes a victory, Odysseus thus represents to Adorno and Horkheimer "a prototype of the bourgeois individual" (1972, 43) restricted to "attaining self-realization only in self-consciousness" (1972, 46). The desiring body is thus subsumed beneath a one-dimensional capacity to work, to dominate nature both inside and outside the self. Within instrumental reason, the body has become abstract: "Bourgeois society is ruled by equivalence. It makes the dissimilar comparable by reducing it to abstract quantities" (Adorno and Horkheimer 1972, 7).

This denial of the sensuous, desiring or erotic body, furthermore, is for Adorno and Horkheimer, the inevitable outcome of the production of a specifically *bourgeois* subjectivity. For it is a subjectivity predicated on the domination of anything considered to be other, including its own desires, its own flesh. The erotic body – the body which *feels*, whose feelings influence thought – falls outside the rubric of instrumental reason and thus becomes characterized as waste, as taboo. "What Odysseus left behind him entered into the nether world" (Adorno and Horkheimer 1972, 32). This netherworld will be shown in this chapter to be the very domain in which Joyce finds his deepest inspiration and in his reconfiguration of Homer's mythic tale the penetrated male body is employed to challenge the hold of instrumental reason.

INDECENT LANGUAGE

Ulysses is a prime example of how the body, when it emerges within discourse, often does so in explicitly erotic or scatological ways. It is as if these two functions were, by virtue of their supposedly secretive or private nature, outside of the public law of language; as if out of sight is out of mind held true for the body. Or, as if the tabooing of certain words not only excised them from so-called decent or proper language, but excised the very body parts and functions to which they refer. To refer to them thus implies discursive impropriety or indecency.

However, Joyce does not present his characters at stool, or micturating, masturbating or copulating, simply in order to shock, but to present life more fully as it is lived. As Joyce himself remarked, "if *Ulysses* isn't fit to read, life isn't fit to live" (cited in Ellman 1982, 537). If there is a shock, it is the shock of recognition, the recognition that nowhere before in literature have characters been presented doing this. As such, the indecency of Joyce's novel remains culturally and politically important. For it not only says the unsayable, but in order to do so it disrupts the neat ordering of language responsible for prescribing what is sayable. The protocols of representation condemn certain body parts and certain bodily acts and functions to the other side, the backside or behind of discourse, which is why the anus becomes a site of panic and must be heavily policed.

Like Freud's repressed, however, those exiled body parts always return. In this sense, the body haunts discourse, the shocking impact of certain (obscene) words bearing witness to the materiality of language – indeed, the *Ulysses* trials provide sufficient evidence that weight, mass and volume are intrinsic properties of words, giving language a physical presence which often goes unrecognized. This material quality of language is most evident in the slang words for those body parts and bodily functions considered unfit for – that is, not fitting into – public discourse. Placing them there is considered indecent. As Genet remarks, the obscene is the off-scene, the not-seen, the unrepresentable *as such*. Joyce includes obscene words in his novel, making them work at installing the body in all its grotesqueness and beauty. His intention is to present humanity in all its facets, including – or especially – those deemed unworthy of literature.

The disturbing quality of what H.G. Wells called Joyce's "cloacal obsession"[47] is indicated by most critics' dismissal or avoidance of it, as if to talk about shit were tantamount to playing with it, as if there were no space, no difference at all, between words and things. Carl Jung called *Ulysses* the "backside of art" (cited in Heath 1984), while Ezra Pound urged Joyce to remove most of the scatalogical references.[48] John Gross avoids the subject altogether, claiming "at this hour in the day there is nothing new to be said on such a topic" (1976, 9).

At the risk of saying something new, then, this chapter will ask why discourse insists on cloaking the cloaca in mystery

---

[47] Wells used this phrase in his review of *A Portrait of the Artist as a Young Man* (cited in Robert H. Deming (ed.), *James Joyce: The Critical Heritage Volume One 1902-1927* (London: Routledge and Kegan Paul, 1970), 86. Joyce's response to Wells was: "'Cloacal obsession! ... Why, it's Wells' countrymen who build water-closets wherever they go'" (cited in Frank Budgen, *James Joyce and the Making of Ulysses*, London, Oxford and Melbourne: Oxford University Press, 1972), 108.

[48] For a detailed analysis of Pound's suggested deletions, see Paul Vanderdam, *James Joyce and Censorship: The Trials of 'Ulysses'* (Hampshire and London: Macmillan, 1998, 20–8).

and shame. By focusing on Joyce's use of the penetrated male body in "Circe", this final chapter concludes with the claim that Joyce's modernism allows for a certain queering of masculinity that doesn't try to avoid or erase that body's penetrability; but rather uses it to critique gender dimorphism in interesting ways.[49]

Ulysses is perhaps the most extreme example of an open literature; Joyce opens the male body to a multi-dimensionality which shatters the binary apparatus by which gender is traditionally constituted, and therefore removes the logic by which that body may even be called male. The multi-dimensionality of Joyce's text reveals a body not tied to the logic of the either/or, but which, in exposing the ruse of logic by which meaning masquerades as truth or knowledge, claims a multi-gendered and rhizomatic multiplicity. This multiplicity – one of modernism's major tropes – suspends traditional logic whilst at the same time registering an essential heterogeneity. This heterogeneity – mapped by the flows of an opened body – is constitutive of the human subject whilst remaining the most persistent threat to that subject's status as a unified totality. As such, it suggests the complex relationship between language and the body.

LANGUAGE AND THE BODY

Because discourse often denies the male body by coding the very concept of body as somehow female, the penetrated male body is often feminized in order to represent at all. It has been argued so far in this book that such feminization is the inevitable outcome of the oppositional logic inherent in the gendered structuration of discourse by which, in turn, embodiment is made intelligible. As such, the penetrated *male* body is in a sense unthinkable, while its representation within a feminine

---

[49] For an account of the anxiety and abjection surrounding the male body in regard to shit, see Calvin Thomas, *Male Matters: Masculinity, Anxiety and the Male Body on the Line* (Urbana and Chicago: University of Illinois Press, 1996).

paradigm has been shown to be a paradoxical confusion of the very polarity of gender it is the intention of such representation to maintain (only women are penetrated). In this sense, language threatens the concept of the male body with erasure at the nodal point or limit-experience of bodily penetration.

As much as language threatens the body, however, the body also threatens language, providing physical and psychological experiences that cannot be represented in words, such as pain. Recall the experience of Des Esseintes, gagged by the dentist's fist, his sense of his body heightened by this breaking off of language.[50] As Elaine Scarry argues, in *The Body in Pain*,

> physical pain does not simply resist language but actively destroys it, bringing about an immediate reversion to a state anterior to language, to the sounds and cries a human being makes before language is learned. (1985, 4)

But as the narrator of Proust's *A la recherche du temps perdu* remarks, upon overhearing two men having sex:

> there is another thing as noisy as pain, namely pleasure, especially when there is added to it – in the absence of the fear of pregnancy ... – an immediate concern about cleanliness. (Proust 1992, 10)

The reference to cleanliness makes it clear what kind of sex is taking place.[51] The representation of the penetrated male body thus has the ability to warp or distort language; the body in pleasure perpetrates a blow against language; like pain, it actively destroys language. Both pleasure and pain thus constitute limit-experiences marked by radical dissolution of

---

[50] For a discussion and theoretical account of the male body in pain, see Kent L. Brintnall, *Ecce Homo: The Male-Body-in-Pain as Redemptive Figure* (Chicago and London: University of Chicago Press, 2011).

[51] That a horror of dirt plays a role in the responses we have to anal sex has been discussed elsewhere in this book.

the self, penetrating the socio-symbolic order and registering within the field of signification as a rupture or breach. As such, it is not strictly anterior to language, as Scarry claims, for there is no such place, once language has been acquired, as *before* language. It is, rather, a state *posterior* to language, behind language, after language has failed. Lost for words, despite being full of them. Pain and pleasure thus gesture towards the behind of language, the infinite, impalpable silence masked by words, the materiality by which those words are contoured.

This chapter focuses on the ways in which language might be embodied. It will argue that thought is always embodied, and that embodiment is thus always erotic; that is, of the sensual, feeling body. Through a reading of Joyce's *Ulysses*, it will be seen how language can be applied to the task of capturing the multi-dimensionality of the body rather than failing it or forgetting it. If the gulf that exists between language and the material world it claims to represent has been the object of enquiry up to now, how that gulf may be bridged, or how it may be employed to disrupt commonplaces of language and the body, is the object of enquiry now. Joyce's modernity gets behind the structure of language, and opens it up at its weakest point, its greatest site of rupture: the penetrated male body. This chapter looks at the passage that obtains between words and bodies, and argues that it is a passage that takes one through the body, an inevitably penetrating experience that recognizes no protocols of socially acceptable behaviour regarding which bodies should and which should not be penetrated.

As Derek Attridge argues, in Joyce's linguistic experiments, "the physical world does seem to come closer than is usually possible in language" (1988, 149). Or as Hélène Cixous remarks, Joyce's language succeeds in "gradually reducing the distance between the word and its appeal to the senses" (1976, 281). Each chapter of the novel (apart from the first three) is allocated a body part that it represents in various ways. So, to take one example, the "Oxen of the Sun" episode, whose body part is the womb, takes place in a maternity hospital, and the gestation of the foetus is represented by a gestation of language. The text itself evolves or grows, from Middle English to Modern English, through pastiche and parody. For this reason, as Richard Ellman comments, Joyce's work represents the "incessant joining of event and composition"; he seems "to come to things through words, instead of to words through things" (1982, 3, 4). In Attridge's analysis of Joyce's use of onomatopoeia, for example, he concludes that

> onomatopoeia ... can be seen as a paradigm not just for all literary language ... but for all languages, indeed, for all representation; its effectiveness lies in the fact that it necessarily displaces that to which it refers. (1988, 157)

For Attridge, then, onomatopoeia is merely the extreme example of what all language does: by the process of naming, it turns sounds into meaning. Whilst this is undoubtedly true, Joyce's use of onomatopoeia signals a multiplicity of language that confuses even this neat correspondence between sound and meaning. For example, to represent the sound Bloom's cat makes, Joyce uses the word "Mrkgnao!" (1992, 65). That 'rkg' presents a sound far different from the traditional English meow – more of a continental accent or inflection (an Italian meow, perhaps; which is the one Joyce would have been most familiar with during the writing of the novel). He thus not only unsettles reality through claiming a fundamentally onomatopoetic nature for language; but by cutting across from one language to another – something he does throughout the novel – Joyce scores through any notion of language as a singular entity, thus registering several levels of reality. For if all language – all representation – necessarily displaces that to which it refers, how can language's necessary displacement of the body be usefully employed to comment upon that body's displacement? How can this *behind* be written? If both displacement of the body *and* a certain proximity to the body can be effected by one and the same language, it is not possible to talk of language in the singular, for, like the body itself, it necessitates multiplicity in our understanding of it. Brian McHale's analysis of *Ulysses* draws attention to Joyce's polyphony or stylistic plurality:

> A discourse (style, register) implies a world – so we have been told, in different ways and with various inflections, by some of those who have thought most profoundly about language in our century ... The categories a discourse carves out, the relations it establishes, and so on – all these encode a particular version of reality, and the different versions of reality encoded by different discourses must inevitably be, to some larger or smaller degree, mutually incompatible, incommensurable. Consequently, discursive parallax, in cases where discourses cannot be attributed to personified sources with the fictional world, implies an *ontological* parallax, a parallax of worlds. In effect, to juxtapose two or more free-standing discourses is to juxtapose disparate worlds, different reality templates. (1992, 54)

Such incommensurability of worlds as expressed in language – or ontological parallax – would have been something that Joyce, as an Irish Catholic, felt very keenly. The language through which he expressed himself, to begin with at least – before he started experimenting and bending it almost beyond recognition, infecting it with other languages – was the language of his oppressors. In *A Portrait of the Artist as a Young Man* Joyce has Stephen Dedalus reflect upon this ontological parallax whilst conversing with the dean of his college, an Englishman:

> The language in which we are speaking is his before it is mine. How different are the words *home*, *Christ*, *ale*, *master*, on his lips and on mine! I cannot speak or write these words without unrest of spirit. His language, so familiar and so foreign, will always be for me an acquired speech. I have not made or accepted its words. My voice holds them at bay. My soul frets in the shadow of his language. (Joyce 1977, 172, original emphasis)

For Joyce, as for Stephen, English is the language of the oppressor, a language he must master and make his own before he can express anything about himself, but in whose shadow his soul frets.

In a similar move – and one which made Joyce's work attractive to Kristeva and Cixous – in order to write *Finnegans Wake*, Joyce had to break up his master's mother tongue[52] and construct for himself a new language: one not immediately recognizable or comprehensible as English, to be sure, but one, nevertheless, not so much unlike as to be utterly alien. Joyce exaggerates the artistic struggle between self-expression and the necessary commonality of language; and he makes it a political struggle. For there is a strong sense in which all language, for everybody, is always already an acquired speech. As Deleuze and Guattari argue in *A Thousand Plateaus*,

> there is no language in itself, nor are there any linguistic universals, only a throng of dialects, patois, slangs, and specialized languages ... There is no mother tongue, only a power takeover by a dominant language within a political multiplicity. (1992, 7)

There is no language in itelf, only a partial – that is, biased and fragmentary – access to something called communication; only a fragmented reality viewed through the cracked lens of a fragmented language. In this sense, Joyce's project of breaking language down and reconstituting it in order to move away from representational protocols is similar to Picasso's attempts with Cubism to fragment the visual field. Both men wanted to disrupt traditional notions of representation and explore a multiplicity or multidimensionality that effected a radical break away from the prevailing tradition of mimetic realism or naturalism in art which had placed enormous emphasis on the belief in objectivity and the logic of identity. Breaking from such mimesis, Joyce fragmented the linguistic plane as Picasso did the visual, suggesting a less direct correspondence between objective reality and artistic representation of that reality. For

---

[52] This use of conflicting genders to describe language is a deliberate prefiguring of Joyce's method of deconstructing binarisms by welding them together.

that correspondence became skewed, waylaid, filtered through culture and passed through the varying absorbancies of the singularly multiple human subject. In Joyce's novel such skewed subjectivity is there in his flux of styles or discourses – from the journalistic to the poetic – juxtaposing, as McHale comments, "disparate worlds, different reality templates". For Joyce, there is a kind of non-clinical schizophrenia at the core of modernity. He presents a modern subjectivity trapped between conflicting worlds, caught in flows of language, all registering alternative – and simultaneous – modes of existence and interpretation: competing discourses, each with its own seductive claim to be the truth. Picasso and Joyce strived for an art that would capture and present such fragmentation.

Unlike Picasso, however, one of Joyce's main targets was the binary logic whereby male=mind/female=body. Joyce refused the separation of mind and body, and in doing so implicitly refused the cultural associations linking the concept of male with the mind and female with the body. In *Ulysses*, the body Joyce installs at the centre of his novel is not only male but penetrable; a body which reimagines gender as something multiple and unfixed to particular arrangements of genitals. It is an open body, sensate and sensitive, registering the fantasies within as much as the realities without. And it shares many of the characteristics of what Bakhtin, in his study of Rabelais (1984), termed the grotesque body.[53]

JOYCE AND THE GROTESQUE

As a pre-Enlightenment phenomenon, the grotesque body can be usefully employed to critique the late nineteenth-century sexological will to taxonomy, while the non-gendered quality of the grotesque throws into relief the modern obsession with gender and its protocols. Bakhtin's work suggests a break that is at once both historical and psychological. For the modern

---

[53] In his introduction to *Gargantua and Pantagruel*, translator J.M. Cohen refers to Joyce as Rabelais' "counterpart and admirer in our own age" (Harmondsworth: Penguin, 1969), 17.

concept of the closed, singular and individuated body is revealed as mythic once its grotesque zones are penetrated and their common ground explored. This revelation of the body's inherent penetrability concludes, for the male body at least, in an act of erasure: it disappears from the scene, and the penetrated body of any sex gets stamped with an abjected and passive femininity. What makes Joyce's proximity of the body and language significantly radical is that the body he chose to place centre stage in his novel is the penetrated male body, Leopold Bloom's body. He thereby immediately rejects the male=mind/female=body binary that has been shown to be so dominant in our culture. Joyce employs the penetrated male body to dismantle the grammar of gender, in order to critique it, in order to present a male body that is multiple and open, and which is, moreover, celebrated for its grotesque qualities. In *Rabelais and His World*, Bakhtin writes:

> The essence of the grotesque is precisely to present a contradictory and double-faced fullness of life. Negation and destruction (death of the old) are included as an essential phase, inseparable from affirmation, from the birth of something new and better. The very material bodily lower stratum of the grotesque image (food, wine, the genital force, the organs of the body) bears a deeply positive character. This principle is victorious, for the final result is always abundance. (1984, 62)

In contrast to the modern concept of the body, then, in which "all orifices ... are closed", the grotesque body "ignores the impenetrable surface that closes and limits the body" (Bakhtin 1984, 318), and dissolves or overcomes the confines between bodies. The orificially closed body, according to Bakhtin, forms "the basis of the image [of] the individual, strictly limited mass, the impenetrable facade" (1983, 320). In sharp contrast, there is "no facade, no impenetrable surface" to the grotesque body. "Neither has it any expressive features" (Bakhtin 1984, 339). The grotesque body refutes and refuses individuality, celebrating instead the bodily functions and drives that are the fundamental basis of our commonality. As Bakhtin argues:

> All these convexities and orifices have a common characteristic: it is within them that the confines between bodies and between the body and the world are overcome: there is an interchange and an interorientation. This is why the main events in the life of the grotesque body, the acts of the bodily drama, take place in this sphere. (1984, 317)

Our sociality is predicated on the universal truth of the orificial body. If the confines between bodies and between the body and the world are to be overcome – that is, if we are going to be able to live together in social groupings at all – we must acknowledge – even celebrate – the acts of the bodily drama, must recognize the events in the life of the grotesque body.

There is, it has to be said, something irreducibly utopian about Bakhtin's vision; a rose-tinted view of more pagan times. It can be found in a different form in the Romantics' view of the countryside as a place of rural purity and beautiful, unbounded nature. But the concept of the grotesque that got taken up by modernity became inflected with a strange cruelty that it turned upon itself. The suffering masculine subject – be it at the hands of *la belle dame sans merci* or of late capitalism – became the modern form of the grotesque.[54]

Although Bakhtin's analysis never directly addresses the ways in which gender played a part in the disappearance of the grotesque body – what Thomas Laqueur calls his "blindness to the brutality of the language directed against women" (Laqueur 1990, 121) – there is nonetheless a sense in which the grotesque body remains radically and specifically *non*gendered. Bakhtin's gender blindness can be viewed

---

[54] In Sacher-Masoch's *Venus in Furs*, Wanda says to Severin: "'It would seem ... that for you love and particularly women are hostile forces; you try to defend yourself against them. However, you are quite overcome by the pleasurable torments and exquisite pain which they afford you. A very modern view'": *Venus in Furs*, trans. Jean McNeil (New York: Zone Books, 1991), 159.

as actively resisting modern principles of sexual categorization. As Simon Williams argues, the non-gendered aspect of the grotesque body provides "a chance to challenge dominant (masculine) notions of the (male) body as a bounded, impermeable entity, and a self that exists by repulsion/exclusion (i.e. unitary and contained) rather than inter-penetration/otherness" (1998, 76). By focusing on body parts such as the anus and the mouth, the grotesque body in a sense *reduces* or bypasses gender difference in ways which highlight its political and historical over-emphasis within the specificities of the dominant models within nineteenth and twentieth century representation. The medieval carnivals that celebrated the grotesque body did so, after all, partly through gender reversals – *travesties* – that destabilized gender roles, if only temporarily. Not only the body, but the whole world was temporarily turned upside down and back to front, and as such reality was rendered affirmatively uncertain, mutable and ambivalent.

For Bakhtin, the grotesque is coterminous with the carnivalesque. During Medieval carnivals what was low was celebrated – just as authority (what was on high) was denigrated and mocked. The aspects of the body termed grotesque are temporarily lauded and celebrated. Peter Stallybrass and Allon White argue that a certain residue or trace of the grotesque has become the *low* against which the bourgeois subject defines and redefines itself; this lowly, grotesque abject body, however, returns as exterior, as Other, marked by nostalgia and fascination (1986, 191).

> The demonization and the exclusion of the carnivalesque has to be related to the victorious emergence of specifically bourgeois practices and languages which reinflected and incorporated this material within a negative, individualist framework.
> (Stallybrass and White 1986, 176)

It is clear, however, that *as a trace* – a symbol of all that is low – the grotesque body becomes marked by notions of exteriority or otherness, and therefore threateningly unknown, even as its proximity is never fully overcome. The body may be denied, or ignored, but it can never be fully and successfully erased from individual subjectivity. As a result, physical pleasure becomes, in the words of Adorno and Horkheimer, "nature's vengeance", an echo of myth which enables men to "disavow thought and escape civilisation" (1972, 105). Thus the body's conceptual associations with baseness, nature, femininity and pleasure serve to render it actively damaging to the ordered, civilized self represented by the masculine, reasonable mind. In this sense, to talk of the body at all is to refer to the grotesque body, something that dangerously dissolves the barriers of individuation upon which modern subjectivity is predicated.

Fear of the body as a fear of madness has come to govern masculinist discourse, as was shown in the case of Schreber in Chapter One. Within the logic of that discourse, risking one is to risk the other. At least one writer has noted the "remarkable similarity between Mr. Joyce's compositions and the prose style of certain lunatics" (cited in Deming 1970a, 251). Indeed, Joyce himself said of *Ulysses*, "that book was a terrible risk. A transparent leaf separates it from madness" (cited in Froula 1996, 23). We have, in a sense, come full circle, arriving at the relationship between the penetrated male body and madness with which this book began. To articulate or (re)present the body's grotesqueness is a form of madness in the shape of a rupture that renders language almost unrecognizable/incomprehensible.

In contrast to the closed modern subject, the grotesque body is "never finished, never completed", but rather "it is continually built, created, and builds and creates another body"; in other words, it is "a body in the act of becoming" (Bakhtin 1984, 317). Mary Russo's work on the female grotesque notes the similarity of this Bakhtinian grotesque body to the one described by Cixous, a "body without beginning and without end" (cited in Russo 1994, 67). Russo remarks on the fact that Joyce is often cited as a model for this approach to the body and text within *ecriture feminine*.

This chapter, however, will argue that the main theoretical value of the grotesque is precisely its inability to be strictly gendered along the lines of either/or. Neither male nor female, the grotesque body serves to critique such demarcations, highlighting their arbitrary nature and challenging the values placed upon them. This logic of the neither/nor, as will be shown, is inherent in Joyce's presentation of the penetrable body. To gender the grotesque as female is to negate its critical potential for disrupting gender categories; it is to align the low that the grotesque manifests with the concept of female, and to reinscribe those pejorative associations the undermining of which is one of the tasks of this book. The grotesque allows us to move beyond the gender dyad and consider bodies whose genders are multiple, or whose experiences cannot fit neatly into the categories of male or female. That is, the grotesque body can harbour within its conceptual parameters a critique of itself, an unstable self-reflexivity similar to that characterizing the modernist moment.

Taking his cue from Rabelais as much as from Homer, Joyce conceived *Ulysses* as "the epic of the human body" (Budgen 1972, 21) with each chapter assigned a different body part. Frustrated at the ways in which the body was often elided in literature, Joyce sought to write of and from the body, and no bodily function – from farts to menstruation – was out of bounds to him. In *Modernism's Body: Sex, Culture and Joyce*, Christine Froula argues that Joyce restores the male body to our understanding of history, affirming it "in all of its senses, inside and out, all day long" (1996, 256). Froula concludes:

> Joyce's analytic self-portraits not only own the male body that Western metaphysics tends at different moments to disavow or univeralize but vivisect the psychodynamics underlying its projections onto and into female forms. (1996, 253)

For Froula, Joyce's modernism is precisely focused on the reinstatement of the male body, informed by a feminism that exposes the discursive strategies by which that body is so often denied. By insisting on the centrality of sensuous male flesh in the making of history, Froula sees Joyce as eschewing the patriarchal culture that hides the male body at the margins in order to centralize female flesh. Froula's argument thus turns on a reversal of the male=mind/woman=body, claiming that a celebration of the (self)paternal body is Joyce's greatest achievement. I will argue that Joyce's text promotes a more multiple understanding of the body that undermines the orthodox heterosexuality of procreative intercourse. For the male body Joyce presents in *Ulysses* breaks with several binaries, including the paternal/maternal one. The sensuality of the male body he explores is so unorthodox as to shatter any categorization of the body along the lines employed by patriarchal culture. The main difference, therefore, between *Ulysses* and the other texts discussed in this book is that Joyce manages to escape the logic whereby flesh=female, whereas the others remain – to lesser or greater degrees – caught within its all-pervasive web.

THIS IS MY BODY

As stated above, the body that is most present in *Ulysses*, the body we come to know most intimately, is Bloom's. From his bowel movements to the sway of his pubic hair in bath water, from his gastronomic preferences to his sexual preferences, it is his body that marks its passage across Dublin and across the pages of Joyce's novel. Joyce's presentation of Leopold Bloom is possibly the most thorough and complete narrativization of the male body in literature: a male body laid open, penetrated, known. More importantly, it is a male body far removed from cultural ideals of masculinity (heroically non-heroic). Bloom is a cuckold, a daydreamer, a poor breadwinner and a bad lover. He is physically unfit (in Nighttown he has to run to avoid getting run over by a car, reminding him that he must take up exercise [Joyce 1992, 567]). He is an outsider, sensitive and empathetic, happy to cook for his wife and do household chores. And he is more sympathetically portrayed than any of the traditionally masculine men in Dublin, who are presented as oafs.

We also get to see how Bloom views his own body. In the "Lotus-eaters" chapter, for example, (scene: the bath; organ: the genitals; technic: narcissism), Bloom narcissistically contemplates his body:

> Enjoy a bath now: clean trough of water, cool enamel, the gentle tepid stream. This is my body. He foresaw his pale body reclined in it at full, naked, in a womb of warmth, oiled by scented melting soap, softly laved. He saw his trunk and limbs, ririppled over and sustained, buoyed lightly upward, lemonyellow: his navel, bud of flesh: and saw the dark tangled curls of his bush floating, floating hair of the stream around the limp father of thousands, a languid floating flower. (Joyce 1992, 107)

This tender contemplation of the male body is an appropriation ("This is *my* body") and an affirmation ("*This is* my body"). The phrase is, of course, from the consecration of the mass, the second half of which Bloom omits: "which shall be given to you". Bloom gives his body to nobody in the novel, and his "limp father of thousands" will later discharge its seed, like Onan, upon barren ground.[55]

Bloom's body is highly sensitive to its surroundings, in flux, sustained within its amniotic bathwater like a foetus; a body full of potentiality, even while reclined. It is located in the present – this is my body, here, now – even as it is an anticipation of the bath to come ("He foresaw his pale body"). It recognizes the ineluctable passing of time: "Always passing, the stream of life, which in the stream of life we trace is dearer than them all" (Joyce 1992, 107). By tracing the stream of life with a stream of words, something is lost, the present passes and is lost. Words remain after the body from which they originated has gone. Aware of this dilemma, Joyce attempts to put the body's multiplicity into the words he writes, and in order to do so the words themselves have to be treated as objects; that is,

---

[55] Joyce is clearly challenging the Catholic church by placing these words in the head of a Jewish masturbator.

they have to be made to perform. This linguistic performance relies upon ambiguity or multiplicity of meaning, and employs puns and portmanteau words by the dozen. If Genet presents all of language as a system of metaphoricity, Joyce presents language as a group of metaphors gone berserk.[56] Again, this is a move designed to challenge the Jesuit teachings of his youth, using words creatively, playing God with language by endlessly and audaciously inventing new words – what Cixous terms an act of heresy or satanic progression.

PERFORMING THE RHIZOME

The chapter of *Ulysses* referred to through the Homeric schema[57] as "Circe" is presented as a playscript, suggesting a certain *performance* or theatricality of language that is both excessive and lacking, both superfluous and impoverished. In "Circe", all the themes of the previous chapters appear, along with many from the chapters to come. In "Circe", innanimate objects speak and words themselves perform. The body part corresponding to the "Circe" episode is the locomotor apparatus: this is writing concerned with movement, transition, flow and experimentation. This is language on the move, metamorphosing into strange, unknown shapes and forms, making a spectacle of itself, drawing attention to itself: language showing off. Like the human body itself, the text itself moved along in tandem, Joyce working on the different parts simultaneously (Wilson 1967, 169). It is an example of

---

[56] "One way of destroying a metaphor is to push its undecidableness to the limit: since a portmanteau word is a coinage, one will never know whether it is metaphorical or not ... Coinages are metaphors gone berserk", Jean-Jaques Lecercle, *Philosophy through the Looking-Glass: Language, Nonsense, Desire* (La Salle, IL: Open Court, 1985), 140.

[57] The Homeric schema appears in Stuart Gilbert's book, *James Joyce's Ulysses* (Harmondsworth: Penguin, 1963). A diagrammatic table of it appears in Declan Kiberd's introduction to *Ulysses* (Harmondsworth: Penguin 1992), xxiii.

an approach to writing by which any text is never more than a work in progress (the working title of what was to become, on publication, *Finnegans Wake*, Joyce's greatest linguistic metamorphosis). Samuel Beckett recognized this when he wrote of *Work in Progress* that it "is not *about* something, *it is that something itself*" (1972, 14, original emphasis). In its uncontainability, its excess, this proliferation of language is characteristic of what Deleuze and Guattari call the rhizome.

In *A Thousand Plateaus*, the second volume of Deleuze and Guattari's two volume work on *Capitalism and Schizophrenia*, they develop a theory of the rhizome as an analytic process predicated on multiplicities rather than binarisms. This helps make clearer what it is about Joyce's text that is so radical. In its botanical sense, a rhizome is an underground tuber that ramifies and diversifies, producing new shoots. Deleuze and Guattari oppose it to what they call arboric systems of knowledge – based on the model of a tree – which solidify in visible and immovable forms (Deleuze and Guattari 1992, 5). The rhizome is therefore both occluded and motional, a network of connections across which things flow and disperse. In this sense, it is a mapping, an inbetween, a becoming. The rhizome oscillates between the lines established by the arboric systems and as such is fuzzy rather than aggregated (Deleuze and Guattari 1992, 505–6). Like the Body without Organs, it disrupts the idea of a unified totality by gesturing to an elsewhere that is both incapable of being represented and constitutive of representation.

The kind of subjectivity suggested by the rhizome, then, is not singular but plural, inhabited by otherness. Likewise, Joyce populates the pronoun 'I' with a myriad of personalities, dispersing the relationship between self and other into a network irreducible to the two terms of any binarism. Joyce has Bloom reflect: "I am other I now"; and refer to himself as, "I, I and I. I" (1992, 242). Furthermore, this rhizomatic subject is in a state of multiplicity contingent upon a shifting body: "Molecules all change" (Joyce 1992, 242), suggesting a constant rearrangement of the self which exceeds the ideality of a stable and unified identity. Having no centre, no structure, no unity, the rhizome exists in an intense (and intensely productive) state of disarray, or becoming, which makes generalization through any act of representation impossible. The rhizome is therefore nonrepresentable, and thinkable only through a concept of multiplicity that shatters the unity of the subject. Rhizomorphosis is a radical state of fragmentation such as cannot be accounted for within existing protocols of representation, such as language, but which nevertheless exists as a kind of chaos or chaosmosis suppurating underneath any representation. The task of Joyce's language is to get closer to that chaos by investing words with an immediacy that bypasses the reductive move of identity thinking.

In other words, if language is to be used to represent the material body, then it must confront those aspects of the body deemed unfit for discursive representation, such as sexuality, or scatology. Moreover, it must present the material body as something not reducible to enforced social categorizations based on anything so crass as mere anatomical difference. Deleuze and Guattari argue that "the rhizome ... is a liberation of sexuality not only from reproduction but also from genitality" (1992, 18). A rhizomatic body thus surpasses and eludes any simple taxonomic move that would confine it to one of two gender groups based on genitalia. By its very nature, its recognition can only serve to disrupt such taxonomic logic.

THE RHIZOMATIC BODY

The rhizome, then, allows us to understand more fully Joyce's claim on the body as ineluctable yet fluid, material yet imaginative, singular yet multiple. The network of passages provided by the rhizome allow for an understanding of bodies as not only full of passages but as themselves a passage, a perambulation through space, through language, through the flesh itself. Joyce writes, "We walk through ourselves, meeting robbers, ghosts, giants, old men, young men, wives, widows, brothers-in-love. But always meeting ourselves" (1992, 273), suggesting that bodies function as dwelling places for all these personages.

These personages constitute a multiple-singularity that has no Other other than its own *dramatis personae*, these we-selves we carry – male, female, hermaphrodite – make of our bodies a rhizome, a nomadic flesh of coexistent multiplicities. The body is thus a singularization of space, but because we are continuously passing through ourselves, that singularity is a multiplicity. As Guattari remarks in his rethinking of subjectivity: "Not only is I an other, but it is a multitude of modalities of alterity" (1995, 96). In this sense, the body is not confined to the either/or of male or female, and neither is it simply both at the same time, but, beyond this, in the occluded realm of the neither/nor, it becomes an essentially multiple and multiply-gendered entity.

This is not an asexual body, but rather, as Deleuze and Guattari argue, fragmentation of the body inevitably leads to sexuality. Similarly, Attridge argues that "sexuality thrives on the separation of the body into independent parts, whereas a sexually repressive morality insists on the wholeness and singleness of body and mind or soul" (1988, 167).

Furthermore, this fragmentation of the body allows intensities their own velocity and texture, their own duration and multiplicity. In *Libidinal Economy*, Lyotard links this to an infinite process of metonymy: "intense passages, tensors, are then no longer singularities, they take on value, as elements, from their continuation, from their opposition, from a metonymy without end" (1993, 27). This endless metonymy is both responsible for the fact that representation works – or that meaning sticks – and indicative of representation's failure. It alludes to the revolutionary potential of poetic language of which Kristeva has written, by lodging a necessary instability within the seemingly stable structure of language.

These *intense passages* refer not only to a movement (as if that word itself didn't indicate something scatological), but to the passages within the body, *as well as* passages, fragments, of text. Their intensity derives precisely from an excess of meaning, something in excess of the straightforward communicative function of language. As such, this intensity is a kind of waste. This connection between faeces and writing will be developed and explored shortly. As Deleuze writes in *The Fold*, bringing out the penetrable quality of matter: "each body contains a world pierced with irregular passages" (1993, 5).

For Lyotard, all systems of exchange are libidinal. As they acquire value within the libidinal economy, these passages become infinitely exchangeable: a metonymy without end. In Chapter Two, penetration of one orifice was shown to conjure the threat/pleasure of alternative openings. Penetration through the eyes, ears and mouth is thus always erotic, always haunted by those other, lower, openings which, by remaining undisclosed, appear all the more seductive, radiating with the promise of transgression. Furthermore, these passages within the body can be made to connect rhizomatically with what Jeanette Winterson calls "the secret passage between body and book" (1995, 132) – that is, with the experience of reading. This would account for why they are more apparent in texts deemed difficult or impenetrable, such as *Ulysses*. Stefan Zweig's 1928 review of Joyce's novel brings together the intestinal and the verbal in a way that clarifies the connections being made here through the word passage:

> Here a man explodes not only in cry, not only in scornful word and in grimaces, but also out of all his intestines, he empties his resentments, he vomits his overdue feelings with a force and a vehemence which makes one sincerely shudder. (Cited in Deming 1970b, 445)

A closed body can only react to the open body presented in Joyce's novel with terror and incomprehension. If the point of language is to communicate, to be transparent and accessible, then what is the point of Joyce's language? His language throws into question the point of language – its supposedly straightforward function as a means of communication. In the words of Declan Kiberd, it is "a sustained meditation on the limits of communicability" (1992, xlix). His language shifts and turns, mutates and morphs, eschewing communication in favour of experience or sensation. The endless nomadism of the subject (in this case, a book) always disrupts the stasis of the object (in this case, also a book) which attempts to represent it.

This multiplicity, this rhizomatic movement that renders the subject objective and the object subjective, brings intellect back to the body from which it sprung, and takes it out again into a world of objects. Or, as Joyce puts it: "So in the future, the sister of the past, I may see myself as I sit here now but by reflection from that which then I shall be" (1992, 249). It is a movement both endlessly in excess of representation, so that, if it is to be shown at all it must be as a deformation or mutation of representation: an indecency or impropriety according to the protocols of representation.

Given that the rhizome is also a characteristic of writing, that "a book [is] all the more total for being fragmented" (Deleuze and Guattari 1992, 6), *Ulysses* becomes even more apposite, for it is probably the most rhizomatic text ever written, not only by virtue of its backward moving tendrils connecting it with Homer's *Odyssey* and Shakespeare's *Hamlet*, but in the way it has multiplied like a virus, inspiring a deluge of critical interpretations in its wake an entire industry of scholars and exegetes; a text generating further texts. Karl Radek refers to the novel's "intricate cobweb of allegories and mythological allusions" (cited in Deming 1970b, 624). Joyce wrote about a third of *Ulysses* during the proofing stage, working his way through six or eight galleys. The publisher, Sylvia Beach, admitted that if real publishers went through this painstaking and expensive process "it would be the death of publishing" (cited in Fitch 1985, 106), recalling later that

> Every proof was covered with additional text ... adorned with Joycean rockets and myriads of stars guiding the printers to words and phrases and lists of names all around the margins. (Cited in Fitch 1985, 106)

As Riley Fitch comments, "No book has ever been written in this way" (1985, 106). As with most aspects of Joyce's life and work, convention went out of the window. According to the Paris correspondent of the *Guardian*, "that *Ulysses* became the sort of book it is is largely due to [Beach], for it was she ... who decided to allow Joyce an indefinite right to correct his proofs. It was in the exercise of this right that the peculiarities of Joyce's prose style reached their novel flowering" (cited in Fitch 1985, 106).[58] Only Proust, whose gargantuan novel *A la recherche du temps perdu* is contemporaneous with Joyce's, would treat the proofing stage in a similarly creative manner: the book as organic matter, spilling beyond the typeset page. Uncontainable words, sprouting shoots of imagination and verbal filigree in an endless, excessive flow. As Stephen Heath puts it:

> the writing opens out onto a multiplicity of fragments of sense, of possibilities, which are traced and retraced, colliding and breaking ceaselessly in the play of this text that resists any homogenization. (1984, 31–2)

This infinite will to heterogeneity that is *Ulysses* is, ultimately, nomadic, taking the reader constantly to somewhere else, to someone else.[59] To read it is to embark on a journey with no map for guidance, although extensive field notes exist in the form of the countless books Joyce's novel has inspired, tracing many entryways into that dense and seemingly impenetrable text.

These two understandings of the rhizome – as body and as text – converge upon *Ulysses*. Whilst Stuart Gilbert's

---

[58] I would refer the reader here to the linking of the anus with the flower in Chapter Three.

[59] Stephen Heath says of *Finnegans Wake* that it is "a work of folding and unfolding in which every element becomes always the fold of another in a series that knows *no point of rest*" (1984, 32, my emphasis). Although Heath's comments are about *Finnegans Wake*, the beginnings of that text can be traced to *Ulysses*, specifically the experimental passages in Circe. Leo Bersani, for example, talks of hearing in the language of Circe, "the anticipatory echoes of things yet to come ... announcing the verbal textures of *Finnegans Wake*" (1990, 165). Heath's comments are, therefore, not entirely out of context in a discussion of *Ulysses*.

schema makes clear Joyce's use of body parts to organize the text, *Ulysses* can also – perhaps should – be viewed without this methodological scaffolding, organless and rhizomatic. Indeed, it could be argued that, without the schema, *Ulysses* is a body without organs, that deleuzeguattarian (non)concept most closely connected to the rhizome. The organs given to the chapters *organ*ize the novel, even as they at the same time demonstrate the textual fragmentation of the body. Moreover, Gilbert's schema – developed in collaboration with Joyce – was central in defending the novel's legal right to be called a work of art rather than pornography. In short, the body parts structuring the novel were made explicit as a reaction to juridical claims against it. *The body/novel was forced to organize in order to represent.*

There is no denying that the body on display in Joyce's novel is large and loud. He plumbs its depths and exposes its more unsightly activities. That he does so in a language both tender and poetic, muscular and coarse, suggests that Joyce is reclaiming the body – with all its orifices, stenches and fluids – for aesthetics, rescuing it from the (off)scene of obscenity. He is presenting the reader with a body at once both familiar and unknown, in a language both familiar and unknown. In this sense, the body Joyce presents to us is not unlike the grotesque Bakhtinian body, full of ambiguity, joyously disorganized.

Attridge argues that one function of language is to reduce the independence of body parts (1988, 160), with the consequence that Joyce's transgressions of the selectional restrictions of English syntax "can be regarded as stratagems that liberate the body from a dictatorial and englobing will and allow its organs their own energies and proclivities" (1988, 167).

Breaking the back of grammatical logic, this asyntactical move is also an asynthetic one, rendering the body/language dialectic productively, transgressively, open and infintely nonsynthesizable. By making fragmentation of the body and fragmentation of language inseparable in this way, Joyce is formulating a materiality of discourse such as Foucault made explicit in some of his work. He is pointing out that seemingly paradoxical "incorporeal materialism" within discourse, the identification and analysis of which can reveal not only the role played by rules and continuity but also that played by chance and discontinuity (Foucault 1972, 231). In *The Order of Things*, Foucault identifies this discontinuity or rupture as a break between language and representation:

> until the connection between language and representation is broken, or at least transcended, in our culture, all secondary languages will be imprisoned within the alternative of criticism or commentary. And in their indecision they will proliferate *ad infinitum*. (1997, 81)

Once language breaks away from its seemingly straightforward connection to an assumed pre-existent reality, once it becomes self-reflective – that is, once it becomes in some sense fiction – it follows a path to infinity. Foucault argues that the emergence of a specific genre of imaginative writing in the nineteenth century which we now call fiction – a genre which, by implication, makes every other discourse non-fictional, or factual – signifies a distinct break between knowledge and language which, paradoxically, impurifies both. "Between the two, the intermediary languages – descendants of, or outcasts from, both knowledge and language – were to proliferate to infinity" (Foucault 1997, 89). Joyce's language is one such intermediary language, marked by a radical proliferation to infinity. Joyce's technique of making language speak – what Bersani calls his "objectified subjectivity" (1990, 161) – works through a metonymy that constantly takes the characters and the readers beyond the text. Bersani points out that "the narrative frequently refers to, say, a Bloom or a Mulligan more real than the Bloom or the Mulligan it allows us to see or hear" (1990, 167). This space beyond or behind the text, where the more real Bloom and co. reside, is the space of literature itself, a fictional space because there is no other kind of space. Fictional because we inhabit language to the extent that language is our reality. That is, what we call reality is no less fictional than what we call fiction. It is not discovered, but created.

"In this sense", writes Foucault, "every work is an attempt to exhaust language" (1998, 19). But, more than that, argues Lecercle, this language of delirium, or what he calls *délire*, is directly "concerned with the relationship between language and the human body" (1985, 95). The task, therefore, is to make these mere words work, in the most physical sense of making them sweat, exhausted, broken and delirious. To push language to its absolute physical limit.

This exhaustive capacity of language[60] – to adjectivize it with the term literary would be to separate it off from what would then be an uncontaminated source of knowledge – is the very quality which makes discourse rhizomatic. For "the text proliferates, grows in unexpected directions, refuses to follow the straight line of demonstration, but on the contrary sometimes changes its course, for no apparent reason", and such "proliferation is always a threat to order" (Lecercle 1985, 96).

Endlessly productive, "a rhizome may be broken, shattered at a given spot, but it will start up again on one of its old lines, or on *new lines*" (Deleuze and Guattari 1992, 9, emphasis added). And these new lines, these experimental, code-breaking nomadic metamorphoses of words, are capable of folding bodies within the very discourse out of which they have been excised. In short: language brings us closer to the material body when it stops making sense, or when it constantly undermines the sense that is being made. Or, rather, the sense made is more rooted in sensation, in sense as an experience, a feeling, a limit, rather than – as it is commonly interpreted – as meaning. Put yet another way, language brings us closer to the material body when it makes us feel rather than think. The performativity of the body is for Joyce inseparable from the performativity of language – and both remain excessively irreducible to a system of representation predicated on the logic of non-contradiction. As Marilyn French argues in her study of *Ulysses*, "if what happens is almost totally contingent on how it is described, act and word are equally potent" (1982, 11). Indeed, for Joyce

---

[60] When Bloom is tired, in the "Eumaeus" chapter, the language also becomes exhausted, lazy, cliched.

words *are* acts, or rather actors, performing and emoting, not in the sense of speech acts, not in the restricted linguistic sense of the performative, but in the magical, incantatory sense of having physical properties, having qualities above and beyond the merely communicative. And nowhere do they perform more than in the Circe or Nighttown sequence of *Ulysses*, in the dark heart of Dublin, in a brothel.

These two meanings of the rhizome – as a textual and a subjective/somatic heterogeneity – come together in Joyce's novel in a language that constantly reinvents itself, thus undermining – whilst also emphasizing – its own production of meaning. This emphasis on the performative aspects of *Ulysses*, its power not just to represent reality but to establish it only to shatter it, was the most difficult obstacle in the critical appraisal of the novel. Confronted with such vertiginous prose, for example, Hugh Kenner opines: "deprived of reliable criteria for 'reality', we have no recourse save to read the text as though everything in it were equally real … even Bloom's change of sex" (1980, 126–7). Conversely, of course, nothing in the book is real, each event happening only within the confines of its pages, its maze of words, and nowhere else. *Ulysses* both performs its own reality and undermines it at the same time. As such, to see Bloom's change of sex in so straightforward a way as Kenner does is to fail to see that there are, as Italo Calvino argues, several levels of reality within a literary text (1987, 101). It is also to fall back on the very gender dimorphism that the text itself is intent on repeatedly problematizing. Bloom does not so much become a woman, as become both male and female at the same time, or, in the words of Dr Malachi Mulligan in the Circe episode: "a finished example of the new womanly man" (Joyce 1992, 613–4).

This diagnosis of Bloom's gender inversion is a parody of sexological taxonomy. As well as allocating a body part and Homeric episode to each chapter in *Ulysses*, Joyce's schema allocates a particular art. For the preceding chapter, "Oxen of the Sun", the art was medicine; for "Circe" it is magic. Not only is science superseded, or counterpointed, by mysticism, but the language of the former chapter is secondhand, whilst the language of the latter is radically new. "Oxen of the Sun" parodies and pastiches past styles; the language of "Circe" is unprecedented. Whilst the one hints at how much language leaves unsaid, the other gestures towards the violence involved in forcing words to articulate the unsayable. The tension between these two chapters contains an implicit critique of modern science, and in particular sexology.

JOYCE AND SEXOLOGY

In "Circe", sexology and pornography – those two nineteenth-century discourses on human sexuality – play against one another, not so much as opposites, more hostile relatives. In Chapter One, we saw how unspeakable the topic of human sexuality was considered for mainstream discourse. Its appearance – which rapidly increased throughout the nineteenth century – took on two forms: the scientific and the pornographic. In Western societies, as Foucault has argued, the *scientia sexualis* predominated, but that is not to say that an *ars erotica* was completely absent. Joyce maintained a keen interest in both, and "Circe" in particular owes a great deal to Leopold von Sacher-Masoch's 1860s classic of flagellation, *Venus in Furs* (with whom Bloom shares a first name). Bloom is an avid comsumer of pornography (as is his wife, Molly), and his domination by Bella Cohen in the brothel plays out scenes from Sacher-Masoch's novel (see Ellman 1982, 369–70).

One of the most consistent themes in *Ulysses* is androgyny. In nineteenth-century sexology, androgyny was not only a physical property of ambiguous gender, such as it is now most commonly understood, but signifed too a more subjective or psychological indeterminacy – an ambiguity over sexuality, or, more often, a clear sign of homosexuality. In *Ulysses*, Joyce presents both Bloom and Stephen as different to the brutish machismo of traditional masculinity, as precursors of a future gender that will acknowledge the femininity in men. The ordinary men of Dublin are presented as the last sad remnants of a dying breed. Whilst this androgyny that characterizes

Stephen and Bloom is not without a certain homoeroticism – and as a result, subject to homophobic responses from the ordinary men – it is in no way straightforwardly homosexual. As Declan Kiberd points out, whilst bisexuality is interpersonal, androgyny is interpsychic (1992, lxiii), a blending of genders not necessarily predicated on desire. Joyce is striving for a model much more complex than the straightforward correspondence of desire and identity that marked most sexology.

Whilst references to Bloom's androgyny appear throughout the novel, it is in the "Circe" chapter that it takes on its most consistent form. And whilst this chapter is a fantasy, a hallucinatory presentation of Bloom's unconscious wishes, one of Joyce's intentions is to confuse the division between the psychic and the corporeal. As such, the events of nighttown are as real as any other events in the novel, for they are manifested, like all the other events, in language.

It is also in this chapter that we find Joyce's most sustained engagement with sexology. Joyce's interest in sexology may be surmised by the accusation levelled against Bloom by the First Watch. Bloom is accused of cutting off a girl's plait, a perversion that appears in case 396 of Richard von Krafft-Ebing's *Psychopathia Sexualis*, the bible of sexology in the 1890s (cited in Deleuze 1991, 135–6). At one point in the chapter, Bloom's father, Virag,[61] appears and refers to a book of his entitled *Fundamentals of Sexology*. The science of sex is linked here not only to the paternal voice, against which the language of "Circe" rebels, but also to the fundament. Later on, Bloom gives his definition of science: "to compare the various joys we each enjoy" (Joyce 1992, 649) – a much more heterogenous approach to understanding human sexuality.

The voice of sexology is also articulated by a group of doctors who appear in "Circe" to pass comment on Bloom's physiognomy. One of them, Dr Malachi Mulligan, is the dreamscape equivalent of Stephen's medical student friend and housemate, Buck Mulligan. As well as being found to be

---

[61] Virag is Bloom's real (Hungarian) name, of which Bloom is the Anglicized version.

"bisexually abnormal" by this hallucinatory doctor, Bloom is also declared both pregnant and *virgo intacta* (Joyce 1992, 613) – recalling once again the Immaculate Conception. According to one of the other doctors, Dr Madden, Bloom also shows marked signs of hypospadia, an intersexual condition in which the scrotum takes on the appearance of labia. In this respect, Joyce is not so much inverting genders as folding them, one within the other, and thereby questioning the taxonomic distinctions upon which much sexology is based. As such, he refuses and challenges the hierarchy that gender imposes on the body by claiming a much more fluid and heterogeneous engagement between desire, the body and the psyche. If the genitals can appear indeterminate, how can any body be classified uncontestedly? Indeed, it is the very condition of what the sexologists termed intersexuality that provides Joyce with the physical image of Bloom's transsexual phantasy. It also provides a means for presenting the penetrated male body that resists the erasure of the masculine so far encountered in the examples explored in this book.

BLOOM'S METAMORPHOSIS

Bloom's metamorphosis in nighttown is one of several transmogrifications throughout the scene/chapter. The chapter is littered with references to animality and transformation: a dog, for instance, wanders in and out of the scene, mutating from one breed to another. Bloom's father appears with "vulture talons" (Joyce 1992, 569); a woman pisses "cowily" (578); Paddy Dignam, whose funeral Bloom attended earlier in the day, appears as a beagle, whilst John O'Connel is described as "toadbellied" (597). There are many, many more examples. And just as the men in Homer's *Odyssey* were transformed into swine by Circe's magic, so Bloom becomes a slavish pig through Bella Cohen's sexual alchemy. The body emerges here as a fold or hinge between fluctuating genders, between mutating embodiments, and such metamorphoses signal not only a radical multiplicity but also a non-human/bestial element or fold to the human which constitutes a direct attack upon the language of reason.[62]

Bloom's metamorphosis takes place in a brothel, thus foregrounding the status of prostitution in its libidinal economy. The brothel is a place where men's sexual dependence upon women is played out, whilst, paradoxically, functioning as a cultural symbol for women's uncontainable sexuality. Bloom's penetration by Bella in her own brothel recalls Querelle's submission to Nono (the brothel keeper) from the last chapter, which also occurs in a brothel: the excess of prostitution and the excess of the penetrated male body are in many ways coexistent. But whereas for Genet the space delineated by this excess lies beyond the representative capacity of language, constituting an outside that can be seen as coterminous with the behind as it is being understood in this book, Joyce opts for a different manoeuvre. Joyce breaks language in order to register that excess. He folds that excess within language and registers the openness of the body – its subjective multiplicity – through an openness of language. The rupture or hole as understood in Chapter One appears in Joyce's text as a linguistic excess that willingly opens itself up to the multidimensionality of the body.

When Bloom initially talks to Bella it is through the synecdoche of her fan. That is, a certain metonymy connects Bella to this folded object. And this metonymy links – in French at least – the event with the object (in French, a fan is *un éventail*).[63]

---

[62] "In spite of all my efforts to convince myself of the contrary, metamorphosis is a morbid subject. Although it is a critique of language (as is evident from the animal or other nonhuman forms that it often employs), it is a critique from beyond the point where language has been forced on one", Irving Massey, *The Gaping Pig: Literature and Metamorphosis* (Berkeley: University of California Press, 1976), 1.

[63] Tom Conley comments in his translator's foreword to Deleuze's *The Fold*, "for Deleuze, an event unfolds from the union of our perception and the duration of a fan ... that unites and disperses a word (an *event*) and an object (an *éventail*) when it swirls the atmosphere": Deleuze, *The Fold: Leibniz and the Baroque*, trans. Tom Conley (Minneapolis: University of Minnesota Press, 1993), xii

Furthermore, it is a metonymy without end, displacing, like a rhizome, any point of origin, as a fan displaces the air it beats.

In *The Fold*, Deleuze suggests that "ultimately the fold pertains to the sensitive side of the fan" (1997, 30). The fold is the fan's *raison d'être*. The movements of a fan are what make its function visible. With its folds moving like lips, that is, as a collective unity or singular multiplicity, Bella Cohen's fan speaks in a multitude of voices that shatters syntax with its schizophrenic personalities, its metonymic mastery. The fan is a fold, opening and closing on the space or hinge (in)between past and present, outside and inside, same and other, subject and predicate, such that "fluctuation of the norm replaces the permanence of a law" (Deleuze 1993, 19). In this bizarre dreamplay chapter, in which objects become subjects and subjects objects, the Fan becomes a character, one that speaks in multiple and disrupted voices: "Is me her was you dreamed before? Was then she him you us since knew? Am all them and the same now we?" (Joyce 1992 642). Such grammatical malfunctioning dramatizes the psychosis present within any attempt to think beyond the categories provided to make the world intelligible. If language is to capture this fluctuation of the norm, it will be in forms not immediately recognizable as logical, not reducible by the unifying process of signification.

For Joyce, masculine submission plays a significant part in this claim to an irreducible heterogeneity of the subject. The Fan/Bella recognizes immediately that Bloom likes to be dominated, calling his marriage a "petticoat government" (Joyce 1992, 642). Bloom willingly succumbs to Bella's domination, wincing as he does so: "Powerful being. In my eyes read that slumber which women love". When Bloom says: "Awaiting your further orders, we remain, gentlemen" (Joyce 1992, 644), he is not only claiming submission on behalf of all men, but also indicating his own status as singular plural: as a singular multiplicity.

This singular multiplicity is, furthermore, presented in its most visible form as the penetrated male body. The domination scene in Circe culminates in Bloom dressed as a woman with Bello trying to sell him/her to prospective male buyers.

To encourage the buyers, Bello plunges his arm "elbowdeep in Bloom's vulva", shouting "There's fine depth for you! What, boys? That give you a hardon? (*he shoves his arm in a bidder's face*) Here, wet the deck and wipe it round!" (Joyce 1992, 651).

At this point in the text, as Bella's forearm slides inside Bloom's vulva, Joyce briefly inverts gender pronouns, referring to Bloom as *she*, Bella/Bello as *he*, making of gender a grammatical technology. *Bella* (beautiful) becomes *bello* (war). Rather than a straightforward representation of the penetrated male body as female, however, this move reduces gender difference to a merely verbal distinction. Within the textual economy of the novel, the discursive switch of gender pronouns carries the body mometarily from one sexed position to another. By becoming she, Bloom suddenly finds him/herself in possession of a vulva, and that vulva functions as an opening onto another dimension, an alternative embodiment: it is a portal, a conduit. As Stephen Dedalus reflects at the start of the third chapter, as he sits on the beach contemplating the ineluctable modality of the visible: "If you can put your five fingers through it, it is a gate, if not a door" (Joyce 1992, 45). And gates and doors lead somewhere else.

But the place this penetration takes Bloom is not the straightforwardly female site of the body that it was for Schreber and Genet. For four pages earlier, upon mounting Bloom in order to ride her like a horse, Bello had squeezed "his mount's testicles roughly" (Joyce 1992, 647). Joyce is clearly not simply inverting Bloom's gender, but rather making male and female coexist within or upon one body. Possessing both vulva and testicles, Bloom emerges as an hermaphrodite, a creature of the folds, his body a hinge between sexed positions. Those body parts referred to/signified by the words vulva and testicles now exist simultaneously on Bloom's body, leaving open the question of his/her gender. It is thus not a question of language or the body, but language *and* the body as an interface of matter itself. Here, the penetrated male body is that body which both holds gender together *and* holds it apart: invaginated *and* testicular, this penetrated body refuses to fall on one side of the dividing line and stay there. It is a body indicated by a space within language that vibrates with equivocality, neither male nor female, such terms being tied to a restrictive technology of language employed to make sense of the human body in terms of socially determined gender roles.

As such, Joyce presents gender not as a polarity, but a multiplicity, or oscillation: a mutable folding of male within female, female within male. Attridge calls it a seepage across the boundaries of gender, a multiplicity which provides "the possibility that gender might be less rigid, less oppositional, less determined by a political and economic system" (2000, 112, 116). For Joyce, that folding is predicated on pleasure rather than biology, anatomy or essence, and is effected through a language rendered uncertain and uncontainable; a language pulled in two seemingly opposite directions (he versus she), only to meet upon the same site, the same body. As Bloom himself reflects, "extremes meet" (Joyce 1992, 622). And later on, in the "Ithaca" chapter, Joyce will offer Stephen "his firm full masculine feminine passive active hand" (Joyce 1992, 788), indicating the full extent of this meeting of extremes and its inherent ambiguity.

Such ambiguity is a refusal of the negating logic of either/or, and an affirmation of the neither/nor. This neither/nor is a multiple simultaneity, an equivocation at the heart of language which Derrida demonstrates in his essay on Joyce's use of the word *yes* (Derrida 1992). This word's equivocality, however – contiguous with the equivocality of all words – is most signally exposed by a response of Bloom's in the brothel, to which Derrida (surprisingly) makes no reference.

Joyce himself considered *yes* to be not only a female word but expressive, in *Ulysses* at least, of the female sexual organ.[64]

---

[64] See Richard Ellman (ed.), *The Letters of James Joyce* (London: Faber & Faber, 1975), 285. Noel Riley Fitch refers to a consultation between Joyce and the French translator Jacques Benoist-Méchin, during which Joyce was convinced of the potency of ending his novel with the word "yes" because it is "the most positive word in the language", *Sylvia Beach and the Lost Generation: A History of Literary Paris in the Twenties and Thirties* (New York and London: W. W. Norton & Company, 1985), 109–10.

Derrida's essay places an affirmation of the flesh firmly within a feminine paradigm, even as it opens up that paradigm to a rigorous deconstruction (1992, 256–309). It is, after all, Molly Bloom who has the last word in the novel, and that last word is "Yes", and it is an invitation to copulation, a willing acceptance of her own defloration, a giving of her body in response to a call. The body, once again, would seem to be a place inhabited by, or a concept represented by, woman. We must remember, however, that Molly's final yes remains unspoken, and exists in thought only.

But there is another yes in *Ulysses* that more pointedly signals this ambiguity. Bloom's response to the Fan's question, "Have you forgotten me?" is the equivocal "Yes. No." (Joyce 1992, 642). Given that the Fan is a synecdoche for Bella, that is, metonymically linked to a female body, such equivocation points to an uncertainty of the status of the body. If Bloom *has* forgotten the Fan's metonymic link to the female body, such oblivion offers his own body an opportunity to inhabit that now vacant space. As such, the affirmation in Bloom's yes is the affirmation of a forgetting or oblivion of the female body, which would allow for a remembering or affirmation of the male body. Such affirmation is, however, immediately denied, negated by Bloom's defeatist *no*, his confession of or concession to remembrance, which is a recognition that he knows the Fan's place, that is, he concedes the status of the female body as body. As such, every subsequent yes – including Molly's final word – carries with it the equivocation of the body's gendered status. As Colin McCabe argues

> Bloom and Bella reflect each other in an endless hall of mirrors. As the text succeeds in giving a voice to the woman in Bloom, it abandons disjunction in favour of a bisexuality which multiplies identity geometrically. (1978, 129)

It is, then, the penetrated *male* body – Bloom's body impaled on Bella's forearm – that ushers in this multiple identity, that acts as a hinge between gendered positions and utters the equivocal yes/no or neither/nor upon which this endless mirroring rests. It is a male body opened and entered in order to undermine the safety of gender polarity, registering as neither male nor female, but instead working against such oppositional logic in order to express a multiplicity of the flesh which the protocols of representation have been structured to deny.

In Chapter Three, it was argued that Genet's construction of an outside to language orchestrated what Derrida has posited as the first phase of deconstruction: namely, a recognition of the violently hierarchical structure of binary thinking, and a subsequent challenging of it by reversing its terms. What Joyce achieves, however, is a movement beyond that straightforward reversal of terms. As demonstrated, the first stage of deconstruction's double movement only reinscribes the hierarchical valuation of the primary term; they are still not equal in value – the second term has merely acquired primary status. In other words, the power structure of the binary apparatus ultimately remains in place. Instead, by making gender a multiplicity, Joyce attains the second stage, which is a refusal of the binaric violence. The hierarchy is smashed, and equality established between both terms in ways which scramble so-called logic. Indeed, this attainment of equality means that two clearly demarcated terms can no longer be discerned. For multiplicity constitutes a form of ambiguity which renders binary thinking deeply unstable. Thus the coexistence upon Bloom's body of both vulva and testicles deconstructs the violent hierarchy of gender. The two terms not only achieve an equivalence of value that makes them interchangeable, but the act of penetration becomes the occasion for such a move. Shuttling between the extreme poles of both at vertiginous speed, rather than settling with one at the expense of the other, Joyce suggests, will reinstate harmony.

VERTIGINOUS GENDER

It should be clear by now how far away this is from what has been expected of a representation of the penetrated male body:

namely, the straightforward inversion of genders. Instead, what Joyce achieves with this coexistence of *he* and *she*, of vulva and testicles, yes and no, is a profound vertigo that undermines traditional gender stability. The reader is presented with a male body made flesh in the most vulnerable and empowering position *simultaneously*. Bloom's fisting thus signals a reconfiguration of the male body beyond the confines of phallic domination. Joyce installs a passive masculinity that avoids an erasure of the masculine and, by so doing, refuses the power imbalance implicated in that hierarchization of gender.

Similarly, Lyotard's *Libidinal Economy*[65] calls for the recognition and affirmation "that there is no insurmountable sexual difference, that each one potentially contains the other's correlate, and so there is the possibility of its crossing over to the 'enemy'" (Lyotard 1993, 207). As such, this crossing marks a point at which the logic of opposition by which sexual difference has been made to make sense – the very idea of a so-called opposite sex – breaks down. The rupture of the penetrated male body and the rupture of the symbolic order are pressed into the service of reimagining gender as a neither/nor.

This extension of the field of masculinity to include the pleasures of submission is, moreover, according to Joyce, something to be desired greatly. The reader is left in no doubt of that when Bello exposes Bloom with the words: "What you longed for has come to pass. Henceforth you are unmanned and mine in earnest, a thing under the yoke" (Joyce 1992, 647). A petticoat government, indeed. That which most terrified and fascinated Schreber – the act of unmanning – is here presented as man's secret desire: to be penetrated, to rotate like a pig on a spit upon a forearm, roasted by pleasure. The concept exceeds itself, and that excess is linked to a process of unmanning that reconfigures and complicates the conceptualization of man.

But to be unmanned – what might that mean, other than to be castrated, as Schreber imagined? Could it also mean to be relieved of the onus of disembodiment, given that man is conceptually associated with a form of radical noncorporeality

---

[65] A book which also ends with the word 'yes'.

associated with the concept mind? Certainly, for Joyce, as for Schreber, unmanning is a process that makes the sensations of the body more salient, more present, by placing male embodiment within discourse and thus removing the traditionally gendered distinction between mind and body, acknowledging a *jouissance* far beyond that bipartite division. For both Joyce and Schreber, unmanning is linked to a bodily penetratation, granting the body's orifices – particularly the anus – a certain discursive validation and erotic presence. Joyce, in particular, and despite his claims to loathe psychoanalysis, would seem to hold that the erotic body and the scatological body are in some sense inseparable, such that denial of the body's excretory functions is a denial of the body's erotic potential.

THE EXCREMENTAL BODY

In *Life Against Death: The Psychoanalytical Meaning of History* (1959), Norman O. Brown develops Freud's theory that the act of sublimation upon which civilization is based inevitably denies and negates the body. For Brown, as for Freud, the transcendental move towards modern bourgeois subjectivity is contingent upon a sublimation of the flesh. As such, he argues that, "to rise above the body is to equate the body with excrement" (Brown 1970, 257). Herein lies the association of anality with death. Herein too lies the strategy adopted by Joyce: namely, to break this equation precisely by highlighting it and, conversely, celebrating the excretory function. Only by reclaiming the body's waste can the body's eroticism be rediscovered, its life affirmed. Brown argues:

> The ever increasing denial of the body is, in the form of a negation, an ever-increasing affirmation of the denied body. Sublimations are these negations of the body which simultaneously affirm it; and sublimations achieve this dialectical tour de force by the simple but basic mechanism of projecting the repressed body into things. The more the life of the body passes into things, the less life there is in the

body, and at the same time the increasing accumulation of things represents an ever fuller articulation of the lost life of the body. (1970, 259–60)

Along with Lyotard, Deleuze and Guattari, Brown's argument must be considered in its context of a 1960s/70s utopian discourse of sexual liberation aimed at refuting the dominant ideology's denial of sexuality and the body. It is nevertheless useful in helping locate the modes of negation by which the body became associated with waste.

Furthermore, if we reread the last sentence from the above quotation but replace *things* with *words*, it becomes clearer to see how Joyce rearticulates the lost life of the body in a way that dismantles this dialectic. Treating words as things, that is, as matter or material, Joyce gives language a substance, a duration[66] within time-space that renders it susceptible to deformation or mutation. Joyce attempts to show this creative evolution or duration of language in the mutating styles of "Oxen of the Sun", revealing it as a peristaltic movement which culminates in Bloom breaking wind (Joyce 1992, 499–561). Such peristalsis connects language to the body, treating words as matter. Explaining his bodily schema to Frank Budgen, Joyce said:

> In my book the body lives in and moves through space and is the home of a full human personality. The words I write are adapted to express first one of its functions then another. In *Lestrygonians* the stomach dominates and the rhythm of the episode is that of the peristaltic movement. (Cited in Budgen 1972, 21)

This peristaltic movement of Joyce's language can be linked to Deleuze's concept of the fold, a move which resists the simple rejection by which an outside is constituted. In his study of Foucault, Deleuze argues that "the outside is not a fixed limit

---

[66] "Duration is the continuous progress of the past which gnaws into the future and which swells as it advances", Henri Bergson, *Creative Evolution*, trans. Arthur Mitchell (London: Macmillan, 1928), 5.

but a moving matter animated by *peristaltic movements*, folds and foldings that together make up an inside" (1992, 967, emphasis added). For Foucault, as for Deleuze, the outside and the inside are not separate spheres – as they were, for example, for Genet – but constitute and create one another, through movements Deleuze characterizes as peristaltic, that is, involuntary, like those of the intestines. The moving fold between outside and inside, like the rhythm of Joyce's writing, its shuttling between extremes, is analogous to the shiftings of digested food and waste matter along the alimentary canal.

For Deleuze, such peristaltic movements or folds connect the soul and the body in the most profound ways imaginable, providing a means of rethinking the promise of a multiple subject offered by Leibniz's writings. The soul and the body are not two distinct levels, but two parts of a multiplicity of turns and folds which form a rhizomatic zone of subjectivity.

> Is it not in this zone, in this depth or this material fabric between the two levels, that the upper is folded over the lower, such that we can no longer tell where one ends and the other begins, or where the sensible ends and the intelligible begins? (Deleuze 1993, 119)

In Deleuze's reading of Leibniz in *The Fold*, the soul and the body are connected in ways that preclude causality of the acts of one in the motives of the other. Rather, both fold into one another in ways so complex that any division or distinction between the two is neither possible nor desirable. In Joyce's almost Leibnizian formula, we "weave and unweave our bodies ... from day to day, their molecules shuttled to and fro" (Joyce 1992, 249). The body is a movement for Joyce, a passage through space and time, a multiplicity made singular by the bounded, though mutable, facticity of the body. These movements inform the formation of subjectivity; indeed, Deleuze suggests that the alimentary characterizes the relationship of self to self much more than the sexual (1992, 102–7). This is apparent not only in the anxiety surrounding sexual use of the rectum and its associative feminization, but also in the penetration through the mouth experienced by Des

Esseintes in Huysmans' *A rebours*. If, as has been argued in Chapter Two, any experience of penetration is reducible to anal penetration, this also makes all penetration an alimentary event.

If embodiment itself is peristaltic, an endless process of foldings between body and soul, men must not only ensure that the colon itself is never colonized by keeping the body impenetrable, but this peristalsis itself is counteracted by a wholesale negation of such movement, such bodily and subjective fluidity, through the promotion of stasis and closure. The colon, as punctuation mark, both breaks and permits a flow of discourse, and Tom Conley's description of Deleuze's style in *The Fold* could be equally applied to Joyce:

> The sentences do not reflect a law, but vary on their implicit norm. They are declarative; often composed of two or three independent clauses *connected by a colon* or conjunctions; unlike a classical concept, they do not seek to recall the origin of a signatory stamp. (Deleuze 1993, xix, emphasis added)

The colon is also the most crucial punctuation mark in a text that is to be performed, linking the characters' names with their speech, allowing a flow of words. It is an opening that also punctuates, a colonization which emancipates, a channel of flowings that also shuts off, like a bodily orifice such as the anus. Like the behind, the colon signals not only an anxious site of bodily penetration, but also an equally anxious site of textual laxity.

Seen in this light, Joyce's cloacal obsession is less the adolescent rebellion of toilet humour, than a demonstration of the irrefutable connection between body and language. The colonization of the body by language, or language by the body. Above all, this is an organic (though by no means organized) phenomenon; this peristalsis is acting on matter, both fecal and textual. Indeed, Joyce seems to have considered it his *raison d'être* to explore this side of human experience, thereby removing the responsibility from other writers, who were freed by this move to remain in the realm of the disembodied ideal.

In his poem "The Holy Office", Joyce writes: "That they may dream their dreamy dreams/I carry off their filthy streams" (1971, 36), suggesting that Joyce saw his role as attendant to those bodily functions art so often denies or negates. Indeed, he implies anality is the basis of all art.

ART IS ANAL

We are now in a better position to understand the importance of what Joyce is saying. Far from being simply a cloacal obsession, Joyce's insistence upon incorporating aspects of the body often deemed unsightly or obscene can be viewed as an attempt to articulate a profoundly philosophical position. That position posits the idea of the fragmentary nature of subjectivity and the contingency of that fragmentation upon a unity that is first and foremost corporeal/libidinal. Joyce asks us to consider that there is present within discourse – whether implicit or explicit – a fundamental relationship between language and the anus.

In Chapter One, I offered an account of language acquisition developed through Deleuze and Guattari's claim that anal sublimation was necessary in order for the subject to acquire language and enter the symbolic order. That is, the field of signification suppresses anality in order to function at all, or, as Kristeva likewise argues, "language acquisition implies the suppression of anality" (1984, 152). In *Revolution in Poetic Language*, Kristeva argues that this suppressed anality and the *jouissance* it harbours nevertheless find their way into the symbolic order, and do so, moreover, by breaking language, much as the roots of a tree might rupture the neat uniformity of paving stones. Poetic formations of language, for Kristeva, such as can be found in Mallarmé and Joyce, serve to disturb the symbolic through their eruption of the semiotic flows. Anality, Kristeva argues, both agitates the subject's body and subverts the symbolic function.

> The jouissance of destruction (or, if you will, of the "death drive"), which the text manifests through

> language, passes through an unburying of repressed,
> sublimated anality. (Kristeva 1984, 150)

This jouissance of destruction – which also goes by the names *semiotic* and *genotext* in Kristeva's work – is none other than the heterogeneous flows of the body. It is, for Kristeva, most locatable in one particular form of linguistic expression: lyricism. She writes, "heterogeneity is gathered up within the most condensed discursive structure of contradiction – the lyric" (Kristeva 1984, 189). This lyricism is an expenditure of language by which the claims of knowledge are revealed as nothing more than the productions of meaning. In this sense, the rejection of waste, that is, the peristaltic movements of both the body and discourse, becomes the precondition of meaning, and what registers as waste is that which is in excess of meaning, but which nevertheless remains meaningful as a challenge to the stability and sovereignty of meaning. What might be called discursive waste is thus in some way equated with human waste, and this equation carries with it a tremendously revolutionary force. These peristaltic movements thus not only shatter the subject's unity, but also reveal that "what passes through the subject's shattering ... is not a known truth but instead its expenditure" (Kristeva 1984, 188). In other words, art – as it is being understood here: at its most revolutionary – is, for Kristeva, the return of abjected anality.

Similarly, Joyce suggests an understanding of the function of the anus as in some sense a model for the production of human culture. In *A Portrait*, Stephen's nascent theory of art is presented through a series of questions such as "*Can excrement ... be a work of art? If not, why not?*" (Joyce 1977, 194, original emphasis). Given that, only several pages earlier, one character is described as "gulping down" a certain phrase, it is clear that one possible form this excretion of art might take is in language: the movement of peristalsis links this process of "gulping down" and excreting out words.

In *Ulysses* language and defecation are constantly and intimately linked. Writing is presented as something expelled from the body. When Stephen rips the corner off a letter on which he has scribbled a poem, the recipient assumes someone was taken short and had to use the letter as toilet paper. In the outhouse, Bloom wipes his backside with a prize-winning short story he has just read. In Nighttown, one of the women accuses Bloom of imploring him "to soil his letter in an unspeakable manner" (Joyce 1992, 593). When the Sins of the Past come to haunt Bloom, they include encouraging "a nocturnal strumpet to deposit fecal and other matter in an unsanitary outhouse attached to empty premises"; "writing in five public conveniences offering his nuptial partner to all strongmembered males", as well as "gloating over a nauseous fragment of wellused toilet paper presented to him by a nasty harlot" (Joyce 1992, 649).

Joyce is asking whether there is a difference between using paper to write upon or using it to wipe ourselves clean, and, if so, in what ways does that difference matter? He is also playfully suggesting that all writing – including his own – is shit. Antonin Artaud, in a short text written around the same time as *Ulysses*, will likewise declare, "all writing is filth" (2001, 23). This contiguity between writing and shit is present in its negative form in the traditional dismissal of pornography as filth. In this sense, only filthy writing – erotic and scatological – can express the multiplicity of the body. Whereas psychoanalysis insists on the separability of the anal from the genital – that is, the erotic from the death drive, *eros* from *thanatos* – Joyce, like Bataille, insists that they are so inextricably bound together as to be radically inseparable. The textual body *is* the sexual body, and the sexual body *is* the scatological body, and vice versa, the scatological body *is* the discursive body, and vice versa. And this *is* is inherently rhizomatic, nomadic, transitive, a no-place place where uncertainty masks itself as certainty. This *is* is a copula because it copulates or permits copulation (a permit allows one to do something, go somewhere, hitherto out of bounds). This *is* is a fold, or in the terms of this book, it is the behind; the domain of the neither/nor, or what Sue Golding has termed "a 'forgotten' homeland, a bleeding land as it were, whose very landscapes circumscribe the nomadic dislocation of the neither/nor" (1997a, 21). It is a place of contradictions left unresolved and irreconcilable, marked by the vertiginous uncertainty of language.

In conclusion, with *Ulysses*, Joyce effects a break from binary logic and promotes a multiplicity which remains modernity's greatest legacy. Kristeva calls it a revolution of poetic language. That multiplicity is apparent not only in the rhizomatic character of the text itself, but also in the presentation of the embodied self found there. Just as Joyce refuses the distinctions of mind/body and reason/madness so too does he refuse the distinction male/female, preferring instead the androgynous space of the neither/nor. The indiscriminate condemnation of the body in *Ulysses* – both its erotic and its scatological properties – expressed by early critics, thus suggests a certain anxiety attending the recognition of those properties which were, for Joyce, inseparable. As this chapter has shown, by refusing the logic of noncontradiction that makes the penetrated male body into a female body, Joyce is allowing that body a place, a spacing, or duration. By making that body a predicate of language, and by making its placing or duration visible as a rupture or fragmentation of language, Joyce signals the fact that representation both *is* and *is not*. For him, the now is both present and absent so that if one is to attempt to (re)present the now – that is, if one is to be modern – one must take into account the shadow or behind of that modernity. But it must be taken into account as an excess, as an example of the concept exceeding itself, and in that overreaching or overflowing it brings about a turn in logic that dissolves binary opposition in favour of a nonrepresentable multiplicity, positing that multiplicity as that which is abstracted in order for representation to take place. Representation, in other words, is the embodiment of erotic thought.

Bibliography

Abelove, Henry (1993), "Freud, Male Homosexuality and the Americans", in Henry Abelove, Michele Aina Barale and David Halperin (eds), *The Lesbian and Gay Studies Reader*, New York and London: Routledge, 381–91.

Adorno, Theodor W. (1978), *Minima Moralia: Reflections from Damaged Life*, trans. Edmund F. N. Jephcott, London: Verso.

— (1996), *Negative Dialectics*, trans. E. B. Ashton, New York and London: Routledge.

Adorno, Theodor W. and Horkheimer, Max (1972), *Dialectic of Enlightenment*, trans. John Cumming, London: Allen Lane.

Allison, David B., de Oliveira, Prado, Roberts, Mark S. and Weiss, Allen S. (eds) (1988), *Psychosis and Sexual Identity: Toward a Post-Analytic View of the Schreber Case*, Albany: State University of New York Press.

Anzieu, Didier (1989), *The Skin Ego*, trans. Chris Turner, New Haven: Yale University Press.

Artaud, Antonin (2001), "All Writing Is Filth", in Brian Singleton and Claude Schumacher (eds), *Artaud on Theatre*, various translators, London: Methuen.

Attridge, Derek (1988), *Peculiar Language: Literature as Difference from the Renaissance to James Joyce*, Ithaca, NY: Cornell University Press.

— (2000), *Joyce Effects*, New York: Routledge.

Attridge, Derek and Ferrer, Daniel (eds) (1984), *Post-Structuralist Joyce: Essays from the French*, Cambridge, London, New York, New Rochelle, Melbourne and Sydney: Cambridge University Press.

Bakhtin, Mikhail (1984), *Rabelais and His World*, trans. Hélène Iswolsky, Bloomington, IN: Indiana University Press.

Bardot, Susan (1994), "Reading the Male Body", in Laurence Goldstein (ed.), *The Male Body: Features, Destinies, Exposures*, Ann Arbour: University of Michegan Press, 265–303.

— (1999), *The Male Body: A New Look at Men in Public and Private*, New York, Farrar, Straus and Giroux.

Barker, Francis (1984), *The Tremulous Private Body: Essays on Subjection*, London: Methuen.

Barreca, Regina (1995), *Desire and Imagination: Classic Essays in Sexuality*, New York: Meridian and Penguin USA.

Barthes, Roland (1979), "The Metaphor of the Eye", trans. J. A. Underwood, in Georges Bataille, *Story of the Eye*, trans. Joachin Neugroschel, London and Boston: Marion Boyars, 119–27.

— (1981), *Elements of Semiology*, trans. Annette Lavers and Colin Smith, New York: Hill and Wang.

— (1991), *S/Z*, trans. Richard Miller, New York: Hill and Wang.

Bataille, Georges (1985), *Visions of Excess: Selected Writings 1927–1939*, Minneapolis: University of Minnesota Press.

— (1987), *Eroticism*, trans. Mary Dalwood, London and New York: Marion Boyars.

— (1993), *Literature and Evil*, trans. Alastair Hamilton, London and New York: Marion Boyars.

Baudelaire, Charles (1972), "The Painter of Modern Life", in *Selected Writings on Art and Artists*, trans. P. E. Charvet, Harmondsworth: Penguin.

— (1982), *Les fleurs du mal*, trans. Richard Howard, London: Picador.

— (1989), *Intimate Journals*, trans. Christopher Isherwood, London: Picador.

— (1991), *The Prose Poems and La Fanfarlo*, trans. Rosemary Lloyd, Oxford: Oxford University Press.

Baudrillard, Jean (1990), *Seduction*, trans. Brian Singer, Basingstoke: Macmillan.

Beckett, Samuel (1972), "Dante ... Bruno. Vico .. Joyce", in Samuel Beckett *et al.*, *Our Exagmination Round His Factification for Incamination of Work in Progress*, London: Faber & Faber.

Benjamin, Andrew (1997), "Curiosity, Fascination: Time and Speed", in Sue Golding (ed.), *The Eight Technologies of Otherness*, London and New York: Routledge, 3–42.

Benjamin, Jessica (1990), *The Bonds of Love: Psychoanalysis, Feminism and the Problem of Domination*, London: Virago.

Benjamin, Jessica and Rabinach, Anson (1989), Forward to Klaus Theweleit, *Male Fantasies Volume II: Male Bodies: Psychoanalyzing the White Terror*, trans. Chris Turner, Erica Carter and Stephen Conway, Cambridge: Polity Press.

Benjamin, Walter (1973), *Charles Baudelaire: A Lyric Poet in the Era of High Capitalism*, trans. Harry Zohn, London: New Left Books.

Bennington, Geoffrey (1988), *Lyotard: Writing the Event*, Manchester: Manchester University Press.

Bergson, Henri (1928), *Creative Evolution*, trans. Arthur Mitchell, London: Macmillan.

— (1991), *Matter and Memory*, trans. Nancy Margaret Paul, New York: Zone Books.

Bersani, Leo (1977), *Baudelaire and Freud*, Berkeley and London: University of California Press.

— (1986), *The Freudian Body: Psychoanalysis and Art*, New York: Columbia University Press.

— (1987), "Is the Rectum a Grave?" *October* 43.

— (1990), *The Culture of Redemption*, Cambridge, MA: Harvard University Press.

— (1995), *Homos*, Cambridge, MA: Harvard University Press.

Blanchot, Maurice (1982), *The Space of Literature*, trans. Ann Smock, Lincoln and London: University of Nebraska Press.

— (1993), *The Infinite Conversation*, trans. Susan Hanson, Minneapolis: University of Minnesota Press.

Bordo, Susan (1994), "Reading the Male Body", in Laurence Goldstein (ed.), *The Male Body: Features, Destinies, Exposures*, Ann Arbour: University of Michigan Press.

— (1998), "Bringing Body to Theory", in Donn Welton (ed.), *Body and Flesh: A Philosophical Reader*, Oxford and Malden, MA: Blackwell.

— (1999), *The Male Body: A New Look at Men in Public and Private*, New York: Farrar, Straus and Giroux.

Boswell, John (1981), *Christianity, Social Tolerance, and Homosexuality: Gay People in Western Europe from the Beginning of the Christian Era to the Fourteenth Century*, Chicago and London: University of Chicago Press.

Bremmer, Jan (ed.) (1989), *From Sappho to De Sade: Moments in the History of Sexuality*, London and New York: Routledge.

Brenkman, John (1993), *Straight Male Modern: A Cultural Critique of Psychoanalysis*, New York and London: Routledge.

Brintnall, Kent L. (2011), *Ecce Homo: The Male-Body-in-Pain as Redemptive Figure*, Chicago and London: University of Chicago Press.

Bristow, Joseph (1995), *Effeminate England: Homoerotic Writing after 1885*, Buckingham: Open University Press.

— (1997), *Sexuality*, New York and London: Routledge.

Bronfen, Elisabeth (1992), *Over Her Dead Body: Death, Femininity and the Aesthetic*, Manchester: Manchester University Press.

Brophy, Brigid (1979), "Our Lady of the Flowers", in Peter Brooks and Joseph Halpern (eds), *Genet: A Collection of Critical Essays*, New York: Prentice Hall.

Brown, Carolyn (1997), "Figuring the Vampire: Death, Desire, and the Image", in Sue Golding (ed.), *The Eight Technologies of Otherness*, London and New York: Routledge, 117–34.

Brown, Norman O. (1970), *Life against Death: The Psychoanalytical Meaning of History*, London: Sphere Books.

Brown, Richard (1992), *James Joyce*, London: Macmillan.

Budgen, Frank (1972), *James Joyce and the Making of Ulysses*, London, Oxford and Melbourne: Oxford University Press.

Burgess, Anthony (1973), *Joysprick: An Introduction to the Language of James Joyce*, New York and London: Harcourt Brace Jovanovich.

Burkitt, Ian (1999), *Bodies of Thought: Embodiment, Identity and Modernity*, London, Thousand Oaks and New Delhi: Sage Publications.

Butler, Judith (1990), *Gender Trouble: Feminism and the Subversion of Identity*, New York and London: Routledge.

— (1991), "Imitation and Gender Subordination", in Diana Fuss (ed.), *Inside/Out: Lesbian Theories, Gay Theories*, New York and London: Routledge.

— (1993), *Bodies That Matter: On the Discursive Limits of "Sex"*, New York and London: Routledge.

— (1997), *The Psychic Life of Power: Theories in Subjection*, Stanford, CA: Stanford University Press.

Calvino, Italo (1987), *The Literature Machine*, trans. Patrick Creagh, London: Picador.

Canetti, Elias (1973), *Crowds and Power*, trans. Carol Stewart, Harmondsworth: Penguin.

Cioran, E. M. (1990), *A Short History of Decay*, trans. Sally A. J. Purcell, London: John Calder.

Cixous, Hélène (1976), *The Exile of James Joyce*, trans. Sally A. J. Purcell, London: John Calder.

Cohen, Ed (1993), *Talk on the Wilde Side: Towards a Genealogy of Male Sexualities*, New York and London: Routledge.

Cohen, J. M. (1969), Introduction to François Rabelais, *Gargantua and Pantagruel*, trans. J. M. Cohen, Harmondsworth: Penguin.

Cohen, Michele (1996), *Fashioning Masculinity: National Identity and Language in the Eighteenth Century*, London and New York: Routledge.

Critchley, Simon (1999), *Ethics Politics Subjectivity*, New York and London: Verso.

Croft-Brooke, Rupert (1967), *Feasting with Panthers: A New Consideration of Some Late Victorian Writers*, London: W. H. Allen.

Davenport-Hines, Rupert (1990), *Sex, Death and Punishment: Attitudes to Sex and Sexuality in Britain since the Renaissance*, London: Collins.

De Grazia, Edward (1992), *Little Girls Lean Back Everywhere: The Law of Obscenity and the Assault on Genius*, New York: Random House.

de Man, Paul (1979), *Allegories of Reading*, New Haven: Yale University Press.

— (1996), "The Epistemology of Metaphor", in *Aesthetic Ideology*, Minneapolis: University of Minnesota Press.

Deleuze, Gilles (1983), *Nietzsche and Philosophy*, trans. Hugh Tomlinson, London: Athlone Press.

— (1986), *Foucault*, trans. Sean Hand, Minneapolis and London: University of Minnesota Press.

— (1991), *Coldness and Cruelty*, trans. Jean McNeil, New York: Zone Books.

— (1993), *The Fold: Leibniz and the Baroque*, trans. Tom Conley, Minneapolis: University of Minnesota Press.

— (1995), *Negotiations 1972–1990*, trans. Martin Joughin, New York: Columbia University Press.

— (2000), *Cinema 2: The Time-Image*, trans. Hugh Tomlinson and Robert Galeta, London: Athlone Press.

Deleuze, Gilles and Guattari, Felix (1983), *Anti-Oedipus: Capitalism and Schizophrenia*, trans. Robert Hurley, Mark Seem and Helen R. Lane, Minneapolis: University of Minnesota Press.

— (1992), *A Thousand Plateaus: Capitalism and Schizophrenia*, trans. Brian Massumi, London: Athlone Press.

Deleuze, Gilles and Parnet, Claire (1987), *Dialogues*, trans. Hugh Tomlinson and Barbara Habberjam, London: Athlone Press.

Deming, Robert H. (ed.) (1970a), *James Joyce: The Critical Heritage Volume One 1902–1927*, London: Routledge and Kegan Paul.

— (ed.) (1970b), *James Joyce: The Critical Heritage Volume Two 1928–1941*, London: Routledge and Kegan Paul.

Derrida, Jacques (1976), *Of Grammatology*, trans. Gayatri Chakravorty Spivak, Baltimore and London: John Hopkins University Press.

— (1978), "Freud and the Scene of Writing", in *Writing and Difference*, trans. Alan Bass, London and Henley: Routledge and Kegan Paul.

— (1979), *Spurs: Nietzsche's Styles*, trans. Barbara Harlow, Chicago and London: University of Chicago Press.

— (1981), *Positions*, trans. Alan Bass, London: Athlone Press.

— (1982), *Margins of Philosophy*, trans. Alan Bass, New York, London, Toronto, Sydney, Tokyo and Singapore: Harvester Wheatsheaf.

— (1987), *The Post Card: From Socrates to Freud and Beyond*, trans. Alan Bass, Chicago: Chicago University Press.

— (1990), *Glas*, trans. John P. Leavey, Jr and Richard Rand, Lincoln and London: University of Nebraska Press.

— (1992), *Acts of Literature*, various translators, ed. Derek Attridge, London and New York: Routledge.

— (1993), *On the Name*, trans. David Wood, John P. Leavey, Jr, and Ian McLeod, ed. David Wood, Stanford, CA: Stanford University Press.

Dollimore, Jonathan (1991), *Sexual Dissidence: Augustine to Wilde, Freud to Foucault*, Oxford: Oxford University Press.

— (1997), *Death, Desire and Loss in Western Culture*, New York and London: Routledge.

Douglas, Mary (1984), *Purity and Danger: An Analysis of the Concepts of Pollution and Taboo*, London, Boston, Melbourne and Henley: Ark Paperbacks.

Dover, K. J. (1989), *Greek Homosexuality*, Cambridge, MA: Harvard University Press.

Eagleton, Terry (1983), *Literary Theory: An Introduction*, Oxford: Basil Blackwell.

Edelman, Lee (1994), *Homographesis: Essays in Gay Literary and Cultural Theory*, London and New York: Routledge.

Ehrenreich, Barbara (1987), Forward to Klaus Theweleit, *Male Fantasies Volume I: Women, Floods, Bodies, History*, trans. Chris Turner, Erica Carter and Stephen Conway, Cambridge: Polity Press.

Ellman, Richard (ed.) (1975), *The Letters of James Joyce*, London: Faber & Faber.

— (1982), *James Joyce*, Oxford, New York, Toronto and Melbourne: Oxford University Press.

Evans, Margery A. (1993), *Baudelaire and Intertextuality: Poetry at the Crossroads*, Cambridge: Cambridge University Press.

Fink, Bruce (1995), *The Lacanian Subject: Between Language and Jouissance*, Princeton, NJ: Princeton University Press.

Fitch, Noel Riley (1985), *Sylvia Beach and the Lost Generation: A History of Literary Paris in the Twenties and Thirties*, New York and London: W. W. Norton & Company.

Fletcher, John (1992), "Forster's Self-Erasure: *Maurice* and the Scene of 'Masculine Love'", in Joseph Bristow (ed.), *Sexual Sameness: Textual Differences in Lesbian and Gay Writing*, London: Routledge, 64–90.

Foucault, Michel (1972), *The Archaeology of Knowledge*, trans. A.M. Sheridan Smith, New York: Harper Colophon Books.

— (1980) (ed.), *Herculine Barbin, Being the Recently Discovered Memoirs of a Nineteenth Century Hermaphrodite*, trans. Richard McDougall, New York: Pantheon Books.

— (1983), Preface to Gilles Deleuze and Felix Guattari, *Anti-Oedipus: Capitalism and Schizophrenia*, trans. Robert Hurley, Mark Seem and Helen R. Lane, Minneapolis: University of Minnesota Press.

— (1985), *Discipline and Punish: The Birth of the Prison*, trans. Alan Sheridan, Harmondsworth: Penguin.

— (1986), *The History of Sexuality Volume Three: The Care of the Self*, trans. Robert Hurley, Harmondsworth: Penguin.

— (1986), *Death and the Labyrinth: The World of Raymond Roussel*, trans. Charles Ruas, London: Athlone Press.

— (1989), *Madness and Civilisation: A History of Insanity in the Age of Reason*, trans. Richard Howard, New York and London: Routledge.

— (1990), *The History of Sexuality Volume 1: An Introduction*, trans. Robert Hurley, London: Penguin.

— (1992), *The History of Sexuality Volume Two: The Use of Pleasure*, trans. Robert Hurley, Harmondsworth: Penguin.

— (1997), *The Order of Things: An Archaeology of the Human Sciences*, trans. Alan Sheridan, New York and London: Routledge.

— (1998a), *Essential Works of Foucault 1954–1984 Volume 1: Ethics*, Harmondsworth: Penguin.

— (1998b), *Essential Works of Foucault 1954–1984, Volume 2: Aesthetics*, Harmondsworth: Penguin.

— (2000), *Essential Works 1954–1984, Volume 3: Power*, Harmondsworth: Penguin.

Frank, Arthur W. (1991), "For a Sociology of the Body: An Analytical Review", in Mike Featherstone, Mike Hepworth and Bryan S. Turner (eds), *The Body: Social Process and Cultural Theory*, London, Thousand Oaks and New Delhi: Sage, 36–102.

French, Marilyn (1982), *The Book as World: James Joyce's Ulysses*, London: Abacus.

Freud, Sigmund (1961), "The Economic Problem of Masochism", in *Pelican Freud Library*, Volume 11, trans. James Strachey, ed. J. Strachey and Angela Richards, Harmondsworth: Penguin.

— (1971), "Psycho-Analytic Notes on an Autobiographical Account of a Case of Paranoia (Dementia Paranoides)", in *Standard Edition*, trans. James Strachey, Volume XII, London: Hogarth Press.

— (1974), *Introductory Lectures on Psychoanalysis* in *Pelican Freud Library*, trans. James Strachey, ed. J. Strachey and Angela Richards, Harmondsworth: Penguin.

— (1977), "Three Essays on the Theory of Sexuality", in *Pelican Freud Library*, trans. James Strachey, ed. Angela Richards, Volume 7, Harmondsworth: Penguin.

— (1985), "Civilisation and Its Discontents", in *Pelican Freud Library*, Volume 12, trans. James Strachey, ed. Angela Richards, Harmondsworth: Penguin.

— (1986), *The Ego and the Id*, trans. Joan Riviere, ed. James Strachey, New York: Norton.

Froula, Christine (1996), *Modernism's Body: Sex, Culture and Joyce*, New York: Columbia University Press.

Gallop, Jane (1988), *Thinking through the Body*, Columbia: Columbia University Press.

Garber, Marjorie (1992), *Vested Interests: Cross-Dressing and Cultural Anxiety*, Harmondsworth: Penguin.

Gay, Peter (1986), *The Bourgeois Experience, Victoria to Freud Volume II: The Tender Passion*, New York and Oxford: Oxford University Press.

— (1998), *The Bourgeois Experience, Victoria to Freud Volume IV: The Naked Heart*, London: Harper Collins.

Genet, Jean (1966), *Our Lady of the Flowers*, trans. Bernard Frechtman, St. Albans: Panther.

— (1969), *Funeral Rites*, trans. Bernard Frechtman, New York: Grove Press.

— (1971), Introduction to *Soledad Brother: The Prison Letters of George Jackson*, trans. Richard Howard, Harmondsworth, Penguin.

— (1972), *Reflections on the Theatre and Other Writings*, trans. Richard Seaver, London: Faber & Faber.

— (1975), *Miracle of the Rose*, trans. Bernard Frechtman, Harmondsworth: Penguin.

— (1982), *The Thief's Journal*, trans. Bernard Frechtman, Harmondsworth: Penguin.

— (1986), *Prisoner of Love*, trans. Barbara Bray, London: Picador.

— (1987), *Querelle of Brest*, trans. Gregory Streatham, London, Glasgow, Toronto, Sydney and Aukland: Paladin Grafton Books.

— (1988), *What Remains of a Rembrandt Torn into Four Pieces and Flushed Down the Toilet*, trans. Bernard Frechtman, Madras and New York: Hanuman Books.

— (1993), "A Reading of *The Brothers Karamazov*", trans. Arthur Goldhammer, *Grand Street* 47: 172–6.

Gide, Andre (1967), *Journals 1889–1949*, trans. Justin O'Brien, London: Penguin.

Gilbert, Stuart (1963), *James Joyce's* Ulysses*: A Study*, Harmondsworth: Penguin.

Golding, Sue (1997a), "Curiosity", in Sue Golding (ed.), *The Eight Technologies of Otherness*, New York and London: Routledge, 10–26.

— (1997b), "Solar Clitoris", *Parallax* 3, no. 1: 137–49.

— (2000), "Singular Multiplicity: The A-radicality Lecture – Second Meditation on Identity, Ethics, and Aesthetics [Or What Does It Mean to 'Inhabit' Technology?]", *The Issues in Contemporary Culture and Aesthetics* 10/11: 286–92.

— (2001), "The Secret (of Seven Deadly Sins and Four Differentiated Vibrations)", *The Issues in Contemporary Culture and Aesthetics* 12: 49–53.

Gross, John (1976), *Joyce*, Glasgow: Fontana/Collins.

Grosz, Elizabeth (1994), *Volatile Bodies: Towards a Corporeal Feminism*, Bloomington and Indianapolis: University of Indiana Press.

— (1995), "Bodies and Knowledges: Feminism and the Crisis of Reason", in *Space, Time and Perversion*, New York and London: Routledge, 25–44.

Guattari, Felix (1989), "The Three Ecologies", trans. Chris Turner, *New Formations* 8: 131–47.

— (1995), *Chaosmosis: An Ethico-Aesthetic Paradigm*, trans. Paul Bains and Julian Pefanis, Sydney: Power Publications.

Hall, Leslie A. (1991), *Hidden Anxieties: Male Sexuality 1900–1950*, Cambridge: Polity Press.

Halperin, David M. (1990), *One Hundred Years of Homosexuality*, New York and London: Routledge.

— (1995), *Saint Foucault: Towards a Gay Hagiography*, New York and Oxford: Oxford University Press.

Hartman, Geoffrey H. (1981), *Saving the Text: Literature/Derrida/Philosophy*, Baltimore and London: Johns Hopkins University Press.

Haver, William (1996), *The Body of this Death: Historicity and Sociality in the Time of AIDS*, Stanford, CA: Stanford University Press.

— (1997), "Queer Research: Or How to Practise Invention to the Brink of Intelligibility", in Sue Golding (ed.), *The Eight Technologies of Otherness*, New York and London: Routledge, 277–92.

— (1999), "Really Bad Affinities: Queer's Honour and the Pornographic Life", *Parallax* 5, no. 4: 9–21.

Heath, Stephen (1984), "Ambiviolences: Notes for Reading Joyce", in Derek Attridge and Daniel Ferrer (eds) (1984), *Post-Structuralist Joyce: Essays from the French*, Cambridge, London, New York, New Rochelle, Melbourne and Sydney: Cambridge University Press.

Hekma, Gert (1989), "A History of Sexology", in Jan Bremmer (ed.), *From Sappho to de Sade: Moments in the History of Sexuality*, New York and London: Routledge.

— (1994), "'A Female Soul in a Male Body': Sexual Inversion as Gender Inversion in Nineteenth Century Sexology", in Gilbert Herdt (ed.), *Third Sex, Third Gender: Beyond Sexual Dimorphism in Culture and History*, New York: Zone Books.

Henke, Suzette A. (1978), *Joyce's Moraculous Sindbook: A Study of Ulysses*, Columbus: Ohio State University Press.

Hocquenghem, Guy (1993a), *Homosexual Desire*, trans. Daniella Dangoor, Durham and London: Duke University Press.

— (1993b), "Towards an Irrecuperable Pederasty", trans. Chris Fox, in Jonathan Goldberg (ed.), *Reclaiming Sodom*, New York and London: Routledge.

— (1999), "On Homo-sex, or is Homosexuality a Curable Vice?", trans. Bill Marshall, *New Formations* 39: 70–74.

Holland, Eugene W. (1993), *Baudelaire and Schizoanalysis: The Sociopoetics of Modernism*, Cambridge: Cambridge University Press.

Horkheimer, Max (1974), *Eclipse of Reason*, New York: Continuum.

Huysmans, Joris-Karl (1959), *Against Nature*, trans. Robert Baldick, Harmondsworth: Penguin.

Hyde, H. Montgomery (1962), *Famous Trials 7: Oscar Wilde*, Harmondsworth: Penguin.

Irigaray, Luce (1985), *This Sex Which is Not One*, trans. Catherine Porter and Carolyn Burke, Ithaca, NY: Cornell University Press.

— (1992), *Speculum of the Other Woman*, trans. Gillian C. Gill, Ithaca, NY: Cornell University Press.

— (1993), *An Ethics of Sexual Difference*, trans. Carolyn Burke and Gillian C. Gill, Ithaca, NY: Cornell University Press.

Jones, Ernest (1951), "The Madonna's Conception through the Ear", in *Essays in Applied Psychoanalysis*, London: Hogarth Press, 266–357.

Jones, David Houston (2000), *The Body Abject: Self and Text in Jean Genet and Samuel Beckett*, New York: Peter Lang.

Joyce, James (1971), *Pomes Penyeach*, London: Faber & Faber.

— (1977), *A Portrait of the Artist as a Young Man*, St Albans: Panther.

— (1986), "Oscar Wilde: The Poet of *Salome*", in Richard Ellman (ed.), *Oscar Wilde: A Collection of Critical Essays*, Englewood Cliffs, New Jersey, London, Mexico, New Delhi, Rio de Janeiro, Singapore, Sydney, Tokyo, Toronto and Wellington: Prentice Hall, 56–60.

— (1992), *Ulysses*, Harmondsworth: Penguin.

Kaite, Berkeley (1988), "The Pornographic Body Double: Transgression is the Law", in Arthur Kroker and Marilouise Kroker (eds), *Body Invaders: Sexuality and the Postmodern Condition*, Basingstoke: MacMillan, 150–68.

Kant, Immanuel (1959), "What is Enlightenment?", in *Foundations of the Metaphysics of Morals*, trans. Lewis White Beck, Indianapolis and New York: Bobbs-Merrill.

Kenner, Hugh (1980), *Ulysses*, London, Boston and Sydney: George Allen & Unwin.

Kiberd, Declan (1992), Introduction to James Joyce, *Ulysses*, Harmondsworth: Penguin.

Kirby, Vicki (1997), *Telling Flesh: The Substance of the Corporeal*, New York and London: Routledge.

Kristeva, Julia (1982), *Powers of Horror: An Essay on Abjection*, trans. Leon S. Roudiez, New York: Columbia University Press.

— (1984), *Revolution in Poetic Language*, trans. Leon S. Roudiez, New York: Columbia University Press.

— (1986), *The Kristeva Reader*, ed. Toril Moi, Oxford: Basil Blackwell.

Kroker, Arthur and Kroker, Marilouise (eds) (1988), *Body Invaders: Sexuality and the Postmodern Condition*, Basingstoke: MacMillan.

Kunzle, David (1989), "The Art of Pulling Teeth in the 17th and 19th Centuries: From Public Martyrdom to Private Nightmare", in Michel Feher (ed.), *Fragments for a History of the Human Body: Part 3*, New York: Zone Books, 28–42.

Lacan, Jacques (1977), *Ecrits: A Selection*, trans. Alan Sheridan, London: Tavistock

— (1982), "The Meaning of the Phallus", trans. Jacqueline Rose, in Juliet Mitchell and Jacqueline Rose (eds), *Feminine Sexuality: Jacques Lacan and the ecole Freudienne*, Basingstoke: Macmillan.

— (1986), *The Four Fundamental Concepts of Psycho-Analysis*, trans. Alan Sheridan, Harmondsworth: Penguin.

— (1993), *The Seminar Book III: The Psychoses,* trans. Russell Grigg, ed. Jacques-Alain Miller, New York and London: Routledge.

Laqueur, Thomas (1990), *Making Sex: Body and Gender from the Greeks to Freud*, Cambridge, MA and London: Harvard University Press.

Lawrence, D. H. (1961), "Pornography and Obscenity", in *A Propos of Lady Chatterley's Lover and Other Essays*, Harmondsworth: Penguin.

Lawrence, T. E. (1952), *Seven Pillars of Wisdom: A Triumph*, London: Jonathan Cape.

Lecercle, Jean-Jacques (1985), *Philosophy through the Looking-Glass: Language, Nonsense, Desire*, La Salle, IL: Open Court.

Lewes, Kenneth (1988), *The Psychoanalytic Theory of Male Homosexuality*, London: Quartet.

Leyland, Winston (1984), Introduction to Oscar Wilde, *Teleny: a Novel Attributed to Oscar Wilde*, San Francisco: Gay Sunshine Press.

Lloyd, Christopher (1990), *J-K Huysmans and the Fin-de-siècle Novel*, Edinburgh: Edinburgh University Press for University of Durham.

Lyotard, Jean-Francois (1988), *Peregrinations: Law, Form, Event*, New York: Columbia University Press.

— (1990), *Heidegger and "the Jews"*, trans. Andreas Michel and Mark S. Roberts, Minneapolis: University of Minnesota Press.

— (1992), *The Postmodern Condition: A Report on Knowledge*, trans. Geoff Bennington and Brian Massumi, Manchester: Manchester University Press.

— (1993), *Libidinal Economy*, trans. Iain Hamilton Grant, London: Athlone Press.

— (1996), *The Differend: Phrases in Dispute*, trans. Georges Van Den Abbeele, Minneapolis: University of Minnesota Press.

MacAlpine, Ida and Hunter, Richard A. (1988), "Translators' Analysis of the Case", Appendix in Daniel Paul Schreber (1988), *Memoirs of My Nervous Illness*, trans. Ida MacAlpine and Richard Hunter, Cambridge and London: Harvard University Press, 369–411.

Maddox, Brenda (1988), *Nora*, Harmondsworth: Penguin.

Marcus, Steven (1970), *The Other Victorians: A Study of Sexuality and Pornography in Mid-Nineteenth Century England*, London: Book Club Associates.

Marcuse, Herbert (1987), *Eros and Civilisation: A Philosophical Inquiry into Freud*, London: Ark Books.

Marshall, Bill (1996), *Guy Hocquenghem: Theorising the Gay Nation*, London: Pluto Press.

Massey, Irving (1976), *The Gaping Pig: Literature and Metamorphosis*, Berkeley: University of California Press.

Martinon, Jean-Paul (2013), *The End of Man*, Brooklyn: Punctum Books.

Mayer, Hans (1982), *Outsiders: A Study in Life and Letters*, trans. Denis M. Sweet, London and Cambridge, MA: MIT Press.

McCabe, Colin (1979), *James Joyce and the Revolution of the Word*, London and Basingstoke: Macmillan.

McHale, Brian (1992), *Constructing Postmodernism*, New York and London: Routledge.

Meyer, Moe (ed.) (1994), *The Politics and Poetics of Camp*, New York and London: Routledge.

Meyers, Jeffrey (1973), *The Wounded Spirit: A Study of the Seven Pillars of Wisdom*, London: Martin O'Keeffe.

Mieli, Mario (1980), *Homosexuality and Liberation: Elements of a Gay Critique*, trans. David Fernbach, London: Gay Men's Press.

Miller, D. A. (1986), "*Cage aux folles*: Sensation and Gender in Wilkie Collins' *The Woman in White*", *Representations* 14: 107–36.

Millet, Kate (1972), *Sexual Politics*, London: Abacus.

Mosse, George L. (1996), *The Image of Man: The Creation of Modern Masculinity*, New York and Oxford: Oxford University Press.

Nancy, Jean-Luc (1993), *The Birth to Presence*, various translators, Stanford, CA: Stanford University Press.

Niederland, William G. (1984), *The Schreber Case: Psychoanalytic Profile of a Paranoid Personality*, New Jersey: Analytic Press.

Nordau, Max (1896), *Degeneration*, London: Heinemann.

Norris, Christopher (1988), *Deconstruction: Theory and Practice*, London and New York: Routledge.

Norris, Margot (ed.) (1998), *A Companion to James Joyce's Ulysses*, Boston and New York: Bedford Books, 1998.

Owens, Craig (1987), "Outlaws: Gay Men in Feminism", in Alice Jardine and Paul Smith (eds), *Men In Feminism*, New York and London: Methuen.

Pia, Pascal (1961), *Baudelaire*, trans. Patrick Gregory, London and New York: Evergreen/Grove Press.

Pile, Steve (1996), *The Body and the City: Psychoanalysis, Space and Subjectivity*, New York and London: Routledge.

Praz, Mario (1962), *The Romantic Agony*, trans. Angus Davidson, Oxford: Fontana Press.

Proust, Marcel (1992), *In Search of Lost Time*, trans. C. K. Scott Moncrieff and Terence Kilmartin, rev. D. J. Enright. London: Chatto and Windus.

Rabain, Jean-François (1992), "Figures of Delusion", in David B. Allison (ed.), *Psychosis and Sexual Identity: Towards a Post-Analytic View of the Schreber Case*, New York: State University of New York Press.

Rancour-Laferriere, Daniel (1979), "Some Semiotic Aspects of the Human Penis", *Versus: Quaderni di Studi Semiotici* 24: 37–82.

Ronell, Avital (1989), *The Telephone Book: Technology, Schizophrenia, Electric Speech*, Lincoln and London: University of Nebraska Press.

— (1994), *Finitude's Score: Essays for the End of the Millenium*, Lincoln and London: University of Nebraska Press.

Rosario, Vernon A. (1997) (ed.), *Science and Homosexualities*, New York and London: Routledge.

Russo, Mary (1994), *The Female Grotesque: Risk, Excess and Modernity*, London and New York: Routledge.

Sacher-Masoch, Leopold von (1991), *Venus in Furs*, trans. Jean McNeil, New York: Zone Books.

Santner, Eric L. (1996), *My Own Private Germany: Daniel Paul Schreber's Secret History of Modernity*, Princeton, NJ: Princeton University Press.

Sartre, Jean-Paul (1963), *Saint Genet: Actor and Martyr*, trans. Bernard Frechtman, New York: Pantheon Books.

Savran, David (1998), *Taking It Like a Man: White Masculinity, Masochism and Contemporary American Culture*, Princeton, NJ: Princeton University Press.

Scarry, Elaine (1985), *The Body in Pain: The Making and Unmaking of the World*, New York and Oxford: Oxford University Press.

Schatzman, Morton (1976), *Soul Murder: Persecution in the Family*, Harmondsworth: Penguin.

Schreber, Daniel Paul (1988), *Memoirs of My Nervous Illness*, trans. Ida MacAlpine and Richard Hunter, Cambridge and London: Harvard University Press.

Sedgwick, Eve Kosofsky (1985), *Between Men: English Literature and Male Homosocial Desire*, New York: Columbia University Press.

— (1993), *Epistemology of the Closet*, Berkeley: University of California Press.

Seidler, Victor Jeleniewski (1995), "Men, Heterosexualities and Emotional Life", in Steve Pile and Nigel Thrift (eds), *Mapping the Subject: Geographies of Cultural Transformation*, London and New York: Routledge, 170–91.

Showalter, Elaine (1992), *Sexual Anarchy: Gender and Culture at the Fin-de-siècle*, London: Virago.

Silverman, Kaja (1992), *Male Subjectivity at the Margins*, New York and London: Routledge.

Silverstolpe, Frederic (1987), "Benkert Was Not a Doctor: On the Nonmedical Origins of the Homosexual Category in the Nineteenth Century", unpublished conference paper, Amsterdam Free University.

Sinfield, Alan (1994), *The Wilde Century: Effeminacy, Oscar Wilde and the Queer Moment*, London: Cassell.

Stallybrass, Peter and White, Allon (1986), *The Politics and Poetics of Transgression*, London: Methuen.

Starkie, Enid (1988), *Baudelaire*, New York: Paragon House.

Stewart, Suzanne R. (1998), *Sublime Surrender: Male Masochism at the fin-de-siècle*, Ithaca, NY and London: Cornell University Press.

Theweleit, Klaus (1987) *Male Fantasies Volume I: Women, Floods, Bodies, History*, trans. Chris Turner, Erica Carter and Stephen Conway, Cambridge: Polity Press.

— (1989), *Male Fantasies Volume II: Male Bodies: Psychoanalyzing the White Terror*, trans. Chris Turner, Erica Carter and Stephen Conway, Cambridge: Polity Press.

Thomas, Calvin (1996), *Male Matters: Masculinity, Anxiety and the Male Body on the Line*, Urbana and Chicago: University of Illinois Press.

Trumbach, Randolph (1993), "The Birth of the Queen: Sodomy and the Emergence of Gender Equality in Modern Culture, 1660–1750", in Martin Bauml Duberman, Martha Vicinus and George Chauncey (eds), *Hidden from History*, Harmondsworth: Penguin

Turkle, Sherry (1992), *Psychoanalytic Politics: Jaques Lacan and Freud's French Revolution*, London: Free Association Books.

Updike, John (1994), "The Disposable Rocket", in Laurence Goldstein (ed.), *The Male Body: Features, Destinies, Exposures*, Ann Arbour: University of Michigan Press.

Valéry, Paul (1958), "Poetry and Abstract Thought", in *The Art of Poetry*, trans. Denise Folliot, London: Routledge and Kegan Paul, 52–81.

— (1989), "Some Simple Reflections on the Body", in Michel Feher (ed.), *Fragments for a History of the Human Body Part Two*, New York: Zone Books, 395–402.

Vanderham, Paul (1998), *James Joyce and Censorship: The Trials of Ulysses*, Basingstoke and London: Macmillan.

Walters, Margaret (1978), *The Nude Male: A New Perspective*, Harmondsworth: Penguin.

Warner, Michael (1993), *Fear of a Queer Planet: Queer Politics and Social Theory*, Minneapolis: University of Minnesota Press.

Weber, Samuel M. (1988), Introduction to Daniel Paul Schreber, *Memoirs of My Nervous Illness*, trans. Ida MacAlpine and Richard Hunter, Cambridge and London: Harvard University Press..

Weeks, Jeffrey, (1977) *Coming Out: Homosexual Politics in Britain from the Nineteenth Century to the Present*, London: Quartet.

— (1981), *Sex, Politics and Society: The Regulation of Sexuality since 1800*, London: Longman.

— (1985), *Sexuality and Its Discontents*, London: Routledge Kegan Paul.

— (1995), *Invented Moralities: Sexual Values in an Age of Uncertainty*, Oxford: Polity Press.

Weir, David (1995), *Decadence and the Making of Modernism*, Amherst: University of Massachusetts Press.

White, Edmund (1993), *Genet*, London: Chatto and Windus.

Wilde, Oscar (1962), *The Letters of Oscar Wilde*, ed. Rupert Hart-Davis, New York: Harcourt, Brace and World.

— (1987), *The Works of Oscar Wilde*, Leicester: Galley Press.

Williams, Simon (1998), "Bodily Dys-Order: Desire, Excess and the Transgression of Corporeal Boundaries", *Body & Society* 4, no. 2: 59–82.

Wilson, Edmund (1967), *Axels' Castle: A Study in the Imaginative Literature of 1870–1930*, Harmondsworth: Penguin.

Winterson, Jeanette (1995), *Art Objects: Essays on Ecstasy and Effrontery*, London: Jonathan Cape.

www.ingramcontent.com/pod-product-compliance
Lightning Source LLC
Chambersburg PA
CBHW071738150426
43191CB00010B/1621